THE MENTOR KING

Pastor Matt & Heather
We are very proud of you
both as our pastors. We
love you very much.
Ron A. Bishop

RON & CHRISTI BISHOP
www.SHEPHERDSHAPERS.com
PO Box 460889, San Antonio, TX 78246
Ron.Bishop@mac.com
(210)774-5353

The Mentor King

Heart-Revealing Days in the Life of King David

Ron A. Bishop

THE MENTOR KING

Printed in the USA

Library of Congress Control Number: 2018910909

ISBN (print): 978-0-9973515-2-1

ISBN (kindle): 978-0-9973515-3-8

Cover Design: Joseph & Doryann Rohrs

Prepared for Publication by www.palmtreeproductions.com

To Contact the Author:

WWW.SHEPHERDSHAPERS.COM

DEDICATION

This book is dedicated to "mentors in worship," all around the world who carry us with them, into God's presence. These are the ones who do not focus on entertaining us, by their talent and performance, but who assist us as we go on our journey to seek God.

We appreciate, those who have just the right blend of big faith, divine anointing, God given talent, and drive to do their best. It seems as if some people are destined to be captains of hundreds, and even captains of thousands in different areas of Christian Service.

Thank you to all of you who have stood up, drawn fire and have worshipped and mentored without abandon. You have led us into the presence of the Lord and have inspired us to be sincere in our time with God, even in public.

Thank you for being warriors first in the heart, then in your feet and then in the walking out of real life. We appreciate you who have dredged deeply into your own hearts and souls to exude your own unique flavor, so that we can grow and mature together in our relationship with the Lord. We honor you as you have been mentors like David.

Thank you for not being self-conscious, or controlled by insecurity, but being bold enough to stand before others, behind microphones, pulpits and on platforms. Thank you for allowing us to be in the room, while you have done some of your worshipping. We have tried to emulate your heart cries, as we have observed you. You enjoyed singing, dancing and worshipping, while challenging us to do the same.

May the Holy Spirit be with you as you continue on your journey.

-Ron A. Bishop

Contents

A Word About the Cover

"David, the Worshipper"

Artist: Dr. La Donna Taylor

The moment I saw this painting, "David, the Worshipper," by La Donna Taylor, I wanted it for the cover of this book. The painting epitomizes David as a minstrel before the Lord. La Donna Taylor is not only an excellent artist on canvas, but also a globally acclaimed violinist, who takes her violin and travels to minister in music and worship to many nations around the world. She was able to express the heart of David in this painting, because she shares a similar passion for bringing people to the heart of God.

www.LaDonnaTaylor.com

Graphic Design by: Joseph & Dory Rohrs

The Graphic design work for the cover of this book was done by Joseph & Doryann Rohrs, of Sarasota, Florida. We are always grateful for their excellent work. They have designed the covers of all three books we have published.

- ***The Joseph Story***
- ***Is There a Grandfather in the House?***
- ***The Mentor King***

ACKNOWLEDGEMENTS

God has been good to me in so many ways. Some of the most significant ways God has shown me gracious benefits is in the relationships He has brought into my life. I must take this moment to name some of those who are close to my heart.

My wife, Christina Reed Bishop, has been a rock in my life for nearly half a century. She came from a small town on the Delmarva Peninsula. She has gone with me to many nations and done so with grace and poise, which I consider almost heavenly. Thank you, Christi, for being my best of all friends. Thank you especially for your help and insight in the birthing of this and all of my books. I love the sparkle in your eyes, your infectious smile and your gentle spirit. Thank you for choosing me.

I would like to acknowledge our son, Cameron, you have made me proud. You devour books and have so much knowledge. You are a true wordsmith and that makes our conversations delightful. Cameron, I appreciate your level of wisdom and often consider you as one of my mentors. Thank you first for choosing Letha, and then for how you both gave us grandchildren; Cole, Lauren and Trent. You and your family are worshippers, you are musical and all are strong contributors to the family core.

I would also like to acknowledge our daughter, Doryann Rohrs. Dory, you always bring joy to my heart. You are by nature a journalist and so inciteful. You often tweak my perspective on things. You are a natural storyteller and have often challenged me to think deeper in every situation. Thank you for bringing Joseph into our lives and then the way you both gave us Gwynne, Cyrus and Cora. We love how they love the Lord, and us, and appreciate their artistic gifts. Thank you, Joe and Dory, for designing the cover of this book as well as the other two books. You are both very good at what you do.

Special Endorsement From My Mentor

I have often been asked, how long have you known Ron Bishop? Years ago, I came into relationship with Ron's family. The Bishops were a good family. Ron was in his teens at the time. The years passed and I moved away and built a church in Maryland and Ron grew up. He had finished his schooling, and was evangelizing, when he came to see me at my church, Spirit and Life Bible Church, Elkton, Maryland. That was when Ron and Christi met for the first time. Christi was a young lady in my church. To make a long story short, they met, fell in love and were married in 1970. It was all God, no doubt about it. When this happened like it did, I asked them to become our young people's leaders, and they agreed. Ron later became my Assistant Pastor.

From the beginning, I knew they would not be staying forever and that God had given me the responsibility to do my part to get them trained for what was ahead for them. They filled that position for the next five years and were always a joy to work with. But the time came (that I always dreaded), because it was time to release them to do the work that God had ordained for their lives. The rest is their history as they followed God's direction. There has never been a time when we have not worked and traveled together.

Ron and Christi Bishop have always been one of the greatest teams that I have ever known. God has used them to touch the lives of thousands around the world.

The books Ron has written have been a blessing to me personally and to everyone who has read them. I encourage everyone to purchase and read these great books.

Pastor Dr. BJ Pruitt
Founder of Spirit & Life Ministries, Elkton, Maryland
Frontline Ministries, Valrico, Florida ~ President

Endorsements

"God has given Ron the ability to ignite your imagination and place you in the story with King David. While you are there you gain insight and understanding of God and David, *The Mentor King,* in a fresh new way. This book encourages, challenges, and inspires you to pursue God and Love people well."

Pastor Jason King

Worship International ~ President
Faith Bible Chapel, Arvada, Colorado ~ Senior Pastor

"As I travel across America working with worship teams, I notice a common thread that seems more prevalent than ever before; churches are preferring character over gifting. The greatest worship experience we can ever have in a public arena is that which reflects the secret place; intimacy with the living God. *The Mentor King* reveals how David's walk with God informed his public life as the leader of Israel. Ron Bishop writes in a way that helps us understand how David's walk with God shaped the character necessary to lead Gods people."

Rachael Hayes
Christian Artist, Songwriter, Worship Leader, Public Speaker, Pastor's Wife
Rachael was born in Wales, UK

"Ron Bishop does a fabulous job on revealing the inner life of the Psalmist David. From the humble beginnings of being a shepherd to becoming king of Israel, David's heart is revealed. Ron gives accurate details and manifold lessons which David learned when he brought the sacred Ark of the Covenant into Jerusalem. There are also beautiful overtones of David's ministry which depict the life and teachings of Jesus Himself. I would heartily recommend the Book, *The Mentor King* for all who long for fresh insights from the Bible and a closer walk with God."

Rev. Dr. Timothy L. Warner
International Ministerial Association ~ President
Northern Lights Christian Center, Hayward, Wisconsin ~ Senior Pastor

"I've loved this book as David is the one character every young Sunday School boy revels in with the great victory over Goliath. Ron Bishop takes us into the mind of David. He brilliantly fills out the background and sets our reading into context. We begin to understand David's thinking and his overriding desire to see God as the true king of Israel. He strips David bare and gets us right into his heart - a heart of worship at its core - a heart after God's own heart. I loved the imagery of the dancing David bringing blessing to everything he touched. This book will make another generation fall in love with the shepherd king once again."

Rev. Kingsley Armstrong
The Joshua Project- President
International Gospel Outreach, Norwich, England, UK - President

"Ron Bishop continues to write with brilliant fashion in his most illuminating work to date—*The Mentor King*—be enlightened and empowered as he unpacks for us this story of David unlike any other. This is a must read for any and all who choose to pursue, practice or produce worship and the leading of it at any level. Masterfully done."

Dr. Mark Holcomb
Awakening Ministries - President
Christian Artist, Songwriter, Worship Leader, Public Speaker
Johnson City, Tennessee

"Ron Bishop captures the true life and legacy of king David as a true worshipper of God. This is a must read for anyone desiring a deeper spiritual relationship with God."

Pastor Jonas Robertson
Church of Abundant Life, Harvey, Louisiana ~ Senior Pastor

"Like his previous work in *The Joseph Story*, Ron Bishop has once again gone the extra mile to introduce us to the flesh-and-blood character and personality of a character from the Bible. Moving beyond historical significance, in *The Mentor King*, Ron breaks open the living heart of David like no other work I have ever read. Every worship leader should make this book part of their library, and every believer who seeks breakthrough will find encouragement and strategy within these pages."

Rev. Wendy K. Walters
The Favor Foundation, Fort Worth, Texas ~ Founder

Prologue

The Shepherd-King who mentored his Nation to love God!

David was a mentor. He mentored his friends, he mentored a king,[1] he mentored hundreds of Hebrew men and their families, and then he mentored a nation.

The Exodus from Egypt had brought many challenges to the Hebrews. Their journey began hundreds of years before David was born. All of Israel could point to the Patriarchs Abraham, Isaac and Jacob, as their founding ancestors. However, they knew very little about Abraham's God, except for the oral traditions passed down to them from generation to generation. Israel was certainly a significant nation but was without an effective central government. At the time of the Exodus, the Hebrews were insecure slaves, pure and simple. Their daily lives and culture, defined them as slaves, and it was apparent that, unless God brought a miracle across their paths, the hundreds of years behind them, as slaves, would continue unabated to become their future. Their mindset was limited and the future looked bleak.

They genuinely needed a deliverer and Moses was the deliverer God had sent to them. Still, a whole generation must arise who would accept new possibilities. As a result of their insecurity and rebellion, the initial generation had to pass on, as they just would not trust the God of Abraham enough to accept His help. The opening up of the Red Sea was a mind-boggling miracle. However, because of their stubbornness, they still refused to accept an all-powerful and benevolent God. When finally, they came to Mt. Sinai, they stood afar off and said, to Moses: "You speak to us, and we will listen. But don't let God speak directly to us, or we will die!"[2] The reason for this response to God was that, they feared God, and were compliant to follow Him, howbeit from afar. Israel needed a mentor, and eventually, that mentor would be David.

> THE HEBREWS WERE IN THE FAMILY OF GOD, BUT DID NOT KNOW THE GOD OF FAMILY.

The Hebrews were not close to their God. They were aware of their historical connection to God but had been a long time coming to Him. In the lives of many Hebrews then, and many in the west today, they have a history of being connected in some ways to Jehovah God, but have never practiced a daily commitment to prayer, personal devotion or sincere worship. To the Hebrews it meant a connection to Judaism, and the Jewish religion.

"In the 21st century, too often it also means a connection to some form of traditional or evangelical denomination or church, and not a strong personal clarity about God, therefore still keeping at "arms-length."[3]

A believer who maintains a "keep at arms-length" relationship with God, will not enhance strength and value in their life, like they would if they read the Bible on a regular basis, repented of their sins and submitted themselves to the dealings of the Holy Spirit. The question must be asked, what value does God bring to the life of a devout follower of Jesus Christ? If a man or woman has a hope for positive things to come from that relationship, then why would he/she think of keeping a distance from God? Is it a lack of trust, or is it a "failure to commit"[4] that is creating reluctance? The first step is to open up your heart and ask Him to forgive your sins.

David was an unusual Hebrew believer. He was the family shepherd, so, from his earliest youth he was awake early and leading the sheep to their grazing areas. He could be seen, not so long after daylight each day, striding across the fields with sheep following behind. In his shepherd's bag would be a simple lunch and a sling shot, while he would be carrying his harp. Perhaps, he was already humming a tune that had come to him in the night. Perhaps, he was reciting a psalm that contained a phrase, which was a simple thought that just kept hanging on.

In David's heart of hearts, he was stronger in his faith than any of his family, or neighbors, or even, for that part, his countrymen. Something had taken root in David's heart… something that others would have allowed to pass on by. But David, would almost grow impatient as he moved toward the place where the sheep would settle in to graze. He had found a quiet place of solitude, which

> WE KNOW DAVID'S HEART, BUT DO WE KNOW HIS HEART OF HEARTS?

spoke volumes to him. That solitude was seldom interrupted but would continue on for hours. It was definitely "life in the slow lane,"[5] but David, as young and energetic as he was, longed, each night, for daylight to come and the journey to begin, so he could get alone with his thoughts, and to worship God, freely and flamboyantly. Each afternoon, David would lead the sheep home to lock them up in their safe corral and get much needed rest. The next morning, he would start his journey all over again.

He was interrupted at times by the forces of nature, by a beast of prey, or perhaps a passing stranger, but more often than not, he spent the full day alone, with his beloved sheep. The sheep were not a distraction to the freedom of a young man, but an excuse to get away from humanity and spend time with deity. He was challenged by an occasional bear, or lion, and these he dealt with quickly and effectively. And then, when the sheep were safe, he would return immediately to what he valued most… time with his Creator God.

As the years passed David's life assignments changed and his circle of involvements were reordered. At last David grew up and found himself assigned to the court of King Saul. Once there, this worshipper just changed audiences. Instead of worshipping God with his beloved sheep, David changed partners and worshipped God before the king. After his experience in the Valley of Elah, and the death of Goliath, he was promoted to serve in a military leadership role. This was more difficult, a bit more of a challenge, but still he worshipped, whenever he could. But finally, the jealousy of the king and national politics altered his status, so he was on the move, from hiding place to caves to the homes of friendly countrymen. Under these circumstances, David discovered that, wherever he went a crowd was gathering.

Eventually a small army had formed in his stronghold, Adullam, and would follow him, as well to other caves and caverns. His first stronghold had been Adullam, but there would be others, scattered all across the land. When David discovered these caves, he could not resist the solitude and the privacy they afforded to him. After a while privacy was not to be his, ever again. But really, David was not worried over his desire for privacy, as long as, all those whom God choose as his audience, did not object to his singing, his playing of his musical instrument, or his demonstrative worship. Those close to David had to realize that, if you are near this man, you must learn to appreciate his lifestyle. Soon their lifestyles blended with his and they began to grow. They found that David would just release his songs aloud and often to God. David had never been shy, or embarrassed, but free to express what he felt toward God. Worship was a part of his thoughts, his dreams, his plans for every day, and in his conversation.

David lived near to a culture, which kept God at a distance, but this young man kept God close to his chest, and near to his heart. He only longed for those around him to experience what he was experiencing. If they could only enjoy God as he enjoyed God, then it would be life changing for them. Never did he think much about mentoring or challenging them. He was, admittedly quite idealistic, and lived to worship, to sing, and to walk as a warrior of faith.

Because of the prophetic declarations of the Prophet Samuel, David knew that someday he would have a larger audience, and that audience would be the entire nation. Until then he would relax and let God take charge of how it would all play out. The one thing David felt deeply about was that, whatever God wanted of him, he would freely and gladly give. This promise came from deep within his heart. It was becoming more and more clear to David that God had selected him to be the next king, but he would leave it all in God's hands. The nation needed what David had to give, and he would eventually get that chance to speak into the lives of the nation.

The day David met Samuel had been a life changing day for him. He had never realized that he was uniquely different than others, but what he did know was that, after the prophet had prophesied to him, and anointed him, the intensity of desire to be alone with God had increased to a crescendo of huge proportions. There was one thing for sure; God was taking charge of his life and he was happy about it.

As the years passed, the 400-600 men and their families had become his audience and slowly he had observed that the mood of his followers had changed. They all, became one very large family and when David was with them, he was at home. They loved him and he loved them. It could be said that David had become, not only their leader, but their mentor, if not their shepherd. They all had moved away from being the distressed, the debtors and the discontented:

> "David therefore departed from there and escaped to the cave of Adullam… And everyone *who was* in distress, everyone who *was* in debt, and everyone *who was* discontented gathered to him. So, he became captain over them. And there were about four hundred men with him."[6]

As a result of this lifestyle change, they had all become the happy, the excited, the fulfilled and the motivated. If David were to want anything, these people would do everything possible to meet that longing. If their leader were to be threatened or attacked, they would move heaven and earth to make the difference for him. Loyalty ran deep in the hearts of all who became David's new audience.

This is the story of David, and you are going to discover David's heart, if you did not already know. Please join me and take a look at those "Thirteen Heart Revealing Days in the Life of King David."

Endnotes

1. 1 Kings 2:2-4 NLT - "I am going where everyone on earth must someday go. Take courage and be a man. Observe the requirements of the Lord your God and follow all his ways. Keep the decrees, commands, regulations, and laws written in the Law of Moses so that you will be successful in all you do and wherever you go. If you do this, then the Lord will keep the promise he made to me. He told me, 'If your descendants live as they should and follow me faithfully with all their heart and soul, one of them will always sit on the throne of Israel.'"

2. Exodus 20:19 NLT

3. www.google.ie - "Keep at arms-length" - "to avoid intimacy or familiarity with something - to avoid intimacy or familiarity with someone - to distance yourself from a person - to distance yourself from an organization - to distance yourself from an issue - to avoid becoming connected with something - to avoid becoming connected with someone."

4. "Commit Phobia" - "Failure to commit" - A reluctance to make a commitment to something important. It may be a failure to commit in a relationship; or it just may be a misunderstanding of how God could bring value into your life, or vocation or society.

5. "Life in the Slow Lane" - This refers to not getting all worked up about the life pressures, which defeat and discourage others. To view every ingredient of a day as significant, is to lose peace, joy and eventually happiness. It can be a pleasure to step off the fast track and discipline yourself toward reducing stress and the pressures of life. Living in a small village, for example, can defuse some of those issues, which city dwellers cannot avoid.

6. I Samuel 22:1-2 NKJV

The Day of David's Prophetic Anointing

I Samuel 16

God had been looking for a worshipper. He could hear the words of a new and rising shepherd whose voice was accompanied by a beautiful harp. This voice came from a young man who was hungry to know God. Day after day this young man would leave his family home, lead his sheep out and into the countryside, passing over hills and through valleys, until he was far enough away and the grass was delicious enough, that the sheep could be nourished and his spirit could find freedom to sing aloud; allowing his heart to release praise heavenward. Young David did not whisper his worship but declared it loudly and boldly. The heavens were moved and the favor of a responsive God was aroused.

Sitting on a grassy knoll, harp in hand, watching the sheep graze, David's worship was rooted so deeply in his heart, that a protective shield began to form around him. It was as if he was attacking life's challenges with the empowerment of the Angelic host, instead of his own. It became clear that this young worshipper had tapped into the realm of "spiritual warfare" and had become committed to whatever it took to invoke a divine attack, against whatever raised its head to reproach God. In a sense, it was as if, when worshipping, he became one with the Lord, for he was enveloped by the Spirit of the Lord. When nothing but divine intervention could quell the storms, his songs moved forward in praise, helping him to win against strong odds. Even from his youth, David learned the art of warfare in the spirit. So often humanity fails to grasp that some battles cannot be won by human weapons. Often the powers of the Angelic hosts must join with us, if we are to prevail. David introduced this level of devotion and spiritual warfare, and later the Prophet Isaiah picked up on this and declared that "No weapon formed against you shall prosper, and every tongue, which rises against you in judgment, you shall condemn." Then Isaiah pronounced a principle by saying, "This *is* the heritage of the servants of the Lord, and their righteousness *is* from Me, says the Lord."[1]

DAVID LEARNED TO WAR IN THE SPIRIT. MOST VICTORIES ARE WON OR LOST IN THE HEART.

Fred Hammond composed a song, which addresses the idea that,

"No Weapon Formed against me shall Prosper":
No weapon formed against me shall prosper, it won't work
No weapon formed against me shall prosper, it won't work
Say No weapon formed against me shall prosper, it won't work
Say No weapon formed against me shall prosper, it won't work
God will do what He said He would do

He will stand by His word

And He will come through

God will do what He said He would do.[2]

David had innocently entered into God's strategy room without fully knowing what was happening in his life. For generations God had been preparing the spiritual climate in Israel for the nation to have a king. Israel had "jumped the gun"[3] and requested a king pursuant to their own desires, rather than waiting for God's timing. It seemed like a good idea, but it had not worked out well.

Judah's sin had an effect when it came to Israel's king.

The patriarch, Jacob, declared in Genesis 49:10, "the sceptre shall not depart from Judah," so we recognize that the Messiah was expected to come through Jacob's lineage. However, his character was significantly flawed, and ultimately, he had failed miserably by selling his brother, Joseph, into slavery and then, after making a move to the region of Philistia, Judah fathered three sons who were wicked. Their iniquity was so flawed that, scripture says that, "God chose to slay them." Finally, Judah's unrighteous bent got so out of control that he, unwittingly, fathered twin sons by way of an illicit relationship with his daughter-in-law, Tamar. In the end, the law delayed "the Lord's anointed" from coming through Judah's lineage until the tenth generation.[4] There were ten generations from Perez to David.[5] Jesus was the offspring of David and that gives significant credibility to David's legitimacy.[6]

God was looking for a Righteous man who could lead Israel.

The Holy Spirit had been brooding and waiting for "the Branch," generation after generation, and now the son of Jesse had arrived.[7] Ten generations had passed since Judah's sin and now God could legally give Israel her king. If God had given Israel a king from Judah in Saul's generation, it would have been Jesse, but Jesse was not the chosen of the Lord; David was the first generation after Judah to qualify, and now David was chosen, and his heart was the perfect one to carry it all forward, redefining the relationship God wanted with his chosen people, Israel.

In Ramah, Samuel heard a clear word from God.

Samuel was at his home in Ramah and was awakened to a stir in his spirit. He felt that this was a different day and things were about to change. He could sense that God was impressing him with an urgency to get an early start, throw open the curtains and look off into the distance for a divine movement for his nation and for his people. This prophet had been entirely too melancholy, for too long, and he felt that God was nudging him, if not commanding him, to get up, move out of the rut and become an instrument of God to change the landscape. The conversation had begun with these words from God, "So, how long are you going to mope over Saul? You know I've rejected him as king over Israel. Fill your flask with anointing oil and get going. I'm sending you to Jesse of Bethlehem."[8]

He could hear the voice of the Holy Spirit deep within saying these words: "I've searched the land and found a son of Jesse. He's a man whose heart beats to my heart, a man who will do what I tell him."[9]

It was clear to Samuel that he must immediately prepare for a journey. This journey would take the Prophet Samuel a distance of 17 kilometers (11 miles) from Ramah to Bethlehem. Of course, this journey in those days took much longer than it would in the 21st century. Still, it was a journey of significance, because it would bring a divine plan together, and launch a new chapter in Israel's history.

Initially, Samuel was reluctant, because he feared Saul would misunderstand his motives. Samuel was always obedient, but the king was unpredictable and likely would see Samuel as an enemy worth destroying. Even so, this prophet knew that God was in charge and that men must walk in obedience as He sees the bigger picture and always moves over the earth in wisdom.

God responded to the concerns of Samuel and gave him a word of wisdom on how to deal with the required task, while allaying his fears. Take a heifer and go for an official visit, for seemingly no other purpose than to draw a local community into a time of consecration, and sincere worship; after all every community needs introspection from time to time. In the meantime, Samuel would begin contemplating his new assignment to "go searching for a heart, unlike before." The last time, it seems like the result, in choosing Saul, was that they settled for a "face," but this time they must change the strategy, by searching for a "heart."[10]

THIS TIME, SAMUEL WENT SEARCHING FOR A HEART... AND HE FOUND DAVID.

The prophet arose from his bed, filled his ram's horn with olive oil and then, went to the enclosure, where he kept sacrificial animals. He carefully selected a heifer[11] to accompany him on his journey.

Samuel then saddled his donkey and made his way down the path in the direction of Bethlehem. It would be a slow walk, taking 4-5 hours, depending on how well the heifer cooperated with the donkey in keeping pace.

He had begun this assignment just after sunrise and should arrive in the village by mid-day. This visit to the people of Bethlehem was not announced or expected. It was spontaneous and calculating, as Samuel was on a mission and had set his face toward the family of Jesse. As reluctant as Samuel had been initially, he was now resolute and determined to fulfill this responsibility and find Saul's replacement. God is always in the details,[12] and this day would be a milestone both for David and for Israel.

The people of Bethlehem, both children and adults, could see the approaching prophet from a fair distance. The road he traveled came from Ramah, bypassing Jerusalem and due south to Bethlehem. There must have been markers, which identified him and sat him apart from so many others who traveled this route. Samuel, a lifelong Nazarite,[13] for example had never ever cut his hair, so this would cause him to stand out differently to so many other travelers. He was currently the most well-known priest of the tribe of Levi; actually, the first prophet in the history of Israel; as well as the last of an era of Judges, having served as "head of state." Men like Samuel were different, unique and focused. Then, given the fact that this old man rode on a donkey, pulled along a heifer on a rope, and had a ram's horn slung about his neck, made this man appear eccentric and very spiritual, to say the least.

To receive a prophet unannounced could send ripples of concern through the town. "The elders of the town came trembling to meet him."[14] Questions and concerns were in the hearts and minds of the people, and especially the officials. Some questions, and comments would have gone like this:

"Why has the prophet come?"

"Is there sin, or a problem that has caused him to make this visit?"

"Has he come to challenge an official?"

They asked Samuel, "What is wrong?[15] Is this a friendly visit?"[16]

"We have not prepared for a visit from the Prophet Samuel."

"If we had only known of his coming we could have prepared a feast, or good accommodations to make him comfortable."

Yes, the city officials felt insecure, but so did Samuel, as he realized he must use his best strategy, to avoid repercussions from the king. The Lord had given Samuel clear direction, but still the human element often feels awkward. Then, Samuel spoke to the people and all their questions evaporated, leaving the people calm. Everyone began to enjoy the moment.

Samuel spoke kindly saying, "Nothing is wrong. I've come to sacrifice this heifer and lead you in the worship of God."[17]

The people were relieved, to hear that only the heifer would die that day.

They watched as this prophet set about to build an altar and to prepare the wood for a fire. After the details were taken care of and the ceremony was soon to begin, Samuel made a request, almost inconspicuously to invite Jesse and his sons to also participate in this consecration to the Lord. The body language of this prophet implied, that he customarily invited significant people from any region, in which he conducted a special service, to join him, but only as a formality. This way of handling details, calmed all concerns and

Samuel was free to pull the family of Jesse aside for a special time of consecration. All this was done outside of ear shot, so there was no suspicion or concern. As far as the citizens of Bethlehem were concerned, this was the way it was always done.

The people of Bethlehem were untroubled and flowed gladly with Samuel, as he led them into a festive consecration to their God. These Israelites did not need to travel to Gibeon to stand outside the tent of meeting, which was the Tabernacle of Moses[18], for this Prophet of God had brought the worship of God to their community. Most of them had never been able to have such an experience. Unless they had made a pilgrimage to the tent of meeting, this was, for them, both a rare moment and the very first time to experience Samuel's service.

Samuel was a conscientious priest with a pastoral heart. He served the entire nation by taking "worship services" to many villages and cities everywhere. On this occasion he had selected Bethlehem, and for good reason. Samuel had brought worship to the people, and the people were ready to celebrate.[19]

Even the fact that Samuel had drawn Jesse and his family out of ear shot, did not bother them, as they savored the moment. Every concern the prophet had felt was now laid to rest and the anointing came strongly upon Samuel to call for Jesse and his sons. "Come to me now, Jesse, and show me your sons, that I might see, which one of these young men is the anointed of the Lord." "In the mind of Samuel, was the plan to view each of Jesse's sons, while listening to the still small voice of God, for His choice as Saul's successor."[20]

As the sons lined up, from the oldest to the youngest, Samuel could see them all, but he hardly paid any attention to the younger sons, as he was so focused on the tallest and eldest son of Jesse. Eliab was tall and handsome. Samuel guessed by his comeliness[21] that he was the person who was to be their future king.[22]

For a moment, it was almost déjà vu for Samuel, as he stared at the height and general appearance of Eliab. He was almost mesmerized at this young man, and instinctively wanted to anoint him. We can see here that even someone as spiritual as the Prophet Samuel, was taken in by the outer man. It is true that appearances can be deceiving.[23] However, God was holding Samuel back and refused this one, because he could x-ray the spirit and nature of the man. After all, God had been looking for a man after His heart for a long time and had already spotted him, out in the bush, out in the grasslands and far away from this crowd of people. God told Samuel, "No, this is not the one." God continued, "Looks aren't everything, don't be impressed with his looks and stature. I've already eliminated him. God judges' persons differently than humans do. Men and women look at the face, but God looks into the heart."[24] Again, it must be noted that on this particular journey, "Samuel went in search of a heart and not a face."

There was little conversation between the Prophet and Jesse.

There had come a point, before the meal was shared, when Samuel called for Jesse and his sons to pull aside for a time of consecration. Jesse was given no explanation, but only that he must parade his sons before the special guest. It appeared almost like "inspecting the troops." Samuel gave no inside information, as to what he was looking for, and no questions were asked. The first hint of anything was when Samuel stood staring into the eyes of Eliab, Jesse's eldest son. For all its brevity, it seemed like time stood still, as Eliab wondered, Jesse quietly observed and Samuel mused. At first, the old prophet seemed as if he had found what he was searching for, having looked up and down the tall young man. Then a strange concern was seen on his brow, as he moved away and toward the second son, Abinadab. It took a moment for all to move their eyes away from Eliab, for Samuel's lingering had sent ideas through the minds of those who observed. There is a principle we know that states, "man looks on the outward appearance, but the Lord looks on the heart."[25] There is another similar wisdom, which we must keep in mind, namely, "Man looks on the outward appearance, and don't you forget it."[26]

Samuel moved slowly away from Eliab; and focused on the other sons who were standing near him. Of course, these sons, in true Hebrew fashion, had lined up from the oldest. Here is the order of their birth. First had come, Eliab, then Abinadab, then Shimea, Nethanel and finally Raddai, and Ozem.[27] A quizzical look came over Samuel as he ran out of sons to consider. "Samuel was blunt, with Jesse, 'God hasn't chosen any of these.'"[28] And then with a questioning look, asked Jesse if he had "some other sons besides these; and when Jesse had said that he had one more, named David, but that he was a shepherd, and took care of the flocks, Samuel bade them to call him immediately, for that, till he was come they could not possibly sit down to the feast."[29]

MAN LOOKS ON THE OUTWARD APPEARANCE, AND DON'T YOU FORGET IT.

PROTOCOL: "No one sits down until this young man comes."

Samuel must have been quite assertive as he addressed his audience[30] with the statement, "Go get him, we're not moving from this spot until he's here."[31] Even as David sang his last song to the sheep, he was not aware of how policies of protocol were being formed. A coronation was about to take place. A "Prophetic Anointing" was about to be given; and yet Israel's future king was not on site. Clouds must have been swirling overhead and emotions must have been running high in the heavens. It must be noted that this anointing was to be the first for David, with two more to come, over the next twenty years.[32]

It must have shocked every member of Jesse's family when it became apparent that everything had come to a halt, for they were now having to wait on the youngest member of the family. If only they had known earlier, then they would have sent a runner to get him, so that he could be present for all that would transpire. Not one member of this family really understood why David was needed, or why his presence was so important. It is quite often a reality, that the youngest members of the family have to wait in line for favor.

It is clear, that a principle is true in this story: Whenever a prophet is present, the entire community is placed on notice, as things will surely change. A prophetic gift is needed to keep a society on track for better things. If a community is negligent, in things that matter, then the presence of a prophet will set everything on its head.

The fact is that David had left the house early that morning, within an hour of daylight, to lead the sheep out to the grazing land. He had been gone several hours before Samuel had arrived unannounced. Of course, everyone had been taken by surprise at how the afternoon's events had been altered by the arrival of the Prophet.

All the women of Bethlehem had quickly put together tables of food, leaving the air charged with electricity. Just out of ear shot, the people could see that the prophet had blessed Jesse and his family one by one. Now things had changed and all were required to stand and wait on another guest to come. Because they could not hear what was being said, they did not know who that guest was, and found it interesting just to watch.

Why was David not at the party?

Some speakers and story tellers have accused Jesse and his family of having intentionally neglected to invite David to this public convocation. It has been said that Jesse, and his family, were clueless and prejudicial against David and had no idea that he could be chosen as the "Lord's anointed."

However, it must be restated that the Prophet Samuel had taken everyone by surprise when he entered the village unannounced about mid-day. David, the young shepherd, had likely departed from home about the same time Samuel had launched on his journey from Ramah. This duty would keep him out for 6-8 hours, before he would begin his slow journey home in late afternoon.

Even in the middle of the "inspection of Jesse's sons" no one, including Jesse, knew Samuel's agenda. It became apparent only after David had been summoned and had actually arrived. Certainly, if you were viewing the events from a distance, you'd be suspicious of how Samuel had lifted the ram's horn over David's head and poured the oil over him. Clearly it was a time of coronation, but for what? They would have no indication of why this young man was being anointed. Without more details, no one would guess that it was to replace Saul.

Why was David the family shepherd?

The reason David was assigned to be the family shepherd was firstly, because owning sheep was one of the family enterprises. Since they owned sheep, someone had to watch them. In every shepherding family, the younger children were usually given this responsibility. Until David was old enough, each older brother had taken turns. In families, the chores tend to shift downward, leaving the youngest children to the more mundane responsibilities. Through the years all the brothers had likely served as shepherds, and even complained about watching the sheep. This particular chore was not the most exciting or prestigious. Unless one was creative to keep the mind from going numb, no one in their right mind would ask for the job. Most would consider it drudgery and boring.

It is apparent that David was of a different mindset. Being a shepherd was his chore of choice. This duty was especially good for him. David was a "take charge" shepherd, using this occasion to "get alone with God," to sing, to worship, to play his harp; making wise use of his privacy by being alone with the sheep. After all, not everyone could grasp the value of singing loudly to God, playing a harp or dancing wildly in circles, especially if they did not have a strong relationship with Him.

This set David apart as a great shepherd. If a poll could have been taken of the sheep, they would poll as "the happiest and most peaceful sheep in the countryside."

I've heard public speakers sermonize of how David was disapproved by his family and thus relegated to an inferior roll, because of jealousy. My suggestion is to take the occasion to closely and slowly read each Bible story, pay attention to every detail, and don't embellish it so much. Just because it sounds plausible, doesn't mean it is true. It is easy to devalue David's position within the family, because so many of us root for the underdog. This makes a feel-good story, but it is not true except for his being the youngest member of the family.

David's story is quite different to Joseph's story.

In the story of Joseph[33], we see that he endured, at the hands of his brothers the evils of treachery and betrayal, but then finally, in God's time, the entire family experienced redemption. The story of David is quite different to the story of Joseph. Just because David was mocked by Eliab in the Valley of Elah[34], doesn't indicate a family relationship of treachery, and betrayal. For the most part David had a good relationship with each member of his family. Later, many of his family members would actually serve with him as ranking leaders and team members.

JOSEPH'S BROTHERS SOLD HIM INTO SLAVERY, BUT DAVID'S BROTHERS BECAME HIS ALLIES.

Now back to the ceremony by the Prophet Samuel.

One of the brothers was sent to fetch David from his duties. Off he had gone to inform David that he was being summoned by the Prophet. This sibling would have to sit this one out, taking over the responsibility of shepherding, while David quickly returned home and to the village.

It must have been a puzzling thing for David, as he rushed back, without full knowledge of why he had been summoned. In the haste of this transition, David would approach the convocation with growing questions and absolutely no clue as to why his presence was required. His brother who provided relief, was not fully aware of why David was even being summoned, so he could not answer any questions.

The Shepherd cautiously approached the festival.

As David came to the gathering he discovered that the common meal was about to begin. It appeared that everyone was actually waiting for him before they would sit together to eat. This was a first for David, as it seemed, being the youngest, that nothing waited on him, but always started just before he could settle in. This was the first of many changes for this young worshipper. From now on, David would discover that his life would change regularly. Upon coming to the gathering, no one explained anything to him, but every moment opened up to the next.

The people were excited and enjoying this impromptu event. However, something took place that left some of them puzzled and in wonderment. Most of them saw what happened, but few had any idea of its significance. From a few feet away, they'd watched as the old prophet had moved toward the approaching shepherd boy. And then it happened, something few would fully understand, and no one, but possibly Jesse and David would wholly grasp.

Samuel stepped forward, removed the ram's horn filled with oil from around his neck and raised it over the young man's head. He beckoned David to kneel to the ground, raised his horn above his head and began to pour. The movies always portray the acts of such men as Samuel, as only pouring a residue of oil upon his head, as if to save oil for future coronations, but this does not seem to have been the case on this day, for David needed to be thoroughly anointed. This was to be the very last coronation this priest would ever preform. He "poured the oil on David's head, while his brothers watched. At that moment, the Spirit of the Lord took control of

David and stayed with him from then on."[35] There seemed to be an aura around him that no one could avoid, and which only God could have explained.

A prophetic anointing came upon Samuel and without abandon, he leaned over and prophesied quietly into the ear of the young man. He spoke in clear and decisive terms, giving both words of knowledge[36] and words of wisdom[37], with these comments:

> "God has chosen you to be Israel's king. God's word to you is to be righteous and obedient to His commands. If you do this your kingdom will continue for a long time, and your house will be of great splendor. If you will do this, you will be celebrated in the world. As Israel's king, you will overthrow the Philistines, and whatever nations you meet in war. You will always be the conqueror and will survive every fight. Finally, while you live, you shall enjoy a glorious name and leave such a glorious heritage to your posterity."[38]

At the very moment when this prophet/priest spoke these words over David, and with the family of Jesse observing, "the Spirit of God entered David like a rush of wind[39], God vitally empowering him for the rest of his life."[40]

Without the Anointing, David could not be Israel's King.

When the anointing oil was poured upon young David, he was "transformed and brought into direct contact with the divine."[41] Without the anointing, David could not have become Israel's king. At that precise moment, he was forever changed; he was bound to God. This ceremony by the old prophet Samuel was clearly prophetic, but it was not the official coronation. It must be understood that this prophetic anointing served the purpose of initiating a commoner, so that he could begin his own orientation, training and conditioning for the throne, which would surely come in just 13 or so years.

While David became empowered by Samuel's pronouncement in this city of Bethlehem, just 13 Kilometers (8 miles) away, Saul had a different experience. It was said that, "At that very moment the Spirit of God left Saul and, in its place, a black mood sent by God settled on him. He was terrified."[42] Often comments are made that, it is not God's way, to send a "black mood" to such a man as Saul. Please realize that, all God has to do is leave the room and withdraw His presence. If and when this happens then blackness and darkness will surely prevail. When the light of God's presence ceases to occupy a life, then despondency, discouragement and depression take over; this will place a drag on the very life of that individual.

Samuel was not a man who craved public affirmation. He was devout to the Lord and perhaps, a bit eccentric. It does not appear that he hung around very long after his assignment was completed. He had taken care of his official responsibility, and apparently gone back home to Ramah,[43] after all, he barely had enough time to arrive home before dark.

How was this a "Heart Revealing Day" in the life of David?

Up to this time, God was displeased with many of Israel's leaders. He was searching for a worshipper, whom He could anoint and then expect to respectfully carry that anointing to fulfill the call upon his life. David was a worshipper, a shepherd, and he enjoyed basking in the presence of God out in the fields, alone, but for the sheep.

From the beginning, he had invited the Spirit of God to reside in him, by opening up his heart to communicate with God. While others were pursuing their own agendas, this shepherd was tuning his ear to the choirs of heaven.

He was a fighter, but his battlefield was more in the spirit world, than with men. It is clear that David, even while in his youth, was able to understand spiritual warfare. He would have enjoyed this verse: "The weapons of our warfare are not carnal, but mighty in God for pulling down strongholds."[44]

GOD IS SEARCHING FOR A HEART. COULD YOU BE THE ONE HE CHOOSES?

That day in the life of David, a portal opened up giving us a peak at the kind of heart God was searching for, when looking for the principal leader for his chosen people. God still searches throughout humanity for people like this to serve in capacities of responsibility in churches, kingdoms, governments and families. If you have such a heart, then it is highly likely that you will be tapped for leadership. However, if selfishness, self-centeredness and self-interests occupy your thoughts, then you may be passed over.

The challenge to you and to all of us is to face our most mundane chores, challenging situations and times of self-doubt, and turn them into treasure troves of opportunity. You and I need to get alone with God, lift Him high in praise and invite the Holy Spirit to infuse us with His gifts. In a world like ours, we must have better leaders, greater levels of humility, and more faith, so that we can develop "hearts like God's heart."

Endnotes

1. Isaiah 54:17 NKJV
2. www.azlyrics.com/lyrics/fredhammondradicalforchrist - Written by Frederick William Hammond, Alvin Lewis Moore • Copyright © Universal Music Publishing Group, Capitol Christian Music Group - For all the lyrics go to the above website.
3. www.idioms.thefreedictionary.com/jump+the+gun - "Jumped the gun" - Etymology: based on the literal meaning of jump the gun (to begin to run a race before the gun that signals the start has been shot). To do something before it should be done.
4. Deuteronomy 23:2 NLT - "If a person is illegitimate by birth neither he nor his descendants for ten generations may be admitted to the assembly of the Lord."
5. Matthew 1:2-6 NKJV
6. Revelation 22:16 NKJV - "I, Jesus, have sent My angel to testify to you these things in the churches. I am the Root and the Offspring of David, the Bright and Morning Star."
7. Isaiah 11:1-2 NLT - "Out of the stump of David's family will grow a shoot— yes, a new Branch bearing fruit from the old root. And the Spirit of the Lord will rest on him— the Spirit of wisdom and understanding, the Spirit of counsel and might, the Spirit of knowledge and the fear of the Lord."
8. I Samuel 16:1 MSG
9. Acts 13:14-22 NKJV - "The Apostle Paul and his party, sailed to Antioch in Pisidia, and went into the synagogue on the Sabbath day and sat down. And after the reading of the Law and the Prophets, the rulers of the synagogue sent to them, saying, 'Men and brethren, if you have any word of exhortation for the people, say on.' … 'Then Paul stood up and motioning with his hand said'" (Saul had been anointed to be king, but displeased God) "… God removed him from office and put King David in his place, with this commendation: 'I've searched the land and found this David, son of Jesse. He's a man whose heart beats to my heart, a man who will do what I tell him.'"
10. *Is there a Grandfather in the House?* By Ron A. Bishop ISBN: 978-0-9973515-0-7 Page 33
11. www.merriam-webster.com/dictionary/heifer - Heifer - a young cow; especially: one that has not had a calf.
12. Proverbs 8:22-31 MSG - The writer of Proverbs quotes "Wisdom" in a monologue, which describes how God has always been in the details. Whatever man says, and whatever our society may believe, we know that God, and not the devil, is in the details. Wisdom was there at creation with our Creator. It was God who carefully formed all that exists and made it conform to His patterns.

13. I Samuel 1:11 KJV- "And she vowed a vow, and said, O LORD of hosts, if you will indeed look on the affliction of your handmaid, and remember me, and not forget your handmaid, but will give to your handmaid a man child, then I will give him to the LORD all the days of his life, and there shall no razor come on his head."

14. I Samuel 16:4 NLT

15. I Samuel 16:4 TLB

16. I Samuel 16:4 CEV

17. I Samuel 16:5 MSG

18. II Chronicles 1:3 NASB - "Then Solomon and all the assembly with him went to the high place which was at Gibeon, for God's tent of meeting was there, which Moses the servant of the LORD had made in the wilderness."

19. www.scheinerman.net/judaism/Synagogue/history.html - History of the Synagogue - The requirement was to go up to Jerusalem when it came to worship. So, during the days of Samuel, and until the days of Solomon, the Tabernacle of Moses at Shiloh, and later Gibeon, was the place to go to worship. The Hebrews were carried into Exile in Babylon by Nebuchadnezzar. This seventy years of exile was a trying and most difficult era for the people, as they recognized their need to practice their faith in God but could find no means of practically carrying it through. During the days of the Exile, the Synagogue was established for a "combination of worship and study."

20. Is there a Grandfather in the House? By Ron A. Bishop ISBN: 978-0-9973515-0-7 Page 33

21. www.merriam-webster.com - Comeliness - "The qualities in a person or thing that as a whole gives pleasure to the senses."

22. Josephus, Book 6, Chapter 8:1:158

23. www.quora.com - "Appearances can be deceiving." An example is found in the story of Snow White. "She ate the most perfect looking ripe red apple that turned out to be poisonous."

24. I Samuel 16:7 MSG

25. I Samuel 16:7 ESV

26. Pastor Ron Willhite, of Roswell, Georgia, a friend of mine, who has been overheard to say, on many occasions. I cannot quote one without quoting my friend as well.

27. I Chronicles 2:13-15 MSG - "Jesse's firstborn was Eliab, followed by Abinadab, Shimea, Nethanel, Raddai, Ozem, and finally David; David was the seventh."

28. I Samuel 16:10 MSG

29. Josephus, Book 6, Chapter 8:1:163-164

30. Evangelist Nate Perry - Several years ago I heard an Evangelist say of this part of David's story, "the roast can get cold and the gravy can congeal, but we're not going to sit down until the King comes."

31. I Samuel 16:11 MSG

32. David was anointed three times over a twenty-year period (age 17-37): Prophetic Anointing: when David was age 17. (I Samuel 16:13) - to be officially crowned later. Kingly Anointing: when David was age 30. (II Samuel 2:4) - Crowned to be King over Judah. Priestly Anointing: when David was age about age (II Samuel 5:3) - Crowned to be King over all the nation.

33. Genesis 37

34. I Samuel 17:28-29

35. I Samuel 16:13 CEV

36. www.en.wikipedia.org/wiki/Word_of_Knowledge - Gift of, or word of Knowledge - "The word of knowledge is often defined as the ability of one person to know what God is currently doing or intends to do in the life of another person. It can also be defined as knowing the secrets of another person's heart."

37. www.christcenteredmall.com/teachings/gifts/word-of-wisdom.htm - Gift of, or word of Wisdom - The gift of the word of wisdom is also the revealing of prophetic future; it is speaking hidden truths of what is not known. It is a supernatural perspective to ascertain the divine means for accomplishing God's will in a given situation and is a divinely given power to appropriate spiritual intuition in problem solving."

38. Josephus, Book 6, Chapter 8:1:165

39. "The anointing came upon David, like a rush of wind" - somewhat like that experienced on the day of Pentecost in Jerusalem, by those who were in the Upper Room. (Acts 2).

40. I Samuel 16:13 MSG

41. www.en.wikipedia.org/wiki/The_Crown_(TV_series) - "The Crown" - This Netflix mini-series (released Nov. 4, 2016) is "a biographical story about the early reign of Queen Elizabeth II, of the United Kingdom." I was struck by the words of King George VI (King of the British Commonwealth during WWII) as he was about to be crowned king of England on May 11, 1937. His words to his young daughter, Elizabeth, were: "When the anointing oil touches me I am transformed and brought into direct contact with the divine: forever changed: bound to God. Without the anointing, I cannot be king." And finally, King George VI said to Elizabeth, "This is the most important part of the ceremony."

42. I Samuel 16:14 MSG

43. *Josephus*, Book 6, Chapter 8:2:166

44. II Corinthians 10:4 KJV

THE DAY DAVID'S FIRST GIANT FELL

I SAMUEL 17

A crisis was brewing in the Royal Palace in Gibeah. The previous day had gone as well as commonly expected, but overnight, and about mid-afternoon, an uneasiness changed the mood of the king. Although no one, on that day was aware of what the Prophet Samuel was doing, all heaven could see it from above. The spirit world had just experienced a divine shift and a young shepherd boy, just eight miles away (13k), had been prophetically commissioned for a future assignment. What happened to Saul on that day in Gibeah, would affect the family of Jesse, within a few short weeks. Something had been roused in the heavens, and earth could not resist what God had in mind. It was clear to all believers that "the whole creation is on tiptoe to see the wonderful sight of the sons of God coming into their own."[1]

God began to affirm His favor over the life of David, giving him a promotion[2] in areas such as destiny, open doors, and opportunities. It must, however, be understood that this favor began by David's heart of hearts being turned toward God in the first place. God responded to David's faith. His response to David was even bigger than David's response to God.

At precisely the same moment when the anointing had come upon David, the anointing was lifted from the King. That anointing was replaced with "a tormenting spirit that filled him with depression and fear."[3]

The scripture describes the mood change that came upon Saul as a "tormenting spirit"[4] or an "evil spirit from the Lord troubled Saul."[5] This is a troubling choice of words to describe what it is like when the "favor of God" is removed from a life. However, it is advisable to realize that a life without the favor of God is a life without grace, a world without warmth and a situation that wreaks more of dilemma than solution. There is a principle that "light and darkness cannot coexist in the same place."[6] If light is removed, then darkness prevails, and darkness is a debilitating existence. The presence of God brings an alignment of hope and peace, as well as an infusion of wisdom and direction. Without these elements in the life of a leader, or any individual, then there is too much frustration and floundering, not to mention the fact that there is no "light at the end of the tunnel."[7]

When an individual shuts God out of His life, then the soul goes dark and God's presence disappears.

Existence is not enough, but when a life exists without the light of God, then that life lacks luster and pleasure. So, it was with Israel's king, on the day when God departed from him. There came upon him a void, which was filled with a lack of light; therefore darkness, or, if you will, an evil spirit.

Some of Saul's servants said to him, "a tormenting spirit from God is troubling you. Let us find a good musician to play the harp whenever the tormenting spirit troubles you. He will play soothing music, and you will soon be well again."[8] Saul agreed and asked if they'd do just as they had recommended. One of the servants said to Saul, "I know someone. I've seen him myself: the son of Jesse of Bethlehem, an excellent musician. He's also courageous, of age, well-spoken, and good-looking. And God is with him."[9]

In response, Saul sent messengers to Jesse to summon David to Gibeah, saying, "Send me your son, David the shepherd. Jesse responded by sending David to Saul, along with a young goat, a donkey loaded with bread, and a wineskin full of wine."[10] "Saul took a great liking to him, and nominated him his armor-bearer, i.e. his adjutant,[11] as a proof of his satisfaction with him."[12] Finally, Saul sent a request to Jesse that he be allowed to stay in Gibeah to serve in close proximity to the King.

Even so, David and Saul did not talk much and Saul did not absorb much of David's story or history. The king was not warm in his nature, not to mention the barriers of age and a lack of spiritual presence in his life. Some would say that Saul was not easily approachable, had serious issues, was often distracted, and did not have a pleasing personality.

Eventually, as the year progressed, there came a time when "kings go out to war."[13] At that time, Saul decided to send young David home to his family. Too much was happening and he did not, for a time, require David's musical services. Jesse was too old to be conscripted into the military, so he remained at home, having sent his three older sons to fight in his stead. Notice that when David was with Saul, serving as a minstrel, his brothers were in Bethlehem with Jesse; later, David was sent home, while his brothers were representing his family on the battlefield. Being home with his father, David had returned to his task of watching the sheep. Keep in mind that David was only about 17, so he was not eligible to be a part of the military.

Go to the front lines of the battle to take supplies to your brothers.

David had been home with his father for several months when Jesse called on him to do him a favor and take supplies to his sons and bring news from them of the battles. He packed a sack of dried grains, and ten loaves of bread for his sons, then he instructed David to: "Carry these ten cheeses to the captain of their thousand, and see how your brothers[14] fare, and bring back news of them."[15] David immediately and responsibly made arrangements with one of his brothers, or a neighbor to act as the keeper of the sheep,[16] while he was on this errand. He arose early the next morning, took the food and was on his way just as Jesse had directed him.

The battle had moved to the Shephelah region, near the village of Shochoh, and specifically, in the Valley of Elah. The tension between the two forces had become quite intense. As David arrived with supplies of food from the family table and word from home, the greetings between David and his brothers were interrupted by the bellowing voice of the giant in the valley below.[17] It would have been good for David, Eliab, Abinadab and Shimea[18] to have had more time to engage in family banter, but it was not to be, as David was on site with these men, for deeper and more profound reasons than just to carry news and supplies from Jesse.

The last forty days had been discouraging days, as the army of Saul had stagnated on this mountain side, being kept there by the threatening presence of their enemies. There had been no movement, and no progress, leaving the result to be forty days without hope of victory. The Philistines had advanced into Judah and captured Shochoh. The Israelites had settled on one mountain facing the Valley of Elah.[19] The Philistines were positioned on the opposite mountain.

David arrived at the camp just as the army was moving into battle formation, while shouting the war cry.[20] Apparently, these men all hoped something had changed during the night. Israel and the Philistines moved into position, facing each other, battle-ready, howbeit from their respective mountains. David left his bundles of food in the care of a sentry, ran to the troops who were deployed, and greeted his brothers.

DAVID HAD "FRESH EYES" TO LOOK AT HOW TO WIN THIS BATTLE.

Just then, one of the Philistines by the name of Goliath, a renowned champion of great stature, for the eightieth time (twice a day for the last forty days) challenged Israel to send out one man who could save Israel's reputation, in a one on one fight. "Goliath stood there and called out to the Israelite troops, 'Why bother using your whole army? Am I not Philistine enough for you? And you're all committed to Saul, aren't you? So, pick your best fighter and pit him against me. If he gets the upper hand and kills me, the Philistines will all become your slaves. But if I get the upper hand and kill him, you'll all become our slaves and serve us. I challenge the troops of Israel this day. Give me a man. Let us fight it out together!'"[21]

There is some dispute over the actual height of Goliath. Primarily, we know that he was a giant, and giants were best known to be aberrant (or at least huge), since their size is not statistically normal. It is clear that David was, as some have said, as short as 5.5 feet tall seeing that he had not grown to full height,[22] and King Saul was likely over 6 feet tall, being head and shoulders taller than other Hebrews.[23] We also know that the giants throughout the Old Testament were known to often be in excess of 8 feet tall, and some even taller. It is also clear that Goliath was extreme in areas of his bulk and strength, especially when we see the details regarding his breastplate, shield, and spear. The weight and size of a spear, or javelin, for the average soldier was only about 2-4 pounds.[24]

> The weight and size of Goliath's weapons and protective gear:
>
> Bronze helmet and a breastplate, which weighed 125 pounds. (57 kg) The shaft of his spear was as heavy and thick as a weaver's beam,[25] and was tipped with an iron spearhead that weighed 15 pounds (7 kg). "A soldier always walked in front of Goliath to carry his shield."[26]

We would agree that the story of David and Goliath reflects on Goliath's "giant status." What seems more significant to me is how Goliath was "a champion" and a "man of war, from his youth."[27] Goliath was certainly more experienced at warring than was David, who was called, a "stripling"[28] by King Saul, and who also referred to David's youth as being, "raw youth."[29]

Throughout the Old Testament there were men who were called giants. We also read that Israel was filled with fear that the people of Canaan were larger than the Hebrews and reported, "we see ourselves as grasshoppers as we look at them."[30]

> "Caleb called for silence before Moses and said, 'Let's go up and take the land—now. We can do it.' But the others said, 'We can't attack those people; they're way stronger than we are.' They spread scary rumors among the People of Israel. They said, 'We

scouted out the land from one end to the other—it's a land that swallows people whole. Everybody we saw was huge. Why, we even saw the Nephilim giants (the Anak giants come from the Nephilim). Alongside them we felt like grasshoppers. And they looked down on us, as if we were grasshoppers.'"[31]

It was easy for the men of Israel to be intimidated by giants. They felt small because the opposition towered over them and bellowed louder than them. They did not take into account who they were fighting for, and that God would give them an edge that their enemy could never have.

In addition to Goliath's being a giant, it is stated that Goliath was six cubits and a span tall,[32] and a "man of vast bulk, and had about him weapons suitable to the largeness of his body, for he wore a breastplate that weighed five thousand shekels."[33] After forty days of Goliath's harassment, Saul's army had become terrified.[34]

David's brothers, King Saul and all who were at the Valley of Elah that day, and for the last forty days had heard the arrogant rantings of this giant and now, once again, Goliath waited in the valley below in plain sight of both armies, issuing threats and cursing Israel, its king and its God. It was obvious that no one was courageous enough to come down to fight Goliath.[35]

What is the reward for the man who slays this giant?

David turned to those in earshot and exclaimed, "What will a man get for killing this Philistine and ending his defiance of Israel? Who is this pagan Philistine anyway, that he is allowed to defy the armies of the living God?"[36] The soldiers answered David saying, "The king has offered a huge reward to anyone who kills him. He will give that man one of his daughters for a wife, and the man's entire family will be exempted from paying taxes!"[37] David's response came as a shock to his brothers and all those who heard him, "I am ready to fight a single combat with this adversary."[38]

David's oldest brother, Eliab, immediately reproved him, scolding him for speaking too rashly and improperly for being such a young man. Rather, Eliab continued, "you really should leave the fighting to us and go back to your flocks and to our father." Eliab did his best to shame his younger brother, saying, "Why did you come down here? And with whom have you left those few sheep in the wilderness? I know your pride and the insolence of your heart, for you have come down to see the battle."[39]

As David walked away, other soldiers had overheard his comments, of how he would gladly fight with this giant.[40] David's words traveled quickly to the ears of Saul. It must be noted that none of Saul's men had, over the last forty days, taken up the gauntlet,[41] which Goliath had thrown down. Every one of them had their ears open, just in case any soldier boasted too much or expressed how glad he would be to take on the adversary. When David was overheard saying, "I'm ready to defeat this man who defies the Lord and His armies," they knew they must inform the king. Someone had to step up and end this stalemate. Quickly David was ushered in before Saul.

ELIAB WAS NOT ANY DIFFERENT TO MOST OLDER BROTHERS. QUITE PROTECTIVE AND FULL OF ADVICE.

Saul was in a stupor, being depleted of energy and hope. It is not even clear if Saul bothered to leave his tent, on those times when Goliath challenged Israel. He seemed to stay in his tent and wait. When Saul had heard that a man wanted to take on the giant he had been hopeful, but when David walked in, and he realized that all he had before him was David, a young man, a musician, a worshipper, who was too slight of build to do a lot of damage to a strapping tall and huge man like Goliath; his countenance fell. Saul had appreciated the manner of David's gift of playing the harp. It was always a comfort to him when this young man took up his instrument and drove the darkness from him. But that was one thing, and to take on an adversary like Goliath would require much more than this artsy, and intuitive dreamer could give.

This king had opinions of David, which confined him to a more restricted role, barring him from consideration in this present circumstance. After all, this was partly why he had sent David home to his father in the first place. This was the battlefield and these were times that require the best of any man. He saw David as young, and certainly not a man of war. He had heard David play songs of warfare, even "spiritual warfare," but to think that David could sing of faith and that translate into his becoming a warrior, in the real world, might be too much of a stretch for an old warrior like Saul.

In Saul's world, men like David didn't have their feet on the ground enough to even speak to Goliath, much less take him down.[42] It was clear to Saul, that David was no match for this fight. While Saul sat, and looked up at David, he thought, "if I were standing, I'd be looking down at this young man." He thought things like: "If David were just taller, or weighed more, if he were older; he could not imagine him standing before that lumbering hulk of a man out there in the Valley of Elah. If I sent David where he wants to go, all of Israel would be the laughing stock of both sides of the valley. David would never meet Saul's standards. It is a fact that "man looks on the outward appearance, and don't forget it."[43]

David jolted Saul out of his stupor: "Don't worry about this Philistine. I'll go fight him!" Saul then replied, "Don't be ridiculous."[44] "You're too young and inexperienced, and he's been at this fighting business since before you were born."[45]

David was first a Warrior in the Spirit; then a "Man's-man warrior."[46]

Few realize a hidden quality, which is present in those who are worshippers, like David. They may not look like they have the spine of a man of war, but when the Holy Spirit works in their hearts, they will be transformed into men of war on the inside. That will always make the difference. It could even be said that, "big things often come in small packages."[47]

David looked back at Saul and told him a story, "I've been a shepherd, watching the sheep for my father. I may look small to you, but I really can hold my own when it comes to facing troubles. I am ready to go into battle, in dependence on God being with me, for I have had experience already of his assistance, for I once pursued after and caught a lion that assaulted my flocks, and took away a lamb from them, and I snatched the lamb out of the wild beast's mouth…"[48] "… and when it rose up against me, I seized it by its whiskers and struck and killed it. Your servant has killed both the lion and the bear; and this uncircumcised Philistine will be like one of them, since he has taunted and defied the armies of the living God."[49]

"I will fight with Goliath and will bring him down, as tall and as great as he is, I will bring him down, till he shall be sufficiently laughed at.[50] Your army shall get great glory after Goliath is slain, by a man like me, who is not seen as a full-grown man, and not fit for fighting."[51] Our enemies may not see me as a man, and certainly not an elder. Give me the chance and you'll see that, "the Lord that delivered me out of the paw of the lion and out of the paw of the bear; He will deliver me out of the hand of this Philistine."[52]

Saul was finally okay with David going to war.

Finally, Saul became convinced and said to David, "Go, and the Lord be with you!"[53] He then said to David, "before you go, I'd like to suggest that you use some of my choice tools of war. I find that, when I use them I am protected and able to do better." He then strapped onto David his own breastplate; then his sword;[54] and fitted his helmet to his head. He then attempted to send David away, having prepared him for battle, outfitted for war. It was meant as a compliment to see how King Saul was insistent that David have the best advantage by using the King's weapons. This was not a small thing, when Saul volunteered his own equipment. David had become somewhat precious to the King, as he had been helpful during his dark moments, by playing the harp and singing. He did not want David to become a casualty of war. Still, Saul did not understand what was really going on here. David understood something the King did not grasp. It is also worthy of note that when King Saul volunteered to give David the use of his sword, he was entrusting him with one of the only iron swords in the land. Only the King and his son, Jonathan, had swords of iron. None of the Israelite soldiers had a sword like this, but only Saul and Jonathan. David knew that he would have the unfair disadvantage by going into the battle without that sword, but he had elected to put his trust in God, rather than weapons of a natural man of war. It would have been almost comical for David to have walked out wearing this equipment; almost like a boy donning his dad's work-clothes. Imagine this: the legs too long, the hat too big and the sleeves hanging down an extra 10 inches.

David tried to move about wearing Saul's armor, but realized immediately that it was not helpful, but rather burdensome, for he had no experience fighting in this way. He had never walked with this armor and found it cumbersome to move freely.

The reality was that the weapons of Saul were good, but they had never been used to bring down a giant before. God wanted to do a new thing and the old ways would not work for him. It is likely that David thought back to the prophetic words of Samuel and how his victories would be assured?[55]

David then said to the King, "Please keep your armor for yourself, for you are able to bear it; but give me the freedom to fight as your servant, and as I desire. Accordingly, David laid Saul's armor aside…"[56]

The battle was now about to become exciting for the troops, for there was movement and for the first time in over a month. With David as the responding challenger to Goliath, it did not look promising for Israel, and the Philistines were certainly in for a surprise. David's entry into the Valley of Elah was unexpected and quite different to what was customary.

David did not gather the troops to cheer him on and he did not wear the normal military hardware. Even his approach was unpredictable, as he sprung from the brook, which was off to one side of the valley. It almost appeared to Goliath that David had jumped into the fray on his own. A lot was at stake. If David's idea of victory was delusional then Israel could be defeated by his overconfidence. On the other hand, if he could bring the big guy down, then it was a fantastic thing. Either way, for these impatient soldiers, it was better than spending another month with a one-sided conversation.

After his latest rant, Goliath, had not returned to his camp, but had lingered, waiting for Israel's response to his boisterous demands. Just when he would have, in disgust, returned to his side of the battlefield, he caught sight of movement in the grass. He could see a youngish looking lad sprinting out onto the field. At first, he thought that this was a youngster who had lost his way. Goliath stepped forward and looked more closely at David, almost passing up his own armor-bearer, who was out in front of him, and carrying his shield.[57] "He took one look down on him and sneered—a mere youngster, apple-cheeked and peach-fuzzed."[58]

David had taken his staff in his hand, then veered off to one side of the valley, so that his steps would bring him near to the brook. He then selected "five smooth stones from the brook, and put them in a shepherd's bag, in a pouch, which he had, and his sling was in his hand. And he drew near to the Philistine."[59]

Over the next few moments Goliath felt the greatest humiliation of his military career. He surmised that David was ill-equipped for serious battle, and was treating this battle with the same urgency, as if he were chasing away unwanted dogs. In the heart of a warrior, like Goliath, this was a colossal embarrassment. This raised his level of fury with Saul and all the Israelites. They obviously did not grasp what damage this defeat would bring to them, and he was now going to show them what he could do to this skinny kid.

He was convinced that Saul had sent David out to mock and belittle him. He saw himself as a serious contender for his nation. He viewed David as a visitor to the field of battle and resented the very idea. He felt that this whole thing was a charade and deep disdain entered his heart. Goliath roared, "Do you take me, not for a man, but a dog? You have not come as if to a fight, but as if you are here to chase away a dog." David came back to him by yelling, "No, not for a dog, but for a creature worse than a dog." This provoked Goliath to anger. Goliath roared back at him, "Am I a dog, that you come at me with a stick?" And he cursed David by the names of his gods.[44] "Come over here, and I'll give your flesh to the birds and wild animals!"[60]

David responded to Goliath: "You've come out to fight me with a sword and a spear"[61] and a breastplate, "but I have God for my armor in coming against you."[62] "I've come out to fight you in the name of the Lord All-Powerful. He is the God of Israel's army, and you have insulted him too! Today the Lord will help me defeat you. I'll knock you down,"[63] "cut off your head, and feed the rest of your body to the dogs."[64] I'll feed the bodies of the other Philistine soldiers to the birds and wild animals. Then the whole world will know that Israel has a real God. Everybody here will see that the Lord doesn't need swords or spears to save his people. The Lord always wins his battles, and he will help us defeat you."[65]

Throughout history, Israel has had other such struggles; for example, during the "Six Day War" (June 5-June 10, 1967) the war between Israel and Egypt, was much like this story found here in I Samuel 17. During the first week of June 1967, I read an interesting comment in my home town newspaper. They quoted Israel's Defense minister, Moshe Dayan. These are his words, which I remember reading: "Egypt comes to this battle with its weapons of war, but we, Israel, come in the name of the Lord and we shall win this fight."[66]

David's descent to the floor of the Valley of Elah evoked a spirit of conflict like nothing over the last few weeks. Each day Goliath had challenged Israel, but that had been from where he stood in the middle of the Valley. Israel had not come down from their vantage point, or moved toward him, because they did not know how they should respond to his words. However, this challenge by David had created an electricity in the air. Although no one had any idea of the outcome, they knew that today would bring about closure of some kind. They moved into position so that David would be given backup, and not be left alone. Perhaps God would smile upon His people and Goliath would fall. Likewise, the Philistines gathered a short distance behind their champion. All were ready for this drawn out offensive to be over and finished.

CONVENTIONAL WISDOM IS BAFFLED WHEN THE LITTLE GUY WINS OVER THE BIGGER GUY.

David continued his debate with Goliath, but from a distance. Goliath had claimed ownership of this battlefield and was incensed that this young man should be trespassing there. David made it clear that his trust was solely in the Lord his God. It was God who would give him the edge, and not a sword, or a javelin. Goliath was big, but God was bigger. David's trust was in God's sufficiency. God was his protector and without God no warlike preparations were enough. Before this battle even began, God was already winning for David. He said, "all men shall learn that God is the protector of the Hebrews, and that our armor and our strength is in his providence; and that without God's assistance all other warlike preparations and power are useless."[67]

Running to the heat of the battle.

David began running with haste toward Goliath, who responded by running toward David. However, it was evident that David was light of foot and erratic in his movements, while Goliath was overburdened by the sheer weight of all that he was carrying. This created a clear advantage for the young man. The harder Goliath ran the angrier he grew at his opponent. As confident as he was of victory, Goliath was put off-guard by the pressure of resentment he was feeling.[68]

David reached into his shepherd's bag and withdrew one of the five smooth stones[69] he'd selected from the brook. He now placed it snugly into the wide part of his sling, so that he could swing it over his head as he continued to run.[70] David thought, "God is with me and He will take this stone to its mark, just as he did with every wild animal I have ever faced." At the next instant, he felt he was close enough to drive the stone hard into the exposed part of Goliath's armor, his forehead. He released it and sure enough the stone went with speed and accuracy, hitting the center of the giant's forehead and "sank into his brain, insomuch that Goliath was stunned, and fell upon his face." David ran and stepped up onto Goliath's body, then pulled Goliath's sword from its sheath, and cut off his head. David had no sword, until he picked up Goliath's sword.[71] "David had triumphed over the Philistine with only a sling and a stone, for he had no sword."[72]

The army of Philistines looked on in total disbelief. They had such confidence that Goliath would win this battle, and yet there had been a total routing of their giant. It was unbelievable. By the time they came to their senses, they were awakened out of their daze by the sound of the advancing Israelites all shouting and running towards them in a full attack. It took them by surprise and so they fled in abject fear. These men were running, but not fast enough, for Saul's army caught them, slew them and injured many. In the end, it was said that 30,000 Philistines were slain and twice that were injured, leading all the way to Gath and even to the gates of Ekron. They came back through the enemy's camp and looted it and burned it to the ground.

Abner, Saul's general, dispatched one of his men to go to the scene of the battle and assist David in carrying his rightful spoils back to his tent; after all there were heavy objects to carry and too many for one man, especially one as slight of build as David. David began to collect Goliath's coat of mail (a garment of metal scales, which was worn as armor), greaves of brass (armor to cover his shins), helmet of brass, spear or javelin, shield and sword.[73] This weaponry would have weighed almost 200 pounds (90 kg). David needed help carrying these items. He deposited them in his tent for safekeeping. David put all of Goliath's armor -- coat of mail, helmet of brass, greaves of brass, target of brass, spear, shield and sword – in his tent.[74] They were part of David's spoil and a memorial to God's mercy and faithfulness.[75]

David carried around his trophy, the head of Goliath.

The rest of the day, David carried around the head of Goliath, as proof of his victory. This scene was one to catch the ire of anyone who had bias in their heart against this rising star. This musician was now more than a musician or a minstrel; he was truly a "man of war," with a developing presence to be reckoned with. God had activated a sure anointing in David's life and he would no longer be relegated to remote places, but to the arenas of public discourse. Such is the discovery in the life of any man or woman, who is willing to give God a chance, allowing Him to activate the Holy Spirit within.

THE BIG QUESTION: IS DAVID A MINSTREL OR A WARRIOR?

David was, all at once, the subject of conversations in everyone's mind. Even Saul and his general, Abner, had a conversation about him, and were in the process of re-evaluating just who he really was. Was David a minstrel or a warrior? Was he weak or strong?

Both Abner and Saul had been caught off guard by this victory. They were still trying to work out in their minds, just who had been serving at Saul's palace as a minstrel. There seems to be much more to David than met the eyes. Saul had been so self-absorbed that he had not bothered to ask enough questions or listen to what David had said. Saul was not a good conversationalist, and thus had never allowed what David said to sink into his memory. We know that he was aware of who David's father was, but we see him asking Abner, even the most basic of questions about David. Neither Saul nor Abner knew the answers to these questions; so, David was summoned to come to the tent of Saul.

There David stood, in the door of King Saul's tent, with a fistful of hair in his hand. Hanging down from that handful of hair, was the huge head of Goliath. It was not a scene the squeamish[76] would like to see, but it certainly did reveal that this man of war had had a busy day. It must have been a sight to see, even for Abner, the leader of Saul's Army. Abner had never seen such a sight, where an average height, 17 years old youth was carrying around such a trophy as the head of a giant man.[77]

Saul began his comments to David, by asking, "Tell me about your father, young man."[78] Clearly, this young man could not be fully appreciated until he had described who his father was. Until the age when a young man becomes recognized in his own rite as a man, he is defined as "the son of," and David was clearly not there yet. If this king is to understand who is standing before him, then he must first understand who Jesse is. Somewhere back in David's life, someone had made a significant deposit in him, so that he had become a powerful young man of drive and character. In Saul's world, it must have been Jesse. What this king did not know was that David had struck out, long ago on his own path, and in his own search to "know God" personally. He had drawn hard fast conclusions that God was "big enough" and "strong enough" to win every battle and succeed in every war. Now this young man had decided to lead others to their own stronger faith. Because of the call of God at work in his life, he was continuing down the road of eliminating every obstacle, which would posture itself as an enemy of God. David's first giants had been from the animal kingdom, a lion and a bear. Next had come the giants of the nations, in first dealing with Goliath. Then would come Philistia itself, as he saw Goliath only as a symptom and not the whole army. His words were prophetic, as he would later face off and totally defeat those who were the nation of the Philistines. Saul would learn details about David on that day, but more understanding would come in time.

How was this a "Heart Revealing Day" in the life of David?

David faithfully followed his father's instructions to take supplies to his brothers at the battle front. His faith in God was such that he was always looking around to see how he could glorify God with his strength, and with his very life.

Within was a strong commitment to be of use to God on a daily basis. As he entered the camp, he had the inner sense that he was always on some kind of Godly assignment. Although he had no idea of how God would use him that day, he always kept his ears open and his eyes alert, to keep a grasp of what was going on around him. David's youth was to his advantage, because he was always full of energy and ready for action. The culture, the environment and all that went on around a man in the early days of the kingdom of Israel were enough to challenge any young man, yet one filled so full of faith and courage made this a very special opportunity.

We see David's heart best when we pick up his interest in the speech being given by the giant, Goliath, in the valley just over the rise, from Saul's camp. David was surprised first of all to hear such a raging challenge, and next that no one in all of Saul's army had stepped up to defend God's honor. David suddenly felt the rumblings of courage rising up within himself. This prepared him to make an immediate response to speak up, then step up and finally to launch out to deal with this raging lunatic. That is just how David saw him, because he saw no man as making justifiable claims against God.

This chapter does show us the heart commitment in David to be a witness for God in a godless world.

Endnotes

1. Romans 8:9 PHILLIPS
2. www.merriam-webster.com/dictionary/promotion - promotion - "the act of moving someone to a higher or more important position or rank"
3. I Samuel 16:13-14 NLT
4. I Samuel 16:14 TLB
5. I Samuel 16:14 KJV
6. Genesis 1:3-5
7. www.idioms.thefreedictionary.com/light+at+the+end+of+the+tunnel - Light at the end of the tunnel. "Something which makes you believe that a difficult or unpleasant situation will end."
8. I Samuel 16:15 NLT
9. I Samuel 16:18 MSG
10. I Samuel 16:19 NLT
11. www.merriam-webster.com/dictionary/adjutant - adjutant/armor bearer - an army officer who helps the commanding officer and is responsible for written communications.
12. www.biblehub.com/commentaries/1_samuel/17-5.htm - Keil and Delitzsch Biblical Commentary on the Old Testament.
13. An example of this is found in: I Chronicles 20:1-3. Apparently, everyone had cabin fever and springtime proved a good time to go and deal with national and cross the border concerns. It appears that, in the model of governing styles of that day, governmental situations were not responded to when issues arose, but after much thought and strategizing took place. At that point in time, kings would take their armies out to settle scores, or offenses.
14. Notice that only three of his brothers (Eliab, Abinadab and Shimea) had gone to war, alongside of Saul's army, leaving David at home with Jesse and his other three sons, Nethanel, Raddai and Ozem.
15. I Samuel 17:18 NKJV
16. I Samuel 17:20
17. I Samuel 17:23
18. I Chronicles 2:13-15 MSG - I Samuel 17:14 "And the three eldest followed Saul." Clearly it states in I Chronicles 2:13-15 MSG the following: "Jesse's firstborn was Eliab, followed by Abinadab, Shimea, Nethanel, Raddai, Ozem, and finally David; David was the seventh."

19. www.biblewalks.com/sites/elahValley - "The valley of Elah is a triangle shaped flat valley, located on the western edge of Judah's low hills... This valley was an important corridor from the coast cities, up to the center of the land of Judah and its cities – Bethlehem, Hebron and Jerusalem."
20. I Samuel 17:20 AMP
21. I Samuel 17:8-10 MSG
22. www.etsjets.org/files/JETS-PDFs/50/50-3/JETS_50-3_489-508_Billington.pdf - "Goliath and the Exodus Giants: How tall were they?" By Clyde E. Billington
23. I Samuel 9:1-2
24. www.en.wikipedia.org/wiki/Dory_(spear) - The Javelin in ancient Greece. "The dory or doru, is a spear that was the chief armament of hoplites (heavy infantry) in Ancient Greece. The Dory (or spear) was about 7 to 9 feet in length and had a handle with a diameter of 5 cm (two inches) made of wood, either cornel or ash weighing 2 to 4 lb. The flat leaf-shaped spearhead was composed of iron and its weight was counterbalanced by a bronze butt-spike."
25. www.answers.yahoo.com/question/index?qid=20110915200609AAQhVqL - Weaver's Beam - It's a cylindrical wooden rod that makes up part of a loom...it looks like the standard size is about 2 and a half inches in diameter and variable length. Considering Goliath is about ten, maybe eleven feet tall in the OT, it wouldn't be outlandish to assume that his spear is about seven feet long, plus or minus a couple feet.
26. I Samuel 17:7 CEV
27. I Samuel 17:33 KJV
28. I Samuel 17:56 KJV
29. I Samuel 17:56 MSG
30. Numbers 13:33 NLT - "We even saw giants there, the descendants of Anak. Next to them we felt like grasshoppers, and that's what they thought, too!"
31. Numbers 13:28-33 MSG
32. I Samuel 17:4 KJV
33. Josephus, Book 6, Chapter 9:1:171
34. Josephus, Book 6, Chapter 9:1:174
35. Josephus, Book 6, Chapter 9:2:177
36. I Samuel 17:25-26 NLT
37. I Samuel 17:25 NLT
38. Josephus, Book 6, Chapter 9:2:177

39. I Samuel 17:28 NKJV

40. Josephus, Book 6, Chapter 9:2:178

41. www.idioms.thefreedictionary.com/throw+down+the+gauntlet - This expression alludes to the medieval practice of a knight throwing down his gauntlet, or metal glove, as a challenge to combat. Its figurative use dates from the second half of the 1700s, as does the less frequently heard take up the gauntlet, for accepting a challenge.

42. Josephus, Book 6, Chapter 9:2:179

43. Pastor Ron Willhite, Roswell, Georgia, USA - Ron responded to the famous line, "Man looks on the outward appearance, but God looks on the heart" by reflecting on the idea that: "Man looks on the outward appearance … and don't you forget it."

44. I Samuel 17:32-33 NLT

45. I Samuel 17:33 MSG

46. www.merriam-webster.com/dictionary/man's%20man - "Man's Man. A man noted or admired for traditionally masculine interests and activities."

47. www.en.wiktionary.org/wiki/big_things_come_in_small_packages - Things should not be underestimated because of their size.

48. Josephus, Book 6, Chapter 9:3:182

49. I Samuel 17:35-36 AMP

50. George Mueller, in one of his sermons made this statement: "Faith does not operate in the realm of the possible. There is no glory for God in that which man can do. Faith begins where man's power ends."

51. Josephus, Book 6, Chapter 9:2:179-180

52. I Samuel 17:37 AMP

53. I Samuel 17:37 NKJV

54. I Samuel 13:19-22 MSG - "There wasn't a blacksmith to be found anywhere in Israel. The Philistines made sure of that, "Lest those Hebrews start making swords and spears." That meant that the Israelites had to go down among the Philistines to keep their farm tools—plowshares and mattocks, axes and sickles—sharp and in good repair. They charged a silver coin for the plowshares and mattocks, and half that for the rest. So, when the battle of Micmash was joined, there wasn't a sword or spear to be found anywhere in Israel—except for Saul and his son Jonathan; they were both well-armed."

55. Josephus, Book 6, Chapter 8:1:165

56. Josephus, Book 6, Chapter 9:4:184-185

57. I Samuel 17:41

58. I Samuel 17:42 MSG

59. I Samuel 17:40 NKJV

60. I Samuel 17:43-44 NLT

61. I Samuel 17:45

62. Josephus, Book 6, Chapter 9:4:187

63. I Samuel 17:45-46 CEV

64. Josephus, Book 6, Chapter 9:4:187

65. I Samuel 17:45-47 CEV

66. I read these words in the Herald Courier Newspaper, Bristol, Tennessee-Virginia. I was employed at that time by the Herald Courier Newspaper. The story was occupying that news cycle, on June 4, 1967. I cannot verify his exact quote, but this is essentially what Dayan said, and I remember it well. I read the quoted words printed by Israel's Defense Minister. At that moment, I just closed the newspaper. I heard my heart say, "Well, this war is over, even before it begins." History records that it took only six days to utterly defeat the Egyptian military that week.

67. Josephus, Book 6, Chapter 9:4:187

68. ibid

69. www.gotquestions.org/five-smooth-stones.html ~ Question: "Why did David choose five smooth stones before going to fight Goliath? Was David doubting God? Was it because Goliath had five brothers? Or, was David simply being prepared?" This essay is worth the read.

70. I Samuel 17:49

71. Josephus, Book 6, Chapter 9:5:189-190

72. I Samuel 17:50 NLT

73. Refer to the ADDENDUM in the back of the book to learn more about "The secrets of Smelting Iron."

74. I Samuel 17:54

75. I Samuel 30:20

76. www.merriam-webster.com ~ squeamish ~ "easily shocked, offended, or disgusted by unpleasant things" ~ i.e. those who are easily sickened or disgusted.

77. wwww.deeperlifemilwaukee.org/wp-content/.../THE_SWORD_OF_GOLIATH.doc

78. I Samuel 17:57-58 NLT

The Day David's Heart Smote Him

I Samuel 18

The battle at the Valley of Elah was over, Goliath was dead, the Philistines had been routed and now everyone had transitioned back to their own homelands. After all that had transpired on the battlefield, things had begun to settle down and take on their normality, thus becoming a part of the local cultures and conversations.

David was no longer just a minstrel, but amazingly overnight, had become a legendary figure in the psyche of all the people. Everyone was talking, both privately and in the public forum. Something about David, had become almost mythological in the mind of King Saul. The favor of the Lord and of all the people came naturally to him during those days. He was not only held in high respect among the people, but also officially within the military. Clearly the favor of the Lord catapulted him to prominence throughout the land. David was quickly becoming a hero of the people and this was a good thing for David, but not in the mind of Israel's king.

Saul began to loathe David, so much that he saw David, not for the benefit he represented as a military asset against the Philistines, but as a possible contender for the throne he himself occupied. In the mind of Saul, David represented his "sum of all fears."[1] Saul was determined to cripple or sabotage David's future.

The King had made promises and pledges to "whomever would face the giant,"[2] but then had reneged on his commitments to this young warrior. He resented the favor all the people had felt in their grass-roots heart of hearts and finally declared that David was "personae non-grata."[3]

If you could have heard the people talk of him in their homes, in their circles of friends, and even on the streets, you would have been convinced that there was a developing romance with this young warrior. This was a high-risk game for David, but he did nothing to stoke the fires of the people's love for him. What made it all so volatile was just one thing: the mental and emotional instability of King Saul.

Soon the climate became infused with rumors, tales and songs, which all spoke of exploits both real and imagined, of David, the young "shepherd warrior." They had heard about his exploits with the lion, the bear and Goliath. This only made the "romanticism" more rich and exciting. No one was more incensed with this upsurge of sensationalism than the king himself. Quite understandably so, the women of Israel unwittingly helped in the matter of this envy and hatred in the heart of the King. It was widely reported that the women of Israel would meet the King and his victorious army with cymbals and drums and all demonstrations of joy, by singing.

The wives would give the call:

"Saul has slain his many thousands of Philistines."

Then the young virgins would give the response:

"… and David has slain his tens of thousands."[4]

This display of fanfare upset Saul and he became very angry. He thought, "The women give David credit for killing tens of thousands of the enemy, and they give me credit for only thousands. A little more of this and they will give him the kingdom itself! So, from that time on, Saul watched David very closely."[5]

Saul began to think about some of his experiences with regard to the crown, and now comes this new and still very young warrior. There had been a time when Saul had gone through a problematic meeting with the Prophet Samuel. On that occasion, he and Samuel had exchanged words. What Saul remembered most were the words that came forcefully out of the mouth of the prophet: "your kingly rule is falling to pieces,[6] and all because of your disobedience, for the Lord has sought out a man after his own heart. The Lord has already appointed him to be the leader of his people, because you have not kept the Lord's command."[7]

WHEN THE WOMEN SANG OF DAVID, SAUL LOST HIS JOY, AND BECAME JEALOUS.

His next thoughts were along the lines of, "could this be the man who will replace me on the throne?" Later, in serious confrontations, Saul will admit to David that he realizes that he will assume the crown after he is gone. Saul had said to David, "I realize that you are surely going to be king, and that the kingdom of Israel will flourish under your rule."[8] For some reason, this reality hit Saul hard and he did not have the grace in his nature to accept it; not now, and perhaps not ever.

Saul became worried over the popularity of this young warrior.

Eventually, Saul was overwhelmed with jealousy and paranoia; so much that David became more and more alienated, causing him, out of necessity, to flee from his place of military prominence in Saul's government and even the royal family. Saul was vexed by David's very presence and agitated by the divine favor, which was clearly at work in his life.

Israel was not really a very large nation, so David employed a lot of effort, in his determination to stay out of Saul's way, while still, for a long time, remaining within the national boundaries.

The days turned into weeks, then months and finally, an urgency prevailed in the lives of David's men, as they realized that the climate was moving from dangerous, to lethal.

The mood over Israel began to change.

David found himself in a dilemma, which grew more toxic by the day. There were close range encounters, and then, as David had fled from Saul's house, more encounters from a distance. Repeatedly, the king threatened David and his very life. Folklore and legends continued to build in the hearts and minds of the people of the land. Most of those tales and stories of David were true, but many were embellished slightly, as is always the case with legends. As a result, David's safety, and that of anyone close to him was more and more at risk. It became evident that God was with David and protected him against those who would bring harm to him. The crown would come to David, so he remained patient to allow God to do it in His own time; after all, David was still only in his early twenties.

David could see the patterns growing in Saul's conduct and concluded that he could not trust that Saul would continue to follow through on his promises to withdraw from pursuing him. Repeatedly, Saul would strike and then recoil, admitting that he had done David wrong. Basically, the king was now more and more unstable, but only God could sort out the problem, and the time for that had not yet come. As time had passed, the king no longer had his minstrel. God had promoted that minstrel, David, into a national spotlight and Saul was left to the demons that invaded his thoughts throughout the days and nights. There was no relief for him.

SAUL WAS WITHOUT A MINSTREL ~ NOW WAS WHEN HE REALLY NEEDED HIM MOST.

Saul went on a killing spree and nothing was sacred to him.

Ahimelech, the priest, had been entrusted the sword of Goliath, for safekeeping. As David fled from the face of Saul, he had found his way alone to Nob, where Ahimelech was serving. During his time there, Ahimelech had given the sword of Goliath back to David, as he had no weapon. Ahimelech, rationalized that the sword actually belonged to David in the first place, and he had been the one who had given it, actually on loan, to this house of God, just as a museum is the recipient of a precious treasure from a benevolent philanthropist. In reaction to this, Saul had accused these priests of treason, and commanded that Ahimelech and eighty-five other priests be slain by the evil Edomite, by the name of Doeg.[9]

What is it like to visit the cave of Adullam?

All caves are not equal. Ask anyone who has been involved with spelunking. The cave of Adullam was unique from many other caves. This one was a serious cave, but not as large as is generally considered a cavern.

The cave of Adullam has been described as a serious cave, much larger than many others. It sits not far from the Valley of Rephaim, and the Valley of Elah, piercing into the side of a hill which rises about 500 feet (150 meters). It is not the only cave in the region, but just one of many. It seems nondescript and easy to miss. It seems apparent that David was drawn to it for a number of reasons.

Friends of mine were taken to this cave several years ago by a former Israeli paratrooper who was serving as their tour guide. My friend, Mark Holcomb, describes his experience at the Cave of Adullam in this way:

> To find the cave, we had to make a treacherous climb from the valley below, up the side of this mountainous area. Upon arriving at the entrance, we could see that it was shaped somewhat like an egg, being about a meter wide and perhaps 3 meters tall. The first thing that struck me was how it was heavily covered with spider webs. It seemed clear to me that no one had entered it for a very long time. The guide took a stick and removed the spider webs so we could enter the cave.
>
> The first thing we saw as we entered was a millstone, which was a little more than a meter in width. At first glance, it would appear that whoever had carved out this millstone had not carried it up and into the cave, but had carved it from the nearby walls of the cave.

We moved around in the cave, exploring the three rooms which increased in size the farther we walked. Some of the ceilings were more than enough in height to raise your hands and even touch the ceiling, while others were not so high. Still there was ample room to accommodate several hundred people if they should choose to camp out there. I would describe it as a "great cave and almost a cavern." When I asked my friend if David's 400 men could have lived there on occasion, he responded, "Yes, I would think so, as well as some of their families."

We had been inside the cave for about thirty minutes when the guide directed us back toward the entrance. He then alerted us that we should look back at how the entrance was now just as heavily covered with spider webs, yet it had only been 20-30 minutes since we had entered. I was amazed at what the guide said about that particular species of spider. He told how Arachnologists (those who study spiders) have determined that this species is actually unique to the area.

This inspired us about how God protected David and his friends, keeping Saul from suspecting that anyone had entered that cave in a very long time.

In considering this cave, it appears to me and to my friend, that God had chosen this cave and that unique spider, from the very beginning of time, to give David protection.

The cave of Adullam became David's stronghold.

David "escaped to the cave of Adullam. His family also became concerned for their own safety and decided that only David, who had his own army, could provide the protection they needed. They saw no other option, but for David's entire family, including his parents, his brothers, and even others who were a part of the extended family, to just show up at the Cave Adullam, asking for asylum.[10] So many other men came, bringing their families.[11] They saw themselves as being in trouble, and vulnerable. These men were in distress, in debt and discontent. They were strong men but came to a place where they felt a need to align with a leader who could become an umbrella over them for their own sakes, and that of their families. Saul would consider them as rogues, but they saw themselves as doing the wise thing to guarantee their own survival.

David made a decision and went to Mizpeh in Moab, where he appealed to the king, "Please allow my father and mother to live here with you until I know what God is going to do for me." So David's parents stayed in Moab with the king during the entire time David was living in his stronghold.

THE KING OF MOAB WAS HAPPY TO HOST DAVID'S PARENTS ~ AFTER ALL HE PREFERRED DAVID OVER SAUL.

There came a point in Saul's search for David that he was so close that he "and David were actually on opposite sides of the same mountain."[12] The Lord, however was on David's side, always giving a way of escape for him. On this occasion "an urgent message reached Saul, that the Philistines were raiding Israel, yet again. So, Saul quit chasing David,"[13] and led his troops to the new battle front.

When Saul returned from following the Philistines, he was told, "Behold, David is in the Wilderness of Engedi."[14] Then Saul took three thousand chosen men out of all Israel and went to search for David and his men in front of the Rocks of the Wild Goats. On the way, he came to the sheepfolds where there was a cave; and Saul went in to relieve himself. Now

David and his men were sitting in the cave's innermost recesses.

David's men said to him, "Behold, this is the day of which the LORD said to you, 'Behold, I will hand over your enemy to you, and you shall do to him as seems good to you.'"

Then David arose [in the darkness] and stealthily cut off the hem (edge) of Saul's robe. Afterward, David's conscience bothered him, because he had cut off the hem of Saul's robe. He said to his men, "The LORD forbid that I should do this thing to my master, the LORD's anointed, to put out my hand against him, since he is the anointed of the LORD." So, David strongly rebuked his men with these words and did not let them rise up against Saul. Saul got up, left the cave and went on his way.[15]

Israel is known as "The land of a thousand caves."

David and his men often found refuge in caves. Certainly, Adullam was the most prominent cave in his life, but there were others, especially in the area of Engedi.[16]

Actually, there are hundreds of caves, and caverns. One of the nicknames given for Israel is "the land of a thousand caves."[17] I discovered in research and in speaking with a friend of mine, who is an archaeologist, working in Israel,[18] that in some areas, as in Engedi, there are actually interconnecting caves and caverns in some parts of Israel. One of those areas is Engedi. It is important to realize that throughout history openings have been made to connect nearby caves. Some of these have been dug out by hand through the centuries, while others were possibly made by David and his men, nearly 3000 years ago. Consider this, David and his men could, quite literally, go underground in a cave, then move through small passages from cave or cavern to others just like it, exiting undetected a distance away. This made the art of illusiveness much easier. As this story continues, you will find that Saul and David meet again, in yet another cave.

A piece of Saul's robe was a prize for a warrior like David.

David's cutting off a piece of Saul's robe was his way of falling in line with the protocol of this world's system. There was nothing unusual about using a fringe from the robe of a defeated king. But David was not to follow this practice because his anointing was based upon a divine opportunity and not his own prowess, or talent. If he wanted God to enable him, and favor him, then he had to conduct himself along the lines of a different paradigm. Instead, and on this one occasion, David had chosen to insult Saul's authority. The still small voice of Holy Spirit accountability began to nudge at David's conscience.

At issue here was David's pride, pure and simple. Other men may rule using such things as the fringe of the robe of a defeated king, but David must rule in ways that reflect "a heart after God's own heart." If pride keeps showing up in his dealings, then, to that degree, the prize is tainted and integrity is compromised.

The Longer the train, the more powerful the King.

Kings of old wore elaborate robes to increase their significance and impress their citizenry. Ancient kings often coveted the fringes of other kings, to increase their own majesty and authority. Upon obtaining these pieces of cloth, they would then sew them to the fringes or the tail of their own robes. Anyone viewing a king's robe would therefore be in awe of the success of the one wearing it.

It was a principle of protocol among royals, or kings, that "The longer the train, the more powerful the king." This seemed to be the normal thought from nation to nation, and culture to culture. If a king were to defeat another king, then, immediately, upon surrender, he would cut off a portion of the defeated king's robe and have it sewn onto the train of his own robe. If a battle took place and soldiers were going through the slain who were laying on the field, then often they would collect the robes from fallen officers or high-ranking leaders, or kings and then deliver them to their king, so that he could add them to the train of his robe. This obviously gave them an aura and raised their sense of self importance. The goal of kings was to pursue majesty and authority, in any way possible. This was one of the methods they employed.

If a king wanted to boast to family or friends, of his many victories and accomplishments, then he would bring out his robe and show them what each piece of cloth represented. David had decided that God's fingerprints were still on Saul, so he would treat him as the Lord's anointed. As a result, his heart had smitten him for cutting off a piece of Saul's robe.

The Story

David had yielded to the opportunity of the moment, having followed his own conventional wisdom, as well as the urging of his fellow soldiers, but was quickly reprimanded by the Holy Spirit. That still small voice had moved on David to reconsider how battles should be won, and how God's favor would be maintained.

Saul had been traveling through the region, searching for David. He seemed to be just one step behind David but could not find him. Finally, he had become unwittingly vulnerable to David.

Saul had come to the rocky crags of the desert of Judah, which reaches from the west toward and descending to the shores of the Dead Sea. This land is a barren area with mostly artistic, steep and very rough rocks and cliffs. Most would consider it fit only for wild goats and the Ibex.[19] He excused himself and walked away from his army and sought refuge for rest and to relieve himself, in the privacy of a nearby cool and dark cave.

The king did not know the cave was already occupied and by the very man whom he considered his arch enemy. The cave was not as shallow[20] as Saul had thought. Rather it reached much deeper and had become a place of refuge for several hundred men who were quietly resting and "on the lam."[21] It came as a shock to them when they heard someone enter their cave, and then to discover that this was the very man they were trying to avoid. But then several of them quietly urged their leader to seize the moment and eliminate their enemy. It was tempting, it was captivating and almost seductive, but not the right thing for a principled man to do.

One of David's men, from deep within the cave encouraged him to see how God had providentially, "given an opportunity of avenging himself of his adversary." He advised David to "cut off Saul's head and so deliver himself out of this tedious wandering condition, and the distress he was in." David said, "it is not right to kill the man who is my master and one whom God thought worthy to be king. Even though Saul is doing evil things to me, I will not do evil things to him."[22]

THE MEN SAID, "CUT OFF SAUL'S HEAD," BUT INSTEAD, DAVID CUT OFF SAUL'S SKIRT.

David thought: "I will not do to Saul what these men have suggested. I will not cut off Saul's head, but I'll just "cut off a piece of

Saul's robe and let him know that he would have been in danger, had it been a real enemy."[23] It is not fully clear how David had access to Saul's robe. However, it seems likely that Saul entered the cave, took off his robe and draped it over a large rock, then continued deeper into the cafe, thinking he was totally alone. This left his personal space compromised, as David was actually hiding in another part of the cave. It was easy for David to slip up to the robe and cut off a portion, which would not be noticed for some time.

While cutting off the corner of the King's robe, David felt uneasy with what he was doing. Gnawing at him on the inside was the feeling that he should not be touching this man or doing this thing. As David stepped away, he felt a twinge of guilt along with the still small voice, establishing a principle in his heart. In years to come, David will write about this incident, reflecting on what God was saying to him: "He suffered no man to do them wrong: yea, he reproved kings for their sakes; Saying, touch not mine anointed, and do my prophets no harm."[24]

David watched as Saul, having taken time to be refreshed, exited the cave to continue on his journey, searching for his prey. After Saul had gone a distance away, but was still in earshot, David also exited, with his men. It was then that David called out to the king. As he uttered the name of Saul, he fell down, with his face to the ground, before the king and said, "My lord the King, why do you believe those who would falsely accuse me and say that I want to hurt you?"[25] "Please do not listen to the words of wicked men, who devise evil against me; and do not honor them by believing what they say, for they are determined to separate friends.

You must judge the dispositions of all men by their actions." David continued by saying, "you must recognize that men's actions demonstrate if there is kindness in their hearts, and I have done nothing that would show that I mean evil to you. Words may be either true or false, but men's actions expose their intentions nakedly to plain view."[26] "Do not believe those who frame such accusations against me, such things as have never come into my mind." David said, "How is it that you have embraced this desire to murder me?"[27] See this piece of your skirt and realize that I could have slain you, I could have as easily cut off your head, but I chose only to let you know that I mean you no harm." By showing Saul the piece of his skirt, David encouraged Saul to agree with him, that he had obviously been in imminent danger, but was shown mercy by David. Saul's very life had been in the hands of David, but he had chosen to do him no harm.[28] David finished his comments by saying, "May the Lord judge between us, but I pledge that I shall never touch you to do you harm."[29]

It was a part of David's core nature to give honor to others. He felt especially inclined to honor those who were elders, or in positions of authority. Saul was, somehow, unable to discern that part of David's heart, because his own heart was so far from God.

WHEN YOU BECOME A WORSHIPPER, YOU WILL GAIN ACCESS TO A DEEP-SEATED WISDOM.

It was out of kindness that David gave Saul the benefit of the doubt, when he was forced to face his fury. David took the approach that Saul had given his ear to advisors who were misjudging him and who were turning the king's heart to fear and distrust of him. In this way, David was allowing Saul to "save face"[30] and blame his disposition on others, rather than himself. We must realize that, in reality, David had become an expert on Saul and his disposition, as he had often, as a minstrel, played his harp and sung to the Lord, while quietly observing the blighted king in a black mood being full of anger and terror. He realized that, because of his spiritual condition, the king had become a toxic and volatile man, and capable of severe mood swings. He was not aware that, as Samuel was pouring the oil over him, the anointing was lifting from the life of Saul.[31] David did not know so much about the timing of the change that had come to the "rejected king,"[32] but he did recognize it for what it had become.[33]

Upon hearing David's appeal, Saul groaned aloud. He then admitted, "You have done me no wrong, even while I have instructed calamity on you. You have done nothing but righteousness toward me." Saul then continued by appealing to David, "And now I realize that you are surely going to be king, and that the kingdom of Israel will flourish under your rule. Now swear to me by the LORD that when that happens you will not kill my family and destroy my line of descendants! So, David promised this to Saul with an oath. Then Saul went home, but David and his men went back to their stronghold."[34]

SAUL WAS NOT A GOOD JUDGE OF CHARACTER, BECAUSE HIS OWN MIND HAD GONE DARK.

How was this a "Heart Revealing Day" in the life of David?

This particular day, in the life of David, demonstrates the genius of who David's was, and how his actions truly reflected the kind of nature that would make him go far. If he would be a "shepherd king," then he must not "think like the herd,"[35] or in the case of sheep, a "flock;"[36] he must be infused with a different mindset. This was one of David's "life lessons" and he passed the test.

When the world reacts from its mind, then you must respond from the heart. The question was asked in a conversation between two young men: "Are you thinking what I'm thinking?" The young man responded, "No, I'm thinking something different."[37] If you want to get different results in life, it is best you start thinking differently than the rest of the population. If you want your life to take on a different flavor then go down a different road. When conventional wisdom expects you to react, then respond, and when it wants you to respond, sometimes you must react. The status quo is generally going down the wrong path.

THE HERD MARCHES BLINDLY! DO NOT FOLLOW THEM. USE YOUR HEART TO BREAK FREE.

David had high morals and deep principles. It showed that David was not interested in retribution. While others would walk down the road of hatred he would not. It also shows that, when God was looking for a righteous and principled man to be Israel's king, he had found it in such a man as David.

David behaved himself wisely.[38] Repeatedly in I Samuel 18, it says of David that "he behaved himself wisely."[39] In one verse, it says he "behaved himself wisely in all his ways; and the LORD was with him."[40] Then it says that, "when Saul saw that he behaved himself very wisely, he was afraid of him."[41] Finally, it says that "David behaved himself more wisely than all the servants of Saul; so that his name was much set by."[42]

Treachery and betrayal were not weaknesses, or deficiencies David would yield to. He had a number of fixed core values, which would not accommodate disloyalty, hatred or disrespect of authorities.

Something had been instilled early in David's life, which had molded his thinking to a "culture of honor."[43] He would honor Saul, because he was the king, whom God had anointed. Dishonoring those who had been chosen and anointed by God was not up for debate.

With him, the essence of the anointing was the most powerful life flow. David was a worshipper and placed more value on God's interest in the bigger picture than he did on the private agendas of mankind. These qualities are not always found in leaders. If a leader will yield his interests, his life-plan, as well as his hopes and dreams to God, much like David, then he or she will come to great success, even in this world. The benefit of embracing God in this way is that the angelic armies of heaven will fight alongside of you against your enemies.

Endnotes

1. www.phrases.org.uk/bulletin_board/46/messages/1035.html - "You probably already know that it's the title of a movie of 2002 based on a Tom Clancy book published earlier in the same year. The book begins with a quote: "Why, you may take the most gallant sailor, the most intrepid airman or the most audacious soldier, put them at a table together - what do you get? The sum of their fears." – Sir Winston Churchill."
2. I Samuel 17:25-27
3. www.vocabulary.com/dictionary - "Persona non-grata" - a person who for some reason is not wanted or welcome.
4. *Josephus*, Book 6, Chapter 10:1:193
5. I Samuel 18:8-9 ERV
6. I Samuel 13:13 MSG
7. I Samuel 13:14 NLT
8. I Samuel 24:20 NLT
9. Read carefully, both chapters of I Samuel 21 and 22
10. I Samuel 22:1
11. I Samuel 22:2
12. I Samuel 23:26
13. I Samuel 23:27-28 NLT
14. The Wilderness of Engedi is an area on the western shore of the Dead Sea, and certainly in the desert. Engedi is one of six towns found in the region. These towns are: Beth-Arabah, Middin, Secacah, Nibshan, Salt Town, and Engedi. Reference: Joshua 15:61-62
15. I Samuel 24:1-7 AMP
16. I Samuel 23:29 KJV - "And David went up from thence and dwelt in strong holds at Engedi."
17. www.israel21c.org/the-land-of-a-1000-caves
18. Dr. Scott Stripling
19. www.ferrelljenkins.wordpress.com - The rocks of the wild goats (Ibex) - The ibex, a type of wild goat, is still found in Southern Palestine, Sinai, Egypt and Arabia; it was known also in ancient times, as is evident from rock carvings. (Fauna and Flora of the Bible, 46).
20. www.merriam-webster.com/dictionary/spelunking - the hobby or practice of exploring caves. Often caves are not a few feet deep but can actually go on to allow for rivers and multiple hiding places.

21. www.dictionary.com/browse/on--the--lam - "On the lam." Escaping, fleeing, or hiding, especially from the authorities.

22. *Josephus*, Book 6, Chapter 13:4:284

23. Ibid

24. Psalm 105:14-15 KJV

25. I Samuel 24:8

26. *Josephus*, Book 6, Chapter 13:4:286

27. *Josephus*, Book 6, Chapter 13:4:288

28. *Josephus*, Book 6, Chapter 13:4:289

29. I Samuel 24:12

30. www.idioms.thefreedictionary.com/save+face - "to keep your reputation and the respect of other people; or to do something so that people will continue to respect you; or to avoid humiliation or embarrassment, to preserve dignity."

31. I Samuel 16:13-14

32. I Samuel 16:13-14

33. I Samuel 16:14-21

34. 1 Samuel 24:20-22 NLT

35. www.en.wikipedia.org/wiki/Herd_mentality - Herd mentality and mob mentality, also lesser known as Gang Mentality describes how people are influenced by their peers to adopt certain behaviors. Examples of the herd mentality include political parties, globalism, stock market trends, superstition, and even home décor..."

36. www.theguardian.com/notesandqueries - "We have collective nouns for numbers of things; flock of sheep and herd of cows for example, but there doesn't seem to be any definition of how many are required before the collective applies. For example, two sheep are not a flock but twenty-three sheep are, so somewhere between two and twenty-three there is a number that is the maximum number of sheep that are not a flock and one more than this number is a flock." Submitted by: Martin Garrod, Southsea, Wrexham, UK.

37. Movie: "August Rush." Arthur asked August, "Are you thinking what I'm thinking?" and August Rust responded with, "No, I'm thinking something different."

38. I Samuel 18:14

39. I Samuel 18:5, 14, 15, 30 KJV

40. I Samuel 18:14 KJV

41. I Samuel 18:15 KJV

42. I Samuel 18:30 KJV

43. www.google.ie/webhp - Culture of Honor. "The traditional culture of the Southern United States has been called a 'culture of honor', that is, a culture where people avoid intentionally offending others, and maintain a reputation for not accepting improper conduct by others."

The Day David Spared Saul's Life Again

I Samuel 26

Word came to David, as it had so many times before, that Saul had, once again, set his face to pursue David, and to have him slain. There were loyalists in Israel, who were friends with Saul and kept him informed of David's whereabouts. David also had spies, or scouts who were loyal to him and would alert him whenever Saul came anywhere close to him. It was clear that many people were choosing sides in this national dispute. It was not easy to keep out of the king's reach, but with God on his side, David was at peace with the daily challenge.

Some friends of Saul who were known as Ziphites, came to inform the king that David was at Hachilah. They offered that, if you will assist us, then we'll search him out and capture him for you. Saul was glad for this offer and came with three thousand armed troops to Hachilah. By that time, darkness was closing in, so they set up a huge camp for the night.

> WHEN GOD HAS YOUR BACK, THE JAVELIN WILL NEVER FIND ITS MARK. WHY? BECAUSE, "NO WEAPON FORMED AGAINST YOU SHALL PROSPER."
> ISAIAH 54:17

David was told where Saul was camped out, with those who were planning to pursue him the next day. Late in the evening he quietly slipped out of his own camp of about 600 men and traveled to the enemy camp. David had purposely taken with him only two of his men: Abishai[1] and Ahimelech[2], the Hittite. He did not plan anything, but to sneak a look at them from a distance. However, he discovered that everyone in Saul's camp was asleep. Saul's inner circle of bodyguards were pulled aside from the rest of his army. With the idea of providing protection for their King, the body guards were sleeping in a circle around Saul, along with Abner, the Commander of his military. No sentries were on watch, so no one was alert. Saul was in a tent alone. At the door of his tent was a spear, which had been driven firmly into the ground by Abner. Abishai, was determined that David allow him to take Saul's life that night. Abishai whispered to David, "God has surely handed your enemy over to you this time! Let me pin him to the ground with one thrust of the spear; I won't need to strike twice!"[3] David answered back, "No, absolutely not. We cannot kill the man who was ordained by God to be the king, even if he is a wicked man."[4] David felt that, "If God's hand had ever been on Saul, then, even if his hand has been removed, His fingerprints are still there."[5]

Everyone in Saul's camp had gone deep into "REM sleep."[6]

As David and his men drew nearer, the camp was quiet, like death, "because a deep sleep from the LORD had fallen on them."[7] David moved easily and smoothly into the very tent[8] of Saul, picked up the cruise of water beside where Saul had laid his head, and pulled his spear from the ground outside of his tent. As quickly and quietly as he had come, so he was gone, before anyone had seen them. If the Lord had not caused everyone in the entire camp to go deeply into sleep, then surely someone would have awakened when David and his two men passed through the camp. Not everyone sleeps on the same level, but if God orders up a dose of sleep for everyone, then that will do the trick.

GOD SENT A STRONG DEEP SLEEP UPON SAUL AND HIS ARMY, SO DAVID COULD STROLL THROUGH THEIR CAMP!

David escaped detection and traveled a good distance away, across a brook, up to the top of a hill, and to a place where he could be easily heard. He then called back to Saul's soldiers and specifically to Abner their commander, awakening them out of their sleep. David called out to the army and to Abner:

> "Hey, Abner! How long do I have to wait for you to wake up and answer me?"
>
> Abner said, "Who's calling?"
>
> "Aren't you in charge there? Why aren't you minding the store? Why weren't you standing guard over your master the king, when a soldier came to kill the king, your master? Bad form! As God lives, your life should be forfeited, you and the entire bodyguard.

Look what I have—the king's spear and water jug that were right beside his head!"[9]

Abner called out, "and who is it who has awakened me?

David said, "Why it is I, the son of Jesse, whom you have made into a vagabond. Listen to me, Abner, you are a man of great dignity and high rank, in the King's court. Why do you take your responsibilities so carelessly, preferring your sleep of more importance than his safety? You deserve to die for your ineptness. You should take your job more seriously. If it were not for my love of the King, then surely I could easily have slain him."

"Look at these items: I hold up the evidence, possessions of your king. I hold up the King's spear and his cruse of water. All this happened while you were on guard, Abner. Send one of your young men over to collect the evidence."[10]

Saul immediately recognized David's voice. He then acknowledged that David had valued his life more than had his own body guards. He said, "David, I owe you thanks, for sparing my life. Please do not think that I shall continue to pursue you further. I believe you must love my life, even more than I love it. You have shown me over and again of your love and respect for me. I have been the cause of your banishment from your own home and your own family. So many times, I was the one in danger, but you have frequently given me back my life."[11]

At this point and directly from the battle field, Saul returned to Gibeah, and to the Royal palace, while David and his men decided they must change base camps, because they did not really trust that Saul was sincere. After all, sometimes men say one thing, and then do another thing. He realized he must remain alert, at least for now.

Time and again this troop of men had become relaxed for a few days, thinking Saul would not continue the chase, then things would change and Saul would appear with his army in tow. The attacks came with too much regularity. When David returned to his camp he decided that he really needed to get out of Saul's sights. He needed to go away, far away and no part of Israel could afford the level of safety he required. He needed to immigrate to another region, perhaps even another nation. Philistia came to mind. It may not sound like a good idea, with his history of having slain Goliath, but it was where he decided he must go, for now.

David and his inner circle of leaders decided that, for a while they should move over into Philistia to see if they could be more elusive and harder to find;[12] after all, with Saul's track record, it did not appear to David that Saul would keep his word.

Receive this word of wisdom to those who have ever suffered wrong.

Sometimes when talking with a friend, and the conversation has tilted toward a bad experience that has been the source of their discouragement, I find myself tempted to step outside and look up to see if the Vultures, or Buzzards are circling the building. When I think my instincts may not be well tuned, I realize that I can always trust the instincts of the undertakers of the animal kingdom, namely the buzzards, and the Vultures. They can always tell the difference as they sense whether something is quite alive and well, or if it is almost dead, or totally and completely dead and starting to decompose.

Therefore, if you suspect that someone is operating out of a wounded spirit, and not seeing clearly, and you don't know which is the case, just excuse yourself and check the skies for circling birds of prey. Then you'll know whether you should lend a sympathetic shoulder, or if you should plug up your ears. Certainly, you should encourage them if you can, but don't just take on garbage from that passing garbage truck.[13]

A dozen buzzards[14] flying in circles overhead is a clear indication that something has died and is beginning to decompose. Those buzzards can smell death, or the spirit of death from great distances. Often you see them circling, as you drive along a highway. It is tempting to stop on the side and see if you see the body. Sometimes, when you hear a friend talking about their struggles in life, you can almost imagine the black buzzards circling overhead. Something is dead or dying. Perhaps a friend is passed, or a relationship is spiraling downward, or a reputation is going down the drain. It may be because of a single comment, or a slanderous tale, or nothing more than having misunderstood a motive. The question is, should you listen in or cry foul.[15]

Revenge is an evil thing, and so is unforgiveness.

Wisdom never allows treachery, betrayal, or even being done wrong to negatively adjust the response given. Revenge is not in the vocabulary of wise leaders or mature Christians. Through the years I have observed such reactions take over the logic and the body language of those whom I have loved and respected, leaving me in prayer that the Holy Spirit will get a memo to my friends before the fateful day of their own demise. Just when I think shepherds, pastors, or leaders know better, I find that they don't. The reality is that all of us have our own blind spots and need to listen to the still small voice of warning that comes from the Holy Spirit. It is easy to be offended, and too easy to become offensive as well. Grace and graciousness are, too often, in short supply.

Saul had taken up issues with David, because of jealousy. The King had gone on the attack, against a well-meaning and quite anointed young man. This caused God to rise up and defend him throughout the process. There were no winners in this story, as much as we must admit that God did remove the attacker and establish a new king on the throne.

Revenge is an evil thing and it could easily have become the reaction of David, thus disqualifying him from assuming the throne. It must also be agreed that un-forgiveness is evil. Nearly every one of us have been at the wrong end of the spear (or javelin) in one way or another, during the course of our lives. Being the object of unthoughtful or unkind words or actions is not uncommon but living a life void of the temptation to exercise revenge is also uncommon. Many times, the offence you experience involves money and you may even feel that you have a strong case for retribution. You have struggled with the temptation to sue or seek payment. This may not be an option, if you're willing to allow the Holy Spirit to fight your battles, and even things up. Imagine, it could be your pride and not the principle of the matter that you are really defending. You may be wise to chill out and allow God to even the score. Your reputation as a wise counsellor may be on the line. We can protest, easily enough, but it might be best to surrender, dodge the spear and even embrace the javelin, rather than to pull it out from the wall and aim at the heart of the one whom you're crossways with. Imagine that you can hear the words of the Lord saying, because you did the right thing, "Well done my good and faithful servant." God is not as concerned about the money as he is about your spiritual currency of soul. Keep in mind, heaven will be grand, but bitterness, could soil your nature, and make others think that there is a skunk in the house. Don't make them look in your direction.

INSTEAD OF REVENGE, LET GO OF YOUR ANGER AND MOVE ON. YOU'LL FEEL BETTER IN A FEW YEARS, AFTER YOU MEET JESUS!

Several years ago, Christi and I were going through a challenge with a church we were pastoring. We found ourselves, while on a road trip, wanting to explain our side of the disagreement. We stopped in Houston, Texas and enjoyed some Mexican food. While reaching for a packet of sugar to sweeten our ice tea, I read this rebuke on one side of the packet. Here is what the Holy Spirit used that sugar packet to say to me:

"Never explain. Your friends don't need it, and your enemies won't believe it anyway."

The idea behind this chapter is "Revenge could not get traction in David's life." It would have been easy for David to remove the javelin from the wall and send it back to the King, in a vindictive manner to do him harm. This reactive nature was not to be found in this young man, because he valued the anointing too much to allow it. To do such a thing would have revealed pride, arrogance and hatefulness in his own heart. To have released Abishai to slay the King would have placed a blot on David's life, which he could never have outlived. It was imperative that David would keep this in mind: The day will come for all of us to face a just God. Remember that He may be keeping a tally of whether you passed the test and showed a forgiving spirit yourself. Just as an exercise, please read and then re-read "The Lord's Prayer," focusing on the word forgiveness:

Jesus said we must pray in this manner:

> Our Father in heaven,
> Hallowed be Your name.
> Your kingdom come.
> Your will be done
> On earth as *it is* in heaven.
> Give us this day our daily bread.
> And forgive us our debts,
> As we forgive our debtors.
> And do not lead us into temptation,
> But deliver us from the evil one.
> For Yours is the kingdom and the power
> and the glory forever. Amen.[16]

One of the things I see in this prayer is that the word debt goes both ways. It is not only possible to face the need of forgiveness from the debt we owe; but also, to face the need of forgiveness, in our hearts, because of the debt owed to us by someone else. It must be considered that when someone offends us, or takes advantage of us, that we owe to them total forgiveness, or even to go so far as to give them absolution.[17] To many this is a foreign word, but only because it seems like only God could be so forgiving. Try it on for size and you may find that it feels good to remove, from your heart, even the hint of disdain for your offender. This means we intercede to God, on their behalf and we must forgive them, unconditionally, before asking God to forgive us.

The big question is, when you face the Father, will you be able to confirm that you forgave everyone who ever offended you? You cannot have it both ways. You desire the Father to forgive you, but have you forgiven the ones who offended you?

BITTERNESS IS WORSE THAN A HORSE-PILL. IT WILL LODGE IN YOUR THROAT & SWELL UP IN YOUR STOMACH.

One more suggestion: Forgive, expecting nothing in return … not even repentance on their part. This brings us again to the word, absolution. Do your own study to see if you're willing to go so far as to wipe away your uncomfortableness with being a forgiver yourself.

If you want to know if you have really forgiven this person, ask yourself this question: would I be willing to give them a friendly telephone call right now, (today, not even waiting for tomorrow), and that you will have a smile in your voice when you talk with them? In some cases, it may have been a year, or a decade, or even longer since you considered a conversation with them.

It is a challenge for us all to forbid revenge from getting traction in our lives. Your challenge is to become a forgiver, if you want to be forgiven.[18]

How was this a "Heart Revealing Day" in the life of David?

David's patience had been tested and his men were tired of running from Saul, year after year. Living a life "on the lam"[19] was no picnic.[20] For one thing, you never know if you will sleep in the same place two nights in a row.

This was not a lifestyle anyone would want, and yet it had been thrust upon David and his six hundred men, as well as many of their families. It would have been tempting and so easy to strike back at Saul, especially, when the anger had been so one-sided. And yet, David had behaved himself wisely time after time.

Revenge is a word capable of mutating and taking on new forms on its own. The culture of toxic reaction can grow, multiply and even explode to unrealistic levels.

David was called the "Sweet psalmist of Israel"[21] and a man after God's own heart.[22] He loved God and trusted Him to bring every problem and each dilemma to a harmonious end but realized that he must be patient. One thing David clearly understood was that it takes time for balance and redemption to get worked out in the lives of so many individuals. In all of our lives there are many people with diverse issues. All these have far-reaching ramifications. To expect that you are the center of it all and that all things must get worked out on your time schedule, and all that conveniently for your sake, is unrealistic.

David was a "Mentor King" and this was one of those times when he mentored by his example. These men learned that they should more likely be surprised when he harbored bitterness, than when he passed the character test, and showed a good spirit. Even so, as we look over his life we see that David was not perfect, and could get riled up over the pressures, which were forming around him; still, he could also become repentant and generous just as quickly.

David knew that he would be king, for the prophet Samuel had said so. He also realized that he was still young, and there would be enough time for him to be king. Life takes a long time to evolve and the forming of a stable, balanced and righteous life must be given a wide berth.

God was engineering the details in David's life. If men are patient, given that God is in charge, then they are releasing God to do it the right way and to bring happier days.

> "Up to the time of Samuel the prophet, God provided judges to lead them. But then they asked for a king, and God gave them Saul, son of Kish, out of the tribe of Benjamin. After Saul had ruled forty years, God removed him from office and put King David in his place, with this commendation: 'I've searched the land and found this David, son of Jesse. He's a man whose heart beats to my heart, a man who will do what I tell him."[23]

David knew that he must yield his life, so that God always had veto power. He would need God's grace to carry the weight of responsibility, and he did not want that responsibility, until God decided he was ready.

The place David was to occupy was that of King of Israel. If this truly was a theocracy, with a Monarch at the top, then David must not tamper with the process. He would have plenty of time to be his own man, with God's approval. He must not be a usurper. He knew full well that he did not want the appointment, unless God had chosen him, and he also knew that until God gave him the crown, then he did not really want it. The weight of the crown would be a job with too much pressure, without the grace of God to go along with it.

David had been a worshipper for a long time. That is what had qualified him for whatever assignment God had chosen for him. Hungering for the throne had not been in David's heart. This had been God's idea from the beginning, and David did not want to have anything unless it was based fully on God's timing for him. He did not long to be a man in authority, but rather a man anointed by God's authority. In other words, he trusted God to make the big choices for his life. He only hoped that he could continue feeling this way.

Endnotes

1. www.biblehub.com/topical/a/abishai.htm - Zeruiah was David's sister. She had three sons: All three sons were listed among David's Mighty Men. (II Samuel 23). These brothers were Joab (David's General), Abishai (Slew 300 Philistines in a single battle with his sword), and Asahel (Celebrated for being swift of foot).
2. www.biblehub.com/commentaries/1_samuel/26-6.htm - Some of the Hittites were among David's most trusted and faithful friends, along with another well-known Hittite, Uriah, (Bathsheba's husband), also a Mighty man.
3. I Samuel 26:8 NLT
4. *Josephus* Book 6: 13:9: 312
5. I heard Evangelist H. Richard Hall (Cleveland, Tennessee) make this statement back in the decade of the 1960s.
6. www.tuck.com/stages - REM sleep is the deepest sleep. it's difficult to wake someone up when they're in REM sleep. "Usually sleepers pass through five stages: 1, 2, 3, 4 and REM (rapid eye movement) sleep. These stages progress cyclically from 1 through REM then begin again with stage 1. A complete sleep cycle takes an average of 90 to 110 minutes, with each stage lasting between 5 to 15 minutes. The first sleep cycles each night have relatively short REM sleeps and long periods of deep sleep but later in the night, REM periods lengthen and deep sleep time decreases."
7. I Samuel 26:12 NKJV
8. Ibid
9. I Samuel 26:14-16 MSG
10. I Samuel 26:22-24
11. *Josephus* Book 6: 13:9: 317
12. *Josephus* Book 6: 13:9: 315-318
13. www.en.wikipedia.org/wiki/Garbage_truck - Some people transport garbage around, like hoarders. Be careful not to allow your ears to become their "depository." "Garbage truck

or dustcart refers to a truck specially designed to collect municipal solid waste and haul the collected waste to a solid waste treatment facility such as a landfill. Other common names for this type of truck include trash truck in the United States, and rubbish truck, junk truck, dumpster, bin wagon, dustbin lorry, bin lorry or bin van elsewhere. Technical names include waste collection vehicle and refuse collection vehicle. These trucks are a common sight in most urban areas."

14. www.straightdope.com ~ Buzzard, "Why do buzzards circle above dead stuff? When you see a vulture circling over that hunk of 'possum tartare on the Interstate, it could be trying to sniff out whether the carcass is still fresh enough to eat. "Rotten enough to gag a vulture" is more than just a saying. Contrary to popular belief, vultures like their food as fresh as they can get it. All three species feed mostly on carrion but will sometimes kill injured or helpless prey. They are generally very cautious in approaching a prospective meal. Perhaps they sometimes circle to be sure that the animal is really dead, and thus no threat, but it's more likely that they are checking to make sure there is no potentially dangerous competitor, such as a coyote, lurking about."
15. www.idioms.thefreedictionary.com/cry+foul ~ "To protest strongly about a real or imagined wrong or injustice." Sometimes you can see a "train wreck" about to happen, and you have to sound off a warning.
16. Matthew 6:9-13 NKJV
17. www.dictionary.com/browse/absolution ~ "Absolution." Act of absolving; a freeing from blame or guilt; release from consequences, obligations, or penalties."
18. Matthew 6:9-13 NKJV
19. www.merriam-webster.com/dictionary/lam ~ sudden or hurried flight especially from the law
20. www.npr.org/2011/10/04/141048472/whats-its-like-to-live-on-the-lam ~ "What's It Like to Live on The Lam." "The Federal Bureau of Investigation estimates there are some 6,500 fugitives on the run from U.S. authorities. Their crimes range from missed child support payments to murder, but most share an ability to live quiet lives under the radar."
21. II Samuel 23:1
22. Acts 13:22
23. Acts 13:21-22 MSG

The Day Terror Came to Ziklag

David was still young, in his early twenties, and had just been relieved from duty as the head of Saul's military.[1] While visiting with Ahimelech, the priest, in the city of Nob,[2] he had spotted Doeg, a Moabite,[3] one of Saul's most trusted servants,[4] and was suspicious as to what evil thing Doeg could be up to. Seeing Doeg had raised serious concern, leaving him unsure as to what he should do to avoid the threats of Saul. It was at that moment that David made a snap decision to escape out of the area quickly. He elected to flee to Gath, which was not far away.

Gath was the nearest Philistine city to the sanctuary of Nob where David was at the moment. It is worthy of note that Gath was the hometown of Goliath, whom David had slain a few years earlier,[5] and also that on this journey, he was carrying the very sword of Goliath, which he had obtained from Ahimelech, the priest.

Upon his arrival in Gath, he was quickly recognized as a man on the run. They also recognized that David was famous in his own right. They brought him before Achish. Those officials who brought David before Achish were not happy with his being there. They said, "Isn't this David, the king of the land of Israel? He is the one the Israelites sing about. They dance and sing this song about him:

> "Saul has killed thousands of enemies, but David has killed tens of thousands."[6]

It is interesting that Israel's enemies, the Philistines, had already begun to acknowledge that David was headed for the throne of Israel, by calling him "the king of the land of Israel."

David saw quickly that he had made a mistake by coming to Gath. The future may bring him here, but for today, this was not a good decision and he had to work his way out of this conundrum, and quickly.

God was with David, but unless God came through with a miracle, he was in deep trouble. Initially, David had thought that perhaps no one would recognize him and that he would be able to just blend into the general population and disappear somewhere in Philistia, but when they immediately recognized who he was, he panicked.

David realized that he had to resort to a creative way of bailing out by whatever way he could. David felt that if he were to act intelligent, it could create a bigger problem for him. After all the important Philistines standing in the court, had already recognized him, and he could literally lose his head in moments. So, there was no way he could negotiate his way out of this situation. It could all blow up in his face.

It came to him that he must lay everything on the line, and act as crazy as his talents would take him. He realized that the Philistine king must see him as a liability, to the point that, he wanted him quickly escorted from his court. This meant that, if he did this right, they would actually help him escape.

David began to spin and gyrate radically. Then he rolled his eyes back into his head. Then he slobbered all over himself and then let out some loud screams. He feigned himself to be loco, insane and out of his mind. But then it was the beating of his head on the walls of the court that alerted the audience that he had lost his mind.

Achish took one look at him and said to his servants, "Can't you see he's crazy? Why did you let him in here? Don't you think I have enough crazy people to put up with as it is, without adding another? Get him out of here!"[7]

David was almost holding his breath, hoping that Achish would not remember him later. It is quite possible that the Lord sent the King of Gath a delusion, so that he hardly realized what his officers were saying, but just focused on his opinions that this man before him was a fool or an imbecile. If this warlord were to have really taken to heart who was before him that day, then things could immediately have gone wrong for David. If Achish had considered that many of Philistia had lost their lives because of this young man, he would quickly have ordered David's execution. And then there is the fact that no one even noticed that he was carrying, on his side, an oversized sword, aka the Sword of Goliath. As it was, God helped David that day and he was able to slip back across the border and back into Israel.

Every leader must censure his own attitudes and paranoias so that fear does not sabotage his legacy.

Saul was jealous of David, because David had God's favor and he did not. The king became so embittered at David that he created a toxic environment to prevent David from being able to live in his home country. As a result, all of those who cast their lot with the young man were also alienated from the land. Neither David, nor his men were able to feel safe to remain with their own families, in their own country. Because of Saul's personal vendetta, the time would come when David and all those who were his loyal compatriots must find residence elsewhere. To put it plainly, Saul made his personal disdain for David, a national struggle, involving everyone who came near to the king.

INTROSPECTION IS LOOKING INTO THE MIRROR TO FIND THE BLEMISHES.

The years passed and, once again, David had met up with Achish.

David was still eluding Saul's capture, but now had an army of 600 men, plus their families. This army had needed to find a place to call their home-base, from which they could come and go. David had led these men back across the border to Gath[8] and met up with this warlord who had managed to become Philistia's king. There seems to be no indication that Achish remembered their first meeting, but rather develops a grace for David that seems to be God given. He was absolutely respectful of David and trusted him as his friend.

David's Army was hiding out in Plain View.

David and his army were given the city of Ziklag to live in and establish their families.[9] In addition, David and his men were assigned the title, by Achish, of "Personal Body Guard for Life."[10] This was no small thing. One year and four months had passed,[11] and they did well making this foreign land a home they enjoyed.

During this time, David created an illusion, drawing in Achish, so that he saw David as loyal to Philistia. It could be said that David created a shadow-impression of working for the interests of the Philistines and by default against Israel.

For those sixteen months everything seemed to be working as planned. David felt that, by living in Ziklag, he was safe from the arm of Saul, and protected by the Philistine border. This had the intended result, which worked for a while. However, it was getting more and more difficult to keep things fluid as planned. As a juggler who finds that he has too many balls in the air and things get out of hand, he could see that his plan was about to start controlling him. David had viewed this strategy as necessary to survive in this hostile environment.

Every morning he would lead his men off in the direction of Israel, which would keep any local spies from knowing his plans. Then he would move his army off into another direction with plans to raid other enemies of Israel, namely those of the "Geshurites, the Girzites, and the Amalekites [the enemies of Israel that Joshua had failed to annihilate]; for they had inhabited the land from ancient times, as one comes to Shur even as far as the land of Egypt."[12]

David had always done his best to avoid touching, Saul, whom he knew was the Lord's anointed. Although Saul was toxic, he felt that the people of Israel were his friends. He had been so adamant to respect Saul, but that had proven quite the challenge. He would never fight against Israel, but Saul somehow always kept the pressure up, and now the situation was recasting itself in a different form, namely as he was still juggling everything with Achish.

However, God intervened and David found himself facing accountability to God. Achish believed David to be on his side, to such a degree that, he built a strategy to call out Saul to war. David had a little game going that worked well for his personal benefits, but he was walking down a precarious path, which was about to catch up with him.

The clouds grew dark overhead for David.

Achish made a decision that things were going really well for his nation and that he should launch a mass campaign against Israel. After all, he had David and his men to back him up. He was convinced that David would go along and was glad to use David's presence as a wedge against Saul.

The armies of Saul and Achish were about to meet on the battlefield. David found himself in a place of uncertainty, in that he did not want to fight against Israel, but also realized that he did not know the timing of the Lord for his own life-plan. God was his counsel, and he must trust God for how God's will would play out for him. Therefore, he stepped up to join Achish in the battle. David and his army were at the back of the full Philistine army standing alongside of Achish,[13] whom they were there to protect.

At that point the other leaders of Philistia, commanders from all over the country, began to feel uneasy with David and his men. They felt that, having David and his men behind them, in the battle, would put them at risk. They did not trust that David would remain loyal to Achish, and not change loyalties in the middle of the battle, to gain back the favor of Israel's king, Saul.[14]

When they arrived back at home base, tragedy had struck.

God was at work in David's life, even during those times when he did not realize it. Had he gone to battle alongside Achish, he would not have been available for many weeks. He would have discovered too late that his family and the families of his men were in danger. God wanted David back in Ziklag because of the horrific surprise they were about to experience. On the same day David was being rejected by Achish, his family was suffering a terror attack.

It took David and his men three days to arrive back home. Approaching Ziklag was a heartrending experience. There were no noises coming from the homes, and no children were playing outside the village. The Amalekites had invaded the region of the Negev, in southern Judah, and the village of Ziklag, in Philistia. They had burned every house to the ground and stripped them of all life, both human and all of the livestock. The shock of the sight before them, weighed heavily upon David and his men. Seeing no immediate enemies to which they could react, left them with grief and sorrow, which bore down upon every man. Some of them just dropped to the ground weeping. All of the men "raised their voices and wept until they were too exhausted to weep [any longer]."[15]

ZIKLAG WAS GROUND ZERO ON THE DAY DAVID AND HIS ARMY RETURNED.

Tensions were running high, as every man looked for someone to blame for this tragedy. Every man had lost his wife and children and was overwhelmed by this intrusion and theft. Because there were no bodies discovered in the fire and destruction, they confirmed that, at this point, all were taken alive, and likely would remain so. At least none of their families had died. All eyes fell upon David and some even voiced shouts of mutiny.

"David was now in great danger, because all his men were very bitter about losing their sons and daughters, and they began to talk of stoning him. But David found strength in the LORD his God."[16] The secret to finding strength in the Lord can be found in the core of your heart of hearts. Some people just don't have it in them to have a deep settled trust in the Lord. But David had always found that, when things go into a downward spiral, then lay hold onto your faith in God and He will work it out for your good.[17] It is likely that David began to think thoughts like these:

> "If God is for me, who can be [successful] against me?"[18]
>
> "If God is on my side, what does it matter who is against me?"
>
> "No weapon turned against (me) will succeed. (I) will silence every voice raised up to accuse (me)."[19]
>
> It is not always easy to face the threats and trials of the enemy, but in the end, God will be (my) "rear guard."[20] In other words, God has my back.

When so many others would have crouched and gone on the defensive, David turned to the high priest, Abiathar,[21] "Bring that sleeveless nightshirt, like the boy Samuel wore, so that I may talk to the Lord."[22] David's actual words were to request the ephod,[23] which we know to be a sleeveless garment worn by the priests. Abiathar, the priest, returned wearing the ephod.

Throughout David's life it appears that he could best worship, when either strumming his harp, or calling for the linen ephod. Later on, when David was bringing up the Ark of God to Jerusalem[24] he shed his kingly robes and slipped on the linen ephod himself to worship. Then he began to dance before the Lord.

It was as if these tools helped him to separate himself from all the issues, which might be swirling about him. David instructed Abiathar to speak to God in a normal voice, and so he did, appealing to God for divine direction.

"Should I go after the people who raided our town?

Can I catch up with them?"

"Go after them," the Lord answered.

"You will catch up with them, and you will rescue your families."[25]

After his appeal to God, Abiathar turned to David and began to prophecy that, not only should they pursue, but they would recover all and successfully rescue their families.

David, immediately turned to his men and told them that all was going to come together quickly, but they must rally and pursue the enemy. They could easily determine the direction the enemy had gone, because of the tracks and markings in the sand around the city.

Off they went toward the brook, Besor. Not far from the Brook Besor they had a breakthrough. When they were near to the brook, they found an Egyptian slave who had been abandoned because of sheer exhaustion, dehydration and hunger. He had been a part of the group of Amalekites, who had attacked Ziklag, just three days earlier, but were in a big rush to leave Philistia, so that they would not be confronted by the Philistines.

David was a patient man and took time to see that the stranger be given food and water, to help him recover. Then he sat down to talk with the Egyptian, who freely shared that three days earlier he had fallen ill and just could not continue trudging along with the others. His master, an Amalekite, had abandoned him there.

The Egyptian slave informed David of all the villages he and the Amalekites had invaded, and even spoke of when they had "burned Ziklag with fire." David asked him if he could lead them to the camp of the Amalekites. He said, "If you pledge not to either kill me, or return me to my former master, then I will help you find them."[26]

IF ACHISH HAD NOT REJECTED DAVID, THEN THEIR FAMILIES WOULD HAVE BEEN LOST, AND CERTAINLY HIS LOVED ONES VIOLATED.

GOD'S TIMING WAS PERFECT.

Upon arriving at the Brook of Besor, it became apparent to David that nearly one third of his men were utterly exhausted and in danger of total collapse, if they continued. As a result, David gave them permission to remain behind to watch after "the stuff."[27] Therefore, 200 of David's men stayed behind at Besor.[28] David and four hundred of the men pressed on, motivated to catch up with the Amalekites.

The Egyptian slave was true to his word and led David and his army to the Amalekite camp. Off in the distance David could see the Amalekites as they were having a grand party and were totally off their guard. Some were passed out asleep and sprawled[29] all over the hillside. Many of them were "entirely drunk with wine,"[30] while others were dancing and celebrating over their great accomplishment of collecting so much spoil from the towns of Judah and Philistia.[31]

David and his men made a sudden and surprising attack and swooped down into the camp. This resulted in a huge victory. The battle waged on for nearly 24 hours, as it began at twilight and continued until the next evening. "Not a man of them escaped, except four hundred young men who rode on camels and fled."[32]

The Plunder taken from the Amalekites, was far greater than the actual losses suffered in Ziklag.

When the battle was over, David had recovered all that had been taken from them, not only from the raid on Ziklag, but also from the other cities and farmlands that had been raided in the region. This represented a bonus for David and his men. They were reunited with their wives and children, having recovered everyone who had been kidnapped. In addition, the sheer increase in cattle and sheep, was phenomenal. Yes, these men were exhausted, but they were also happy with the results. The spoil, which they seized was so much larger than they had lost, that these men felt prosperous.

In addition to recovering their wives and children, and their own flocks of sheep and herds of cattle, there was additional livestock, which were taken from the defeated Amalekites. All of these additional animals were separated from those that had been recovered from Ziklag, and then driven back to Ziklag exclaiming, "this is what belongs to David."[33]

In addition to all they recovered of their own, they captured also other captives who had been stolen from the areas of the Cherethites and other cities nearby. These Amalekites had been on a raiding rampage, and other remote areas of Judah had fallen victim as well. David rescued them and set them free so that they could return to their homes. Later, after David would become king of Israel, some of these people served David as body guards and special forces under the command of Benaiah, David's lower general.[34] They were grateful for David's efforts to set them free from this bad experience.

David proves to be a benevolent leader.

The army of David, along with the huge entourage, returning from the battlefield found their way back to Besor. There they found those two hundred warriors who had been too exhausted and famished to continue their journey.

As soon as David's entourage came face to face with the men who had remained behind, he gave a respectful salute to them.[35] There were some of the men with David who were troublemakers and began to mock those who had been unable to continue the journey. They were in an emotional high from the recent victory, and some of David's men failed to see these 200 soldiers as compatriots. Rather they saw them as losers and unworthy of participating in the victory.

David rebuked those men for their selfishness and turned their attention to the Lord. He had overheard their words, as they said, "These 200 men didn't go with us, so why should we give them any of the things we took. These men get nothing but their own wives and children."[36]

David could not believe what he was hearing, and immediately rebuked his men, and branded this attitude to be "evil and unjust."[37] He said, "Don't even go down that road, in light of the fact that God has been so good to us. Think about it, he has given us a great victory against those Amalekites who attacked and burned down our town. He has saved our wives and our sons and daughters, protecting them from danger. It has been inconvenient for all of us, but He has restored to us our possessions and given us the opportunity to deliver this host of people."

David continued, "Do you really want to be remembered for this selfish attitude?"

Then David defused the situation by saying, "This is the way it will be, both now and in the future. Soldiers who stay behind to guard the camp get as much as those who go into battle."[38]

From that time onward in Israel, it became a common practice that those who stood guard over the "stuff," such as the supplies, would receive an equal share with those who fought in the heat of the battle.[39]

Upon arriving in Ziklag, while his men were rebuilding their homes, David took advantage of the generous supply, which God had brought to him and his men, by sending couriers with gifts of portions of the spoils to friends all over Israel. David did not forget his friends who had been kind to him but sent gifts to many of those who had shown the courage to express favor, during dangerous times. Certainly, the Elders of Judah had always stood by David, even when Saul had not appreciated it. They often had to show their kindness to David in quiet ways, using diplomacy. but still they had always remembered this young man, as a part of their tribe. Beyond Judah, and all over the nation, there were so many other cities and small communities which had been kind to David and his men, as they had been on the move to avoid Saul: cities which had shown kindness and had given provision to them. Many of those David chose to honor had been officials in high places of government, while so many others were simple people who were purely grassroots people of the land. David wanted to give back to them in loving ways and this was the way he wanted to show it. His message, which the couriers carried, simply stated: "We took these things from the Lord's enemies. Please accept them as a gift."[40]

This story of the attack upon Ziklag, ended positively. David had learned to take his challenging times and turn them into acts of kindness.[41]

Why were these warriors so exhausted?

David's men were justifiably exhausted, because of the sheer energy they had used up. Consider the rigorous schedule they had been through for the week that led up to their arrival at the Brook of Besor. These men had walked all day every day, on a three-day, 50-mile journey from north of *Aphek* to *Ziklag.*[42]

Keep in mind that, until the Romans came to the Middle East, and built roads[43] centuries later, there were no roads, only paths, but more often than not, it was across fields, navigating through uneven terrain, and across streams of water. There were no "superhighways anywhere in the world," in those days.

Initially, these men had walked that 50 miles from their families in Ziklag, to the scene of the coming battle, in Aphek. They had stayed a day, then had a short night of rest, before setting out to return to Ziklag, on a three day walk to cover the 50 miles back to Ziklag. Upon arriving they were shocked, at their village being burned with fire, robbed and their families taken. This left them emotionally drained. They were devastated.

They searched frantically, through their homes, to confirm that no lives of their families had been lost. David went to prayer and then they devised their strategy to recapture their families from their captors. They walked then, about 20 miles to the Brook of Besor.[44] They met up with the Egyptian slave, spent the necessary time to allow him to recover and then walked onward to meet up with the Amalekite army. This walk was laborious, exhaustive and long. None of the rest times in this story were very restful. This week was almost without the sort of rest that helps you recover from weariness. Every night was short and every day was long. Although these men kept going, there were those times, when they were trudging and having difficulty putting one foot in front of the other. Adrenalin was the fuel they kept using up. There is also the issue of adequate food supply. These men had little opportunity to eat, and they did not have modern granola bars, or beef Biltong,[45] or jerky.

I'M SO WEARY I THINK MY HEART WILL JUMP RIGHT OUT OF MY CHEST, BUT I MUST CONTINUE ONWARD!

Just to meet up with the Amalekite army, they likely had to walk, at least 40 miles from Ziklag, before they spotted them camped out on the hillside. Upon finding the Amalekites, they launched into a spontaneous attack, which was a total surprise to their enemy. Then the battle raged on from twilight one evening through the night and up to the following late afternoon.

Somewhere over those days, they had minimal snatches of rest or sleep, but all in all, these men were short on rest, low on energy, high in adrenalin, short on food supply, until they spoiled the enemy's camp. This all went on from Aphek to Ziklag and then on to the camp of the Amalekites to total about 100 more miles, or a total of walking time to about 4-5 days. At that point then they fought throughout the night, through the next day and a total of 24 hours, in a fight for their lives. It is worthy of note that an ancient army could walk only about 20-25 miles in a day.[46]

The 200 men had been so exhausted they could not carry on, so they had stopped to recoup at the Brook of Besor, so they had been saved from walking the last 20 or so miles to the enemy camp, as well as the 24 hours of fighting.

I do not doubt that all 600 men were weary, but I can also understand why the 200 men, who stayed "by the stuff," just could not go onward.[47]

How was this a "Heart Revealing Day" in the life of David?

When David and his men came within view of the city of Ziklag, they realized smoke was still rising up from their smoldering homes. Tragedy had struck and fear for their families gripped them sorely. This turned to anger in the hearts of some, and then spiraled further until mutiny filled the air, and some of his men even spoke of stoning David. Confusion was taking over that army.

At that time David was faced with a decision. He could either go into a defensive posture, or he could turn to God. He chose the latter and asked the priest Abiathar to go get the linen ephod. Abiathar went to where he kept the ephod, slipped it over his own garments and returned to join David for what would come next.

THE BEST WAY TO ASK GOD FOR HELP IS SIMPLY ... START WORSHIPPING! BUT DON'T FORGET TO ASK FOR HIS HELP.

David realized that only God could help him at that moment. When Abiathar came back, wearing the ephod,[48] David turned his heart upwards and began to worship. David called out to God to help he and his men find the answers during that moment of despair.

Not only his men but also David himself was in grave danger of despair. They all needed to hear what to do next, and how to go to the aid of their families. There were no bodies in the fire, so it seemed evident that all of their loved ones were still alive. God was above and could see far away and into the situation, which had brought such great concern. God knew who had done this, and where they were at that very moment.

David called out to ask God for direction, and the word of the Lord was swiftly given to Abiathar, who spoke in prophetic response that he must follow quickly after the enemy and God would grant them victory.

If David had not chosen this path of action, then they would have had no solution, and confusion would have continued to prevail. As it was God was faithful and the families were restored. This shows how David had such depth of love for God and always gave the Lord opportunity to affect his decisions. That always makes the difference in our lives.

David took time to patiently speak with the Egyptian. It was apparent to David that he was a wounded soldier, depleted of energy and near death, if someone did not care for him. He also realized that a man in his circumstance might have evidence that could help in their search for their enemies. Anyone involved on the battle field would know the value of such a man, and with his years of experience David knew that he should take time to listen to the words of a man like this.

David gave him water to drink, as he was dehydrated, and food to eat, as he had been given no food for at least three days. His body was stressed and deficient and must be treated kindly. Again, David patiently began to question him, so that he could test him on how he was relevant to their search.

David felt no despise for the men who had been weary and unable to continue in the fight. Those who work in the support of the troops, or who "stand by the stuff," or who are weak and weary from the struggle, will be given kind consideration when they must rest. All of these would receive equal pay when the battle is finished. This shows how David had core values in his heart of hearts, which would pass the test of integrity and character all the way to the end.

This was one of those heart revealing days in the life of David, the man who would soon become the king. He established these attributes deep within, and had proven himself to be benevolent, just and kind.

Royalty is overrated if your heart is not filled with the sort of integrity and character as to make the common citizen feel proud and respectful. It is becoming clear that David was worthy of such respect.

Endnotes

1. I Samuel chapters 19 & 20 - Here it shows that David's time with Saul was over, and he must leave his position over Saul's military, as Saul was determined to slay him.
2. Nob, a city of priests, just outside of Jerusalem, and near the Mount of Olives.
3. I Samuel 21:7
4. Ellicott's Commentary for English Readers, in comments on I Samuel 21:7
5. I Samuel 17:48-51
6. I Samuel 21:11 ERV
7. I Samuel 21:12-15 MSG
8. I Samuel 27:1-3
9. I Samuel 27:5-6
10. I Samuel 28:2 NLT
11. I Samuel 27:7
12. I Samuel 27:8 AMP
13. I Samuel 29:2
14. I Samuel 29:3-7
15. I Samuel 30:4 AMP
16. I Samuel 30:6 NLT
17. Romans 8:26-28 MSG - "Meanwhile, the moments we get tired in the waiting, God's Spirit is right alongside helping us along. If we don't know how or what to pray, it doesn't matter. He does our praying in and for us, making prayer out of our wordless sighs, our aching groans. He knows us far better than we know ourselves, knows our pregnant condition, and keeps us present before God. That's why we can be so sure that every detail in our lives of love for God is worked into something good."
18. Romans 8:31 AMP
19. Isaiah 54:17 NLT
20. Isaiah 58:8
21. Josephus Book 6, Chapter 14:6:359 - Abiathar was the son of the high priest, Ahimelech, the priest of Nob. Upon the death of Ahimelech's at the hands of Doeg, Abiathar had escaped and fled Nob. Now he served in the capacity of his father, as the high priest, who traveled with David.
22. When Samuel was a child, serving with Eli, his mother, Hannah,

23. Ephod - In David's day, the ephod was a loose fitting sleeveless garment worn by Jewish priests. It was much like a night shirt. When he was a young boy, "Samuel was ministering before the LORD, as a child dressed in a linen ephod [a sacred item of priestly clothing]." In II Samuel 6:16 AMP, it was a garment worn by David as he worshipped, while bringing the Ark of God into Jerusalem.
24. II Samuel 6:16
25. I Samuel 30:8 CEV
26. I Samuel 30:11-15
27. Josephus Book 6, Chapter 14:6:365 - and also: I Samuel 30:24 KJV
28. I Samuel 30:9
29. https://en.oxforddictionaries.com/definition/sprawl - sprawled: "sit, lie, or fall with one's arms and legs spread out in an ungainly or awkward way."
30. Josephus Book 6, Chapter 14:6:362
31. I Samuel 30:16
32. I Samuel 30:17 NKJV
33. I Samuel 30:20 NLV
34. II Samuel 8:18
35. I Samuel 30:21 KJV
36. I Samuel 30:22 ERV
37. Josephus Book 6, Chapter 14:6:365
38. I Samuel 30:24 CEV
39. Josephus Book 6, Chapter 14:6:367
40. I Samuel 30:26 CEV
41. Ibid
42. www.jesuswalk.com/david/06_david_strengthens.htm - The distance David and his army had to walk from Ziklag, to join Achish's army was about 50 miles (80 K). Then they had to walk back, making it a total of 100 miles (160 K).
43. www.ancient.eu/article/758/roman-roads - The long straight roads built by the Romans wherever they conquered have, in many cases, become just as famous names in history as their greatest emperors and generals. Building upon more ancient routes and creating a huge number of new ones, Roman engineers were audacious in their plans to join one point to another in as straight a line as possible whatever the difficulties in geography and the costs in manpower.

44. www.theseason.org/1Samuel/1Samuel30.htm - The distance from Ziklag to the Brook of Besor was approximately 20 miles (32 K).

45. http://www.dictionary.com/browse/biltong - "(in South Africa) strips of lean meat dried in the open air."

46. www.quora.com/How-far-could-a-medieval-army-march-in-a-day - It is likely that an ancient army could walk up to about 20 miles or as much as a maximum of 25 miles per day, based on about 3 miles per hour of sustained walking.

47. IBID

48. *Josephus* Book 6, Chapter 14:6:359 - "David desired the priest Abiathar to go put on his sacerdotal garments, and to inquire of God, and to prophecy to him, whether God would grant, that if he pursued after the Amalekites, he would overtake them, and save their wives and their children, and avenge himself on the enemies?"

The Day God Gave David a Breakthrough

II Samuel 5

Saul and three of his sons had been slain in battle on top of Mount Gilboa. At first the Hebrew nation was divided by the conflict that arose between those who were loyal to the house of Saul, and those committed to the house of David. This conflict went on for seven years. Finally, the disputes were settled and eventually came to an end, with the deaths of both Abner[1] and Ishbosheth.[2] The tribal leaders all gathered in Hebron, to anoint David as king of their unified nation.[3]

Israel's enemies felt shock waves as David was crowned king.

When there is a change of a national leader, nearby nations are also affected. When the Philistines heard that Israel was now unified under their new king, the shock waves rippled throughout the region.

THE NEIGHBORS SAW DAVID'S CORONATION AS A BIG PROBLEM FOR THE REGION!

The Philistines saw this as a strengthening of Israel and decided to diminish the effect by a full-on attack. They rallied their troops in an attempt to capture David. They came to the "Valley of the Giants"[4] and spread out across this wide expanse of land.[5] From this vantage point they were determined to defeat David, so that he would not enjoy the momentum of success. Two battles were fought from this valley, one right after the other. It must be noted that the Philistines did not come alone. Josephus states, "Let no one suppose that it was a small army of the Philistines that came against the Hebrews."[6] When reading the Bible account, it is easy to conclude that these events, being covered in only nine verses, are the stories of two minor battles.[7]

However, we must understand that these were significant "front page"[8] events in Israel's history.

> "When the Philistines heard that David had been anointed king of Israel, they mobilized all their forces to capture him. But David was told they were coming, so he went into the stronghold. The Philistines arrived and spread out across the valley of Rephaim. So, David asked the Lord, "Should I go out to fight the Philistines? Will you hand them over to me?"
>
> The Lord replied to David, "Yes, go ahead. I will certainly hand them over to you."
>
> So, David went to Baal-Perazim and defeated the Philistines there. "The Lord did it!" David exclaimed. "He burst through my enemies like a raging flood!" So, he named that place Baal-Perazim (which means "the Lord who bursts through"). The

Philistines had abandoned their idols there, so David and his men confiscated them."[9]

The northern kingdom of Israel had just experienced the assassination of their king,[10] and then by popular demand of the citizenry, had merged with the southern kingdom of Judah under the leadership of Judah's king, David. The assassination of Ishbosheth had been a regional tragedy. However, what the people chose to do, by aligning under David's command, proved to be quite redemptive. It fostered unity and stability in their respective nations. Although these two Hebrew nations had a common history, no one in the region saw this merger coming. This unification of the two nations sent ripples of fear to their enemies. To complicate things for those who objected to this amalgamation, it must be admitted that David would be nobody's puppet; nor would he be inconsequential or weak. David always left a "big footprint"[11] wherever he went.

The defeat of this coalition of nations, established David as a force to be reckoned with. "Syria, Phoenicia, and many other nations who were known as being warlike nations came to the assistance of Philistia, to share in this war. Although Philistia had lost tens of thousands of their men, in previous battles, they still came upon the Hebrews with three times as many soldiers as before. They even chose the same spot of ground, as in previous battles to set up their camp."[12]

When the dark clouds rise, it is definitely time to go to prayer.

A giant threat on the horizon drew David into prayer. He decided that the best place he could go to collect his thoughts, and get alone with God was Adullam, his favorite stronghold. It took effort to get to the cave and then to slip inside, without being noticed, but it was worth it for David. He knew that the enemy threat was imposing, but he also knew that, if he could gain the assurance that God was on his side then the dark clouds would be transformed into spring rains, for him. This confirms the fact that David was a "man of power" working under God's authority, and not just self-reliant. David needed God in his corner and this was the way he would do the bidding of his "heart of hearts."[13] The Cave of Adullam, had become not only a stronghold for him, but a secure place to which he could retreat when he needed to talk to God. This is exactly what the new king did on that day. He knew that if he could go to this familiar place he could hear from God on what he should do next. This worshipper had long since learned that few battles can be fought in your own strength. He had also learned that there are some struggles, which require a higher power, and that "divine insight" generally will make the difference.

The road to becoming King over all twelve tribes of Israel had been a long journey of more than twenty years for David. He had been between the ages of at least 14 and 17 when Samuel had anointed him prophetically, as the future king. When Saul died, David was age 30, but did not get the crown, for an additional seven and a half years, because of the divide between those who sought power. Now at past the age of 37, he had finally been crowned king of all of Israel.

Only God can see the outcome, but if God is in your heart, you can too!

The anointing of the Lord had been a powerful force in David's life. He had known all along that this day would come. He remembered well the prophetic words of the Prophet Samuel.[14] As a matter of fact, he had grown dependent on hearing from God before he moved forward in major decisions, especially, when it involved matters of human life. David generally was not agenda driven. Rather, he would stop, pray and listen. Sometimes that word came from within, but more often than not, it came from the mouths of those who were servants of the Lord, standing near to him. It was said of David, that "he never permitted himself to do anything without prophetic insight, and the command of God, because he knew that he must depend on God as his security for the time to come."[15] The famed historian, Josephus said that David sought out the high priest to ask for divine insight.[16] On this day, it would be no different. David sought the Lord, and the Lord responded, "Go up; for I will doubtless deliver the Philistines into your hand."[17]

A MAN OF COURAGE & PRAYER CAN ALSO BE A MAN OF FAITH & POWER!

David was confident that God would sustain him, and on this day would take a major step in permanently overthrowing the yoke of the Philistines.

The Lord had answered, and now it was time for David to act!

David became confident in his heart, that God would take every attack, and each circumstance and turn it to his favor, giving to him the victory. When men and women receive a divine guarantee that they have God on their side, it makes a difference. This leader had no fear of failure, because God was overshadowing every detail of the upcoming challenge.

What would you do if you had the "rock solid assurance," to such a degree, that you experienced "no fear"? Would you charge

IF YOU HAD NO FEAR OF FAILURE, WHAT WOULD YOU ATTEMPT?

forward without abandon? Is your faith as strong as David's faith? If you will learn to: pray first, then secondly listen for His "word," then trust, and finally charge forward in obedience, you will get the same kind of results that David experienced. If this level of strength is buried deeply in your heart of hearts, even in the 21st century, then your life will take on a different fragrance and an amazing aura.

God, is a "God of Breakthrough," and He can give one to you.

With the word of the Lord echoing in his brain, David, while charging forward to engage his enemy, observed how God was already making a difference in his thinking, just like he had on the day his first giant fell. When the battle was nearly finished, he began to utter these words, "The Lord broke through my enemies like water breaking through a dam."[18] So David "named that place, Baal-Perazim (which means "the Lord who bursts through").[19]

In life, we must make sure the god we serve is the right God. Some gods are spelled with a little "g". Those gods are unresponsive and made of inordinate or inferior stuff. The gods of the Philistines and all the surrounding nations were usually made of wood, stone or some kind of metal. Those gods are stuffed with other materials, or just hollow, thus filled with air.

The Philistines discovered that their gods were not able to give them victory over Israel's God, so they abandoned them. As a result, they did what history has often shown us; if their gods did not give them what they wanted, then they were cast aside. It was the same in the wilderness, when Israel realized that "their rock is not as our Rock, even our enemies themselves being judges."[20] The Philistines had left their idols at Baal-Perazim. After a battle, a parade, or a public event, it is customary to collect the garbage and to dispose of it. In this case, David ordered his men to collect the discarded, useless idols and to burn the idols with fire.[21]

When the curtain closed, the defeated called for an encore.

It was not enough to be summarily defeated by Israel. The armies came back for more and David was instructed by the Lord to go after them using a different strategy.

David had gone back to prayer. The stage was again at, "The valley of the Giants."[22] This time the Lord said to David, "Your enemies think they have figured out what you will do in this battle. This time you must surprise them by changing your strategy. They will expect you to engage them in a full-frontal attack. However, you must move your army quietly into position, and wait until I give you a command. This is how it must be: Keep your army in the forest, and not out in the open. Stay in the groves of the trees, which is located behind them. They are facing one way and will not expect you to come from that direction. This place is called 'the Groves of Weeping', and will provide for you, protection from being detected."[23]

THE SOUND IN THE TREES WAS A SUPERNATURAL SOUND ... NOT JUST THE WIND IN THE LEAVES.

"Neither the Philistines, Phoenicians, Syrians or the other neighboring armies will suspect your advance from that direction. In addition, this grove is really close to them, albeit from the back of their ranks. Just before you are to begin the ambush, the air will be still, and without wind. Then you must listen closely, for I will cause a fresh wind to make a sound in the leaves of those trees that sounds a lot like the feet of soldiers marching."[24]

"You will realize that I am sending my heavenly army ahead of you to set the stage for the defeat of your enemies. At that moment, and without delay, you are to advance, fully aware that I have prepared an obvious victory for you and your army."[25]

David and his army routed those armies completely. The first thing that happened was that all the neighboring armies were so surprised by this change in expected strategy, and went "A.W.O.L.,"[26] fleeing for their lives, only to be followed by a portion of David's men. The balance of the armies, including the Philistines, fled in the direction of Gaza and were followed by all of the fighting men of Israel.[27]

The final assignment for David and his army was to return to the camp of their enemies, which had been abruptly abandoned. It seems that when many ancient armies traveled into battle, they took more than their bedroll and weapons of war. They carried all kinds of relics and riches, not to mention the precious metals and jewels, which were used in creating their idols. These spoils of war became the property of David and his army. Then, once again, David and his men were faced with the duty of collecting all the "junk gods" of their enemies, which they had discarded. These had no more personal value to the pagans as they fled for their lives.[28]

TODAY LOTS OF PEOPLE HAVE "JUNK GODS" AND NEED TO DISCARD THEM.

How was this a "Heart Revealing Day" in the life of David?

The day had begun with a celebration in David's heart, as finally the Crown was his. It had been more than twenty years in coming, but, in reality God had always been in the details. David's heart was prepared, and so, the angelic host was placed on alert. David and God were in alignment. Now every individual and even the neighboring nations had to consider doing the same. There is an often-repeated idiom that suggests that "the devil is always in the details," but David became convinced early in his life, that God is an intervening God, and thwarts the devil's schemes. God had ordained David to be Israel's king, and so, the backlash from the realm of darkness would try to bring him down. It is funny how those things work. Whether in your day to day challenges, in church life, in business, or in politics; the fact is, that there is always someone who feels compelled to be the opposition.

Chaos loves to run things. It must, however, be understood that God is a master of taking hold of chaos, and all unpredictable forces and bending them into subjection to his divine order. For those who demand "order" to every strategy, may I introduce you to the way God will take your order, and temper it with chaos.[27] This is a provocation God loves to bring, so that we remain humble in His presence. We are merely clay and He is the master craftsman.

DAVID RECOGNIZED THAT GOD'S SPIRIT WAS HIS BEST SCOUT IN THE FIELD!

On the day when David was crowned king, word went out to the entire region that Israel was now about to get back on track, with their new king having been installed. The unction of anointing, the aura of divine grace, and the energy generated when we are in righteous order were now about to lead Israel into a time when sustained victories would become the "norm."[30] As long as Israel and their king walked in step with their God, they would enjoy the favor of God, every time they went into the field of battle. It did not matter who their enemy was, or how big their war machine stood; God would rout out the enemy and sustain Israel, carrying them to triumph.

The way this day revealed David's heart was, in how he faced every challenge in prayer. Certainly, all would agree that David was able to use his military experience to face-off with his enemies. But David, as a worshipper, saw the need to make God the leader of Israel. He recognized that the Holy Spirit was his best scout, in the field. God saw things from above, so His vantage point gave Him the advantage. He could see around every corner, through every obstruction, and into the hearts of every opposing force. If God was the "Commander of the Lord's army," then there would be no surprises. In the story of the fall of Jericho,[31] Joshua yielded to allow God to be in charge.[32] As a result, and for many years, Israel experienced a period of sustained victories. Like Joshua, David could depend on the faithfulness of God, and he knew it. This reveals a lot about David's heart.

From the heart of David, we could easily hear him say it this way, "God showed me that it wasn't my job to do the heavy lifting. No. That was something that only He could do. It was my job to seek Him, to trust Him, and to stand on His Word."[33]

God gave David a breakthrough, and then He did it again; a second breakthrough within a short window of time, by giving him a winning strategy of surprise. David had learned how spiritual warfare works. He learned that you must pray first, believe next, and then stand back and give God a chance to address the problem. The problem with so many is that they cry out in fear, instead of entering into a strategic prayer focus; then they hope, instead of believing; and finally, they doubt that God will do anything for them. This is not the way this king was thinking. He was operating on a different level. David stood on the promise that God would give him sustained victories, one after another. Still he must prime the pump[34] by having a fresh approach to God. David would never have agreed with the idiom we occasionally hear in the 21st century: "You cannot always succeed. You win some, and you lose some."[35]

David's heart was totally aware that God was for him and not against him. He also realized the difference between, just being an adherent[36] and a "believer". Adherents have merely joined the movement, but a believer has learned to activate faith, so that victories are imminent.

One of our discoveries about David's heart is that he trusted God to give him a prophetic word, and then that He would come through for him in times of trouble. In the twenty-first century, there are many who have never been introduced to a faith that works. Their experience with religion, or church, in particular is so traditional that God is neatly and tightly, if not firmly kept in a box, and unable to get free to work in their lives. They have become merely adherents, and not believers, with a personal constitution of trust in God. David was a worshipper, a dancer, an aggressive believer in his God. Never would he describe God as unresponsive, or uncaring. He saw God as his friend, his catalyst for change, and the one upon whom he could trust, without hesitation. God would always come through for him.

David believed that no giant and no storm could withstand the power of God, or even slow God down. He also realized that God

IS YOUR FAITH INACTIVE? ... OR DO YOU HAVE EXTREME FAITH?

could see his heart. Yes, David failed on a number of occasions, but the strongest part of his heart was a willingness to bend his knee and repent, quickly; and that as soon as he became aware of his infraction. God was "boss" and David was a compliant believer.

The good news is that what worked for David, will work for you. If you move away from just being an adherent and pick up the torch of total trust in God, entering into a lifestyle of aggressive faith, then you will have your breakthrough. Of course, David's arena of breakthrough was huge, but yours can be huge too. Here are some good words to try as you learn to more strongly describe your response to faith:

You have heard of extreme sports,[37] why not extreme faith? Connect with God on a personal level and establish your own prayer life. When you pray, don't forget to also believe.

Total faith can give you ginormous results. Try fitting these words into your mind and see if you can envision stronger results. Begin by challenging your thoughts to bigger, more exciting words, which could describe your new road to a stronger faith:

- Enormous – greatly exceeding the common size, or extent.
- Ginormous – extremely large
- Humongous – huge, enormous.
- Aggressive – strong or emphatic in effect or intent

You could even call it: "outrageous faith."

Endnotes

1. II Samuel 3:26-30
2. II Samuel 4:5-8
3. II Samuel 5:1-5
4. Josephus Book 7, 4:1: 72 - Also called, "The Valley of Rephaim" in II Samuel 5:18
5. II Samuel 5:17
6. Josephus Book 7, 4:1:74
7. II Samuel 5:17-25
8. www.oxforddictionaries.com/definition/front_page - "The first page of a newspaper, containing the most important or remarkable news of the day. Used to draw attention to an important or noteworthy fact or occurrence."
9. II Samuel 5:17-21 NLT
10. II Samuel 4 tells the story of the assassination of Ishbosheth at the hands of two usurpers, who thought to get reward from David, the king of Judah.
11. www.merriam-webster.com/dictionary/footprint - "a marked effect, impression, or impact". Some people leave a small impact, while others a much larger impact, or foot print.
12. *Josephus* Book 7, 4:1:74-75
13. www.shmoop.com/shakespeare-quotes/heart-of-hearts/meaning-now.html - Society has changed Shakespeare's phrase to mean that we're choosing one of our many hearts. Hamlet refers to the core of his heart, and that's essentially what we're saying when we use it today. 'It's something we're really certain about. We know it in our heart of hearts.'"
14. *Josephus* Book 6, Chapter 8:1:165
15. *Josephus* Book 7, 4:1:72
16. The high priest at that was Abiathar, who also a trusted counsellor.
17. II Samuel 5:19 NKJV
18. II Samuel 5:20 ERV
19. II Samuel 5:20 NLT
20. Deuteronomy 32:31 KJV, II Samuel 22:32 KJV
21. 1 Chronicles 14:12
22. Josephus Book 7, 4:1:72 - Also called, "The Valley of Rephaim" in II Samuel 5:18

23. *Josephus* Book 7, 4:1:76-77 - I have taken the content of this account and reworded it to include the ingredients of Josephus' story.

24. Ibid

25. Ibid

26. www.dictionary.com/browse/awol - A.W.O.L. - "In the service of the military. To be absent without leave; to be absent from one's post or duty, without official permission, but without intending to desert." absent without leave; absent from one's post or duty

27. Ibid

28. Ibid

29. Is there a Grandfather in the House? - by Ron A. Bishop - "Chaordic – Life is a blend of both chaos and order". Page 255-260

30. "Norm" - When the outcome is so predictable that it becomes par for the course.

31. Joshua 6:1-22 - The miraculous fall of the city of Jericho.

32. Joshua 5:13-15 ESV - "When Joshua was by Jericho, he lifted up his eyes and looked, and behold, a man was standing before him with his drawn sword in his hand. And Joshua went to him and said to him, "Are you for us, or for our adversaries?" 14 And he said, "No; but I am the commander of the army of the LORD. Now I have come." And Joshua fell on his face to the earth and worshiped* and said to him, "What does my lord say to his servant?" And the commander of the LORD's army said to Joshua, 'Take off your sandals from your feet, for the place where you are standing is holy." And Joshua did so.

33. Movie - Quote by Chris Fabry, Movie: "War Room – Prayer is a Powerful Weapon" - A 2015 American Christian drama film.

34. www.wisegeek.org/what-is-pump-priming - Prime the pump - If you have seen an old water pump, but on the first pump, no water is produced. To prime that pump, means to begin by lubricating the mechanics and then it will work properly. "In order to prime the pump, often all that is needed is another source of the liquid being sought. This is usually accomplished simply by pouring some of that liquid down the well. Once that is done, simply turning on the pump or using a hand crank, depending on the type of pump, is usually all that is required. In most cases, once water starts to flow from a pump, more priming in the future should be unnecessary."

35. idioms.thefreedictionary.com/You+win+some%2C+you+lose+some

36. www.google.ie/search?q=adherent - Adherent - "someone who supports a particular party, person, or set of ideas."

37. www.wikipedia.com - Extreme sport. Extreme sports are recreational activities, perceived as involving a high degree of risk. These activities often involve speed, height, a high level of physical exertion, and highly specialized gear.

The Day David Poured Out Water as a Sacrifice to God

II Samuel 23

David and his band of soldiers lived stressful and complicated lives and that for year after year. Sometimes they were avoiding detection from Saul and his army; often they were making a living providing cover and security for a wealthy farmer or rancher, who recognized his assets were in danger from the threat of rustlers, marauding bands of soldiers just passing through, but often and nearly always in battles that kept them tired and in need of refreshment. Often, they just needed to be at home, wherever that could be, resting, or with their wives and children.

"Once during the harvest, when David was at the cave of Adullam, the Philistine army was camped in the valley of Rephaim. The

Three (who were among the Thirty—an elite group among David's fighting men) went down to meet him there. David was staying in the stronghold at the time, and a Philistine detachment had occupied the town of Bethlehem.

THE CAVE OF ADULLAM WAS SECLUDED JUST ENOUGH THAT NO ONE NOTICED. IT WAS THE PERFECT HIDEAWAY FOR DAVID'S ARMY.

David remarked longingly to his men, "Oh, how I would love some of that good water from the well by the gate in Bethlehem." So, the Three broke through the Philistine lines, drew some water from the well by the gate in Bethlehem, and brought it back to David. But he refused to drink it. Instead, he poured it out as an offering to the Lord.[17] "The Lord forbid that I should drink this!" he exclaimed. "This water is as precious as the blood of these men who risked their lives to bring it to me." So, David did not drink it. These are examples of the exploits of the Three.[1]

They risked all for one cup of water.

This story is about an incident, which took place during the wars fought by David and his men but is not easily placed in the chronology of events. The story is one selected as an interesting human-interest story, and one which gives us a portrayal of the courage and loyalty, which occurred after one of their military expeditions. Notice that in both times this story is named, it is merged with a collection of stories about the others of "David's Mighty Men."[2]

David, and his men needed to be refreshed in body and spirit, after being involved in another battle. They found that the cave of Adullam was the perfect place for the rest they needed. A relatively large army of Philistines had settled nearby in the Valley of Rephaim, while a large garrison[3] was established in Bethlehem.[4]

Apparently, with so many caves throughout Israel, no one seemed to notice this one, so David and his men, with a little effort, were able to come and go, without being detected. There was a village by the name of Adullam,[5] but then there was nearby, the cave Adullam. On the outside Adullam appeared like an insignificant hole into the mountain, however, once inside, it opened up into quite a larger room which was able to accommodate many of David's army. This was where David and his men, on many occasions sought refuge, as well as a place where he would go to hide out and seek God in prayer. Really, it appears that, God designed this cave just for David, as there is no mention of it earlier and not much about it later in history.

THE CURIOSITY OF SPELUNKING WAS NOT A TRENDY HOBBY OF THE AVERAGE HEBREW 3,000 YEARS AGO.

David came out of the cave, and was looking longingly off to the east, in the direction of Bethlehem. This was somewhat of a sentimental moment for a young man who was missing home, and missing its warmth, comforts and flavors. From his mouth, and in the hearing of at least three of his warriors, he allowed to slip these words: "Oh, how I would love some of that good water from the well, by the gate in Bethlehem."[6]

This was not likely an intentional hint, but a casual, if not an idle remark to his friends. It was certainly not a command, or a directive, but merely his thinking out loud from his heart. He really was thirsty, and no water in all the earth could quench his thirst like the water from that particular well. Lots of water has a flavor, and water with a familiar flavor is always especially tasty to the one who recognizes it.[7] Water from that particular well was almost sacred in David's memory.

This comment was void of personal expectations, as he had taken steps to deliver his parents to the care of his friend, the King of Moab, for as long as it would take to settle the issues between he and Israel's king. David had been a fugitive, running from Saul for several years and he knew full well that, if he traveled to Bethlehem, he would not be able to see his family, but only draw water from the well. So, this truly was only a personal longing for water from his home town well.[8]

David's mighty men were "warriors extraordinaire."[9] It has been assumed that the three men who overheard David's comment, were the same three whose stories had just been chronicled, namely Jashobeam[10] (whose nickname was Adino), Eleazar[11] (the son of a man named Dodo), and Shammah.[12] They were just three of the thirty-seven listed of David's Mighty Men.[13]

These men who had come to David in Adullam were grass roots men,[14] who had no false pride, or unrealistic expectations. However, if they pledged their loyalty and support, they'd give their lives in the performance of it. When David made that simple wish, they looked at each other and without uttering even a word, slipped out of the stronghold and fearlessly headed in the direction of Bethlehem.

To these men, it did not matter whether their journey would be in daytime or nighttime. It did not matter if they were to encounter a host of Philistines, or if there was nothing but wildlife spread out over the countryside. There were so many stories of their dynamic exploits that their persona was both fearless and intimidating. To be on the other side of the line, facing these approaching men was to tremble, quake and seek refuge, regardless of how many were in your rank. These men of David had each been known to slay as many as eight hundred men, and even worse. It was difficult for the opposition to separate truth from legend and the Philistines refused to take a risk just to confirm that the stories were untrue.

Adino, Eleazar and Shammah did not sneak through the countryside, or wait until nighttime to travel, or allow their eyes to dart this way and that. No, they were fearless men of profound courage, so they took the most direct route, because of who they were and the level of confidence they each had that God would help them accomplish the task at hand. David had taught them that God was with them and would be there always to assist them from point A to point B.

David was a man of prayer and his men had been transformed on the idea of how the wars they fought were not theirs but God's. I am confident that David had shared his own personal stories of his exploits with the men. After all, around those camp fires somebody was always talking and sharing of their personal "fish stories." David would surely have motivated his men with his own stories of when God had intervened for him.

When a sports coach faces his team just before going into a major game, where more than a trophy is on the line, but perhaps an entire season, he will engage in the best motivational speech he can muster. Sometimes they'll even bring in a specialist in motivation, just to get the team pumped and ready to defeat the opponent. David did not need to do that, because, when he and his army faced the opposition they did so reminding themselves that:

> "No weapon formed against you shall prosper, And, every tongue, which rises against you in judgment you shall condemn. This is

> the heritage of the servants of the LORD, and their righteousness is from Me," says the LORD.[15]

Those warriors went on a Long Walk and the Philistines stepped out off their way.

The scripture says that the three men broke right through the Philistine lines, and that they penetrated the Philistine camp,[16] as if daring anyone to stand in their way. Certainly, there were those Philistine solders who did not even recognize who they were, but in that case, we must realize that there had to be another element to make up the difference. It had to be the aura of anointing.

These men had stood against formidable odds before and that day would be no different. It is amazing when you have a history where, just one of you could stand up and chase a thousand of the enemy; then along comes one of your teammates and you find that the odds multiply, allowing you to put ten thousand to flight. The problem the enemy has, is that they do not understand the power of God that stands with you, enables you, empowers you and pushes you on to absolute victory. These men had learned, in following in David's shadow, that the gods of the enemy are nothing but wood, stone and manmade materials. They are not like our God.[17] And after all the millennia, many of them have had to agree that their god sold them out and left them sweltering in defeat. The God whom Adino, Eleazar and Shammah served was the same God David served, and so they pressed onward, in the direction of Bethlehem.[18]

> "So, the Three broke through the Philistine lines, drew some water from the well by the gate in Bethlehem, and brought it back to David."[19]

Water is to earth like blood is to the human body.

Adino, Eleazar and Shammah returned to the camp, part way up the mountain and into the cave. Some may have noticed that they were absent, but nothing seems to be said about it. They had silently slipped out, perhaps partly because they did not want a crowd going on this water run. Oh, yes, a couple dozen of the men would likely have enjoyed going along on this rowdy adventure, just because they were all rambunctious and always up to some fun. But this had really been a sober commission, as self-imposed as it was. These three men just did not want to make a fuss. They had heard their hero express a desire for water from that particular well, and they decided it was something they could do, and so they had ducked out and taken care of it before anyone even knew they were gone.

Upon their return, a small crowd gathered around David along with the troupe of three, just to see what was going on. They could all see their leader standing there glaring at the jug of water, muttering something like, "But I just cannot drink this water. As wonderful as it would be to quench my thirst, and as wonderful as it would taste, I can only think of the risk you took to bring it to me."

All of David's men who were present watched as word had gotten out what those three heros had done for David. It was as if silence prevailed. It was expected by all that David would be so honored, so grateful that he'd value their gifts to such a level, that he would tilt his head slightly, savor the moment and sip that room temperature water from his childhood well. They expected that then he would smack his lips in delight, as he slapped them on the back and complimented them for their kindness. It took longer

THEY REALIZED THAT DAVID'S THOUGHTS WERE A CUT-ABOVE.

than any had expected for David's response. Then it happened, the unthinkable, the unpredictable. Any other man would have gulped it down, almost licking the damp container when all would be gone… but no, not David. In total disbelief, they had observed as David looked around, at his audience… and then at those three men of valor.

FROM THAT MOMENT, THEY KNEW WHY HE HAD BEEN CHOSEN TO BE ISRAEL'S KING.

He then said, "Thank you my friends. You have done me a great service, and something I did not expect. Your blood could have been spilled, and you could have lost your lives. This was a great risk, and I am honored by your gift, but I consider this gift too sacred for me to drink. As blood is to the body, so is water to the earth. Thank you, but I must pour this water out, as a sacrifice to God, for bringing you back again to me."

At that moment, everyone realized why their leader was blessed by God. They realized that David was so highly principled that he did not fit the normal paradigm. His devotion to God surpassed anything they had ever observed in the life of any man.

David's way of thinking was different to the status quo of the day. It became clear that if you are a leader, you must live more by principle than just good ideas.

These men all knew the gist of what was going on in that cave. Although they had never observed a scene like this played out before, they all knew David's heart and they all knew that he was the mentor, the teacher, and certainly their fearless leader. They did not always understand what drove him forward, but they did make it a practice to listen to whatever he said, because he was so clear in his wisdom and perspective.

Now they could overhear David saying, "How could I drink this water with God watching me? I could not drink the blood of my three strong warriors who risked their lives to bring it to me, so I will not benefit from their sacrifice."[20] There are some sacrifices, which are not to be benefited by men, but left only to God, and as a man, I will offer this to God.

What was the result of David's big pour in the cave of Adullam?

Through the years, David had been teaching these men about the nature of God. He was determined not to cross the line and do anything, which would compromise his core values. God meant so much to this worshipper, and he had no intention of stealing God's glory in any area of his life. Leaders must learn the distinction between, that which belongs to God, and that which is acceptable for those made of flesh. The jury was not out, it was now time to make a pronouncement and David was ready to begin the "Big Pour." This water belonged to God and he was prepared to make an offering to God, that which belonged to Him.

These men were not small men, but Mighty Men and all those who were joint believers stood there watching and listening. They were, once again, impacted with a "Life Lesson," which they would never forget. Loyalty was strengthened on that day and every man grew a few centimeters taller, and a whole lot wiser. When David tipped the jug and began to pour, a gasp was heard throughout the cave of Adullam.

DAVID WAS NOT OFTEN CONFUSED ON WHAT BELONGED TO HIM AND WHAT BELONGED TO GOD!

"David refused to drink it. Instead, he poured it out as an offering to the Lord... This water is as precious as the blood of these men who risked their lives to bring it to me." So, David did not drink it."[21]

Some have said, "Why is God so silent?"

God is not silent but speaks daily through His Word and through the lives of those who are believers in Him. "Clearly, you are a letter from Christ showing the result of our ministry among you. This letter is written not with pen and ink, but with the Spirit of the living God. It is carved not on tablets of stone, but on human hearts."[22]

David was determined to be a "living epistle" so that the eyes of every man could see an unmistakable message coming straight from the heart of God. He did not live life in such ways as to embolden himself just because he could, but he lived it so that all could know God better just by watching him. The Atheist does not know God because he is not looking for God. David, however, saw the handiwork of God in everything.

How was this a "Heart Revealing Day" in the life of David?

David's heart was always exposed to those around him. If you lived and worked with David you could easily see what kind of mettle he had on the inside. He was not complicated, and people could always say, "What you see is what you get."[23] Lots of people are complicated, unpredictable and prideful. David was simple, he was humble, and followed his core values meticulously. He was not without fault, but one thing, which all could say is this: If he did wrong, he would admit it and repent quickly.

In this story, we see that David was not often confused on what belonged to him and what belonged to God. Watch David and you will learn that some of his most basic character traits were that he loved God, was a worshipper, and always kept in focus his own need for intimacy with his Creator. As a result, he successfully had a lot of followers who were loyal to him and to God and were especially strong in their faith.

The fact is that all things belong to God. He takes everything which is left behind, after your death, and carries your assets, heritage, legacy and inheritances from generation to generation. Whatever assets you collect or accrue in this life are only a reflection of His grace and favor. The reality is that God is your father, even if you don't know how to acknowledge Him. He owns everything, because he existed before you, created you and will transcend past your life to future generations and into eternity. Every material thing you possess, is merely on loan temporarily and actually is on "loan from God."[24]

Humility was a part of David's inner core, or spiritual DNA. He had focused on worship and humility for so much of his life that it was one of his most highly developed fortes. He knew the world did not revolve around him, so he was able to easily bend the knee to a higher power.

It is a fact that those who are super-talented are often promoted and highly favored. As a result, accolades are often cast at their feet; which makes them feel really good and "special." If you are one of those highly esteemed individuals, and your talent is so obvious it is over the top, then you have to make a conscious decision to be humble, and always point to God, when the awards are being handed out. If you are consistent in giving the glory to God, then we, in the audience will take notice and appreciate what we see in you.

WHAT DAVID REALLY WANTED WAS "LIVING WATER," NOT JUST WATER FROM BETHLEHEM.

David decided that he was flesh, and what he really wanted was "living water," not just water from Bethlehem. That is why he decided to give God the glory. Therefore, he poured out the container of water as an offering to God.

Leave room in your life for the Holy Spirit to provide you with the sparkle. It is not you, your personality, or your creativity that gives you the sparkle. It is the Holy Spirit inside of you. Let Him place the light over your head that brings opportunity and blessing to your life, your career and your relationships. Your future will be bright if you are willing to "pour out the water" when all around you are chanting, "drink it, drink it!"

Endnotes

1. II Samuel 23:13-17 NLT

2. II Samuel 23 and also in II Chronicles 11

3. www.en.wikipedia.org - "garrison" - "the collective term for a body of troops, stationed in a particular location, originally to guard it, but now often simply using it as a home base.

4. I Samuel 16:1 - Remember that Bethlehem was the place of birth for David. He grew up here with his father, Jesse and his family. So, the well was a familiar place for them to get their water.

5. en.wikipedia.org/wiki/Adullam - Adullam is an ancient ruin, built upon a hilltop overlooking the Elah Valley, south of Bet Shemesh in Israel. In the late 19th century, the town was still in ruins, and called by the Arabic name, `Eîd el Mieh

6. 1 Chronicles 11:17 NLT

7. www.en.wikipedia.org/wiki/Amanzimtoti - Amanzimtoti, Kwa Zulu Natal, South Africa – Ron & Christi Bishop and their children moved from the USA to live in this village in 1985 to take the lead in a Zulu Bible College. "Legend has it that when the Zulu King Shaka tasted the water in 1828, he said 'Kanti amanza mtoti', meaning 'So, the water is sweet', from where the name of Amanzimtoti originated, and also marks the start of its colourful cultural heritage."

8. I Samuel 22:3-4 MSG - "David went to Mizpah in Moab. He petitioned the king of Moab, "Grant asylum to my father and mother, until I find out what God has planned for me. David left his parents in the care of the king of Moab. They stayed there all through the time David was hiding out."

9. www.english.stackexchange.com - "warriors extraordinaire." Generally, use of the word, extraordinaire occurs if you want to put the adjective after the modified noun, and want to make the noun sound more like a title, so as to add a touch of French flavor to the sentence. It seems that the French purposely choose to use such words, since (English being an additional language), they select a nicer word, than just an ordinary word. It does sound better than just "extraordinary."

10. Jashobeam, aka Adino - II Samuel 23:8 and I Chronicles 11:10-11

11. Eleazar - II Samuel 23:9-10 and I Chronicles 11:12-14

12. Shammah - II Samuel 23:11-12

13. www.gotquestions.org/mighty-men-David.html - The full list of the mighty men of David is located in II Samuel 23. There you will see 37 men listed.

14. www.dictionary.com - "grassroots men" – The common, or ordinary people, especially as contrasted with the leadership or elite of a political party, social organization, etc.; the rank and file."

15. Isaiah 54:17 NKJV

16. I Chronicles 11:19 MSG

17. Deuteronomy 32 - Read carefully the entire chapter, focusing especially on the word, "Rock."

18. God is Israel's Rock. Without Him, they will always be defeated. If they are defeated, it is because they trusted in their own strength. God will only depart when man thinks he can win without Him.

19. Deuteronomy 32:30-31

20. 1 Chronicles 11:15-19 NLT

21. I Chronicles 11:19 VOICE

22. I Chronicles 11:19 NLT

23. II Corinthians 3:3 NLT

24. www.dictionary.cambridge.org - WYSIWYG is an acronym for "what you see is what you get." This means "nothing is hidden". Originally attributed to comedian: Flip Wilson.

25. www.RushLimbaugh.com - Rush Limbaugh is often boastful as he says, his "talent is on loan from God". You may think you do not like that statement, "Talent on loan from God." but if you will, just take a moment to consider that, all you have material and personal gifts, are "on loan from God." Everything in this life is temporary. If you have talent, it is also "on loan from God."

THE DAY DAVID REALLY LEARNED TO DANCE

II SAMUEL 6

David was well aware that Saul had not been a spiritually sensitive leader, and now he must fortify the nation, so that they would develop a strong faith. In many ways, this nation was like a blank page, ready to be written upon. David was just the man, because of his personal relationship with God.

The fact that David was exuberant, full of faith, loved God with all his heart, and was able to lead aggressively, made him the best man to lead this nation. From this point, God had set the stage and now, David was prepared to lead as a "man after God's own heart." David was "the sweet psalmist of Israel." He gave them music, inspiration, romanticism, integrity, victory after victory and history. David was not perfect, but he made positive deposits

ISRAEL WAS LIKE A BLANK PAGE, AND DAVID WAS GLAD TO WRITE UPON IT!

in people's lives on every stratum, giving them hope like no other leader they'd ever had. He did not see himself as only responsible to be the head of state, but as interested in the spiritual well-being of the people. This went a long way toward building strong faith and forging an enduring allegiance to God and King.

What was the back-story of this day?

Three months earlier.

Saul had been dead for seven years and the kingdom had been divided for all that time. Now, finally, the kingdom was reunited as one nation, under the rule of David.

David took strategic steps to make Israel strong and unified. One of his first steps was to capture Jebus, rename it Jerusalem, and to set Israel in order by making Jerusalem[1] Israel's capital city. After that, David determined to establish Jerusalem as the spiritual capital as well, by bringing the Ark of the Covenant out of storage, and then to place it strategically in that city.

David realized that he must step out in faith to lead the nation to God. It was not that Saul had caused the nation to backslide, as much as it was that they were still weak in their faith and had never really understood what a nation of faith looked like. They had a long history, but the history of Israel had not matured far from the original state of "slave nation status," with meager perceptions on spiritual matters. As a people, no one seemed to understand how they could have a personal faith in God. They were distant and had never been attached to God. They taught their children traditions and culture, but never really taught them faith and trust, because they did not understand such things. In reality, they were untrusting, because they had never been taught. Now was the time and it was David's job to show them the way.

DAVID'S BIGGEST CHALLENGE WAS TO TEACH ISRAEL TO PERSONALLY, LOVE GOD!

Just three months earlier David had gathered the elders together and discussed his grand idea to bring the Ark of the Covenant from its resting place at Kiriath-Jearim (Baale-Judah), where it had been kept in isolation and out of service for all the years of Samuel's reign as judge and then throughout the 40 years of King Saul's reign, as well as 7.5 years of Ishbosheth's reign in Mahanaim.[2]

David had gained agreement from the elders to send a contingent of young and strong soldiers from all over the land, along with the priests and Levites. He challenged them to go with him to Kiriath-Jearim to bring up the Ark of God, and to carry it to Jerusalem, and there to keep it, and offer before it those sacrifices and those other honors with, which God used to be well pleased.[3]

David, the Ark of the Covenant, and Uzzah

David mobilized thirty thousand[4] of his best soldiers to accompany him on the journey from Kiriath-Jearim, a distance of nearly 12 miles (17 Kilometers) to Jerusalem.[5] Accompanying him were many priests and Levites, so that there was a very great contingent to endorse this effort. Coming to the house of Abinadab, which sat on a hill overlooking the city, they began by having the priests[6] place the Ark onto the bed of a new oxcart. The two sons of Abinadab, both Levites, directed the cart. Ahio was walking out in front, while his brother, Uzzah walked alongside the cart.[7]

This great procession went well for the first half of the journey, but suddenly tragedy struck. The road was not always smooth, and at one point a rough place threatened the stability of the cart, causing concern that the Ark would actually slide off the cart. Within arm's length was Abinadab's son, Uzzah. When the oxen stumbled, Uzzah reached out to steady the Ark, so that it would not fall.

> "And when they came to Nachon's threshing floor, Uzzah put out his hand to the Ark of God and took hold of it, for the oxen stumbled. Then the anger of the LORD was aroused against Uzzah, and God struck him there for his error; and he died there by the Ark of God."[8]

The famed historian Josephus states clearly that, "Now, because he was not a priest and yet touched the Ark, God struck him dead."[9]

Instantly, David became defensive, as he did not understand why this tragedy had taken place. Why had God slain this man and in this way? He felt that God was, for this moment, being unreasonable; after all they had no ill intent, but were trying to do a good thing, by restoring worship of God back to the public arena. In David's mind, there could be no justifiable reason for Uzzah's death. David began to think irrationally, while thinking God was the one who was being unreasonable. It took a few weeks before David began to get a focus on what had really happened.

EVEN GOOD MEN CAN STEP OVER THE LINE AND SUFFER CONSEQUENCES!

David's immediate reaction was to stop the procession. He then turned around to get his bearings and to make a decision as to what his next move should be. Immediately, he saw another Levite by the name of Obed-Edom.[10] This man had come as a part of the procession, to stand close to the Ark. For some reason, David felt relief that this man was so conveniently nearby. When he checked closer, he discovered that Obed-Edom lived nearby and very convenient to where this tragedy had taken place.

David was afraid of the Lord that day, and said, "How shall the Ark of the Lord come to me?"[11] He asked, "'How can I ever bring the Ark of the Lord back into my care?' So, David decided not to move the Ark of the Lord into the City of David. Instead, he took it to the house of Obed-Edom[12] of Gath."[13]

The mood of this grand throng of people was somber as they all broke from the celebration and made their way back to their homes, all over Israel. This meeting would not reconvene for three months, and even that meeting was not, at this point, definitely on the docket for now. David was in a pouting mood and disappointment was in every heart. Nothing is said about Uzzah's funeral or what comments were made by all the people on that occasion. One thing is for certain, David's heart was now distancing itself from concern about all the grand plans he had had for pomp and ceremony. It would be a few weeks before he would address issues regarding spiritual matters. The next move was in God's court, for sure, and that came about immediately.

Obed-Edom, on the other hand, was delighted to have a new guest in his home, namely the Ark of the Covenant. This was the guest he needed, but never realized how much he wanted. After the breach of Uzzah, you can be sure that every member of Obed-Edom's household gave the "Ark of the Covenant" a wide berth, taking great care to respect its space and give it the place it deserved. From the first day, things changed in his home. He had eight sons:

> "Obed-Edom's sons were Shemaiah, the firstborn, followed by Jehozabad, Joah, Sacar, Nethanel, Ammiel, Issachar, and Peullethai—God blessed him with eight sons."[14]

Obed-Edom recognized that the overall disposition of himself and every member of his family was improving and stronger in every way. It seemed that everyone was happier, healthier and kinder. He saw improvements in his business affairs, his community relationships and even life itself. This seemed to transpire immediately, but it also became crystal clear over the next few weeks. He noticed that the entire neighborhood was talking about it, as it was obvious even to strangers. Word began to leak out and spread in the form of rumors, which morphed into legends, making it all the way to the king's home and back again.

THE ANOINTING COVERED OBED-EDOM'S HOME. EVERY DAY WAS A GOOD DAY!

While David sat at breakfast, he would be interrupted by friends who just stopped by to let him know what was going on in the part of the kingdom, where Obed-Edom lived. Leaders on various levels would just drop in to give him a heads-up on the spiritual weather patterns, which were forming over the area around Nachon's threshing floor, just down the road from Obed-Edom's home. And then there were the couriers who had been sent by the security forces, to inform him of strange and positive things that were happening to Obed-Edom and seemingly everything he touched.

King David was told, "The Lord has blessed the family of Obed-Edom. He has also blessed everything that belongs to him. That's because the Ark of God is in Obed-Edom's house."[15]

These reports caused David to develop a sense of suspicion. At first, he had questions, and then he found himself envious, as he felt that it just wasn't right, that Obed-Edom was enjoying all these blessings and he felt out in the cold[16] and separated.

It was at that point that David recognized that he had done something amiss but did not yet know what transgression he had made. He put the scribes to work to discover what details he was missing, which would make all the difference the next time. After all, David had longed for so long to reintroduce God to the children of Israel, as he knew Him.

David had written of his love and devotion to God, and how he had longed to bring the symbol of God's presence, to the capital of the nation. The Ark had never physically been to Jerusalem. David spoke in Psalm 132 of how they had searched the land and found the Ark of the Covenant in Kiriath-Jearim.

Obed-Edom was a man of no means. His family was poor and he had little to make him happy, except for what God might do in his life. This man, however was devout and always ready to do, for God, what he felt he should. When the opportunity presented itself, as it had the day Uzzah died, this man of the tribe of Levi, was ready to step up and do what he could. Days later, it was reported, that Obed-Edom was "exceedingly happy, and the object of envy to all those that saw or inquired after his house."[17]

SOMETIMES YOU MUST REHEARSE THE DETAILS TO SEE WHAT YOU DID WRONG!

David had heard enough of the divine favor, prosperity and good fortune that had descended upon the world of Obed-Edom. He felt that those blessings should well be upon every man who is determined to live in the shadow of God's presence, but he would do his best to make sure that, before many days passed, he would call for them upon his own house and upon his own life.

It had been many years since the Ark of the Covenant had been a topic of discussion. No one David knew had even addressed the subject of "how to deal with the protocol surrounding 'the Ark of the Covenant.'"

Three months after the national tragedy, they had done the research and discovered that there were legitimate reasons for Uzzah's death. It had become apparent that Israel's failure had been in repeating the Philistines' methods for transporting the Ark of the Covenant. Actually, to say it bluntly, Israel had followed the example just as the pagan priests of Dagon had prescribed to the citizens of Ekron. This failure had taken them down a wrong road and corrections had to be made. Not only that, but he had not respected the occasion enough and had commissioned the transport of that Ark to unqualified men.

David was horrified and had faced the fact that the Philistine method of "transporting the Ark" was not the plan Israel should have followed. He thought, "Why did we just assume that we should carry the Ark of the Covenant on an oxcart?" He began to realize that, he had been irresponsible, by only focusing on taking the Ark from "point A to point B." Of course, sacred assignments must require their own protocol, and be handled with utmost respect and reverence. David realized, now that the reason for this tragedy had not been the Lord, but his own failure to know the law and to treat the sacred things with greater respect.

One more thing he had learned:

"All priests are Levites, but not all Levites are priests."[18]

Uzzah was of the tribe of Levi but had not been consecrated to function as a Levitical priest, for the house of the Lord. There was a difference and all of Israel had been given an object lesson on protocol. Uzzah had grown up around the Ark, as it had been a guest of his parents' home for all of his life; and so, he had become quite familiar and perhaps even possessive of its aura, but that could not enter into the picture, as the Ark of the Covenant was "God's treasure Chest" and not owned by any man. For Uzzah, it must have become second nature to secure and protect the Ark on the first day he had ever seen it in danger. Without realizing it, Uzzah, like a big brother, had embraced a sense of personal responsibility to protect and secure the Ark of the Covenant as it traveled from the sanctity of his own home to Jerusalem, and the place it would now rest. In the mind of Uzzah, this was his way of being a good host, but it was out of line with the way God expected things to be done. As unfortunate as it is, for Uzzah to pay with his life, it also must be understood that all things that pertain to the holiness of God must be considered holy ground and not to be trifled with by mere man. Keep this in mind: God is holy and more perfect than perfect, while men are flesh and will never rise to that level of perfection. Even if we are able to achieve the perfection we're challenged to seek,[19] it still is only by the grace of God, and not because we are so bright, or good.[20] There is a principle we must embrace: "God can touch man, and all is improved, but the fingerprints of man must never contaminate the things of God."

UZZAH STEPPED OVER THE LINE! HE HAD BECOME TOO FAMILIAR WITH THE SACRED THINGS.

Every time a human being touches anything, he leaves his mark (fingerprint).[21] Holy things must not be touched by flesh, or it will contaminate, sabotage and compromise even the holiness it touches. God is big and our touch will never improve or compliment anything, which comes from heaven. The scribes came back to David, as they had discovered a scripture, which would change things:

> "Make four gold rings and fasten one of them to each of the four legs of the chest. Make two poles of acacia wood. Cover them with gold and put them through the rings, so the chest can be carried by the poles. Don't ever remove the poles from the rings. When I give you the Ten Commandments written on two flat stones, put them inside the chest."[22]

When the researchers discovered this scripture, regarding the holy furnishings of the Tabernacle, they knew exactly why Uzzah had died:

> "The camp will be ready to move when Aaron and his sons have finished covering the sanctuary and all the sacred articles. The Kohathites will come and carry these things to the next destination. But they must not touch the sacred objects, or they will die. So, these are the things from the Tabernacle that the Kohathites must carry."[23]

David made a decision. We will do God's business in God's way and follow His patterns to the detail. He then began making plans accordingly.

There was one more matter, which David felt he must take care of now. Because of their kindness in taking care of the Ark, David embraced Obed-Edom and his sons, by giving them the responsibility of guarding the door of entrance to the Ark, while it stood in the Tabernacle, which David had placed in the Capital city of Jerusalem.[24] This reflects the kindness and the shepherd-like care

David felt for all the people of Israel. He was always observing how he could serve the people in considerate ways. It could be said, that he had their backs, and would never take advantage of them, thus determining to always do the responsible thing.

GOD CAN TOUCH MAN, AND ALL IS IMPROVED ~ BUT THE FINGERPRINTS OF MAN MUST NEVER CONTAMINATE THE THINGS OF GOD.

The Day David Began to Dance

The day began with euphoria, like David had not experienced in quite some time. He had experienced victories, strong faith and divine favor, so many times before, but this day was starting off with an inner happiness, because he knew what was about to transpire. A lifelong dream of his was to show that the Lord is "the true King over Israel, and once again in the midst of his people."[25] He was a leader and today, David would lead.

> "The Ark of the Lord remained there in Obed-Edom's house for three months, and the Lord blessed Obed-Edom and his entire household.Then King David was told, "The Lord has blessed Obed-Edom's household and everything he has because of the Ark of God." So, David went there and brought the Ark of God from the house of Obed-Edom to the City of David with a great celebration. After the men who were carrying the Ark of the Lord had gone six steps, David sacrificed a bull and a fattened calf. And David danced before the Lord with all his might, wearing a priestly garment. So, David and all the people of Israel brought up the Ark of the Lord with shouts of joy and the blowing of rams' horns."[26]

David summoned the priests to come to see him. The meeting, on that day involved Zadok and Abiathar, as well as several others of the Levitical leaders. David admitted that they had all made a mistake just three months earlier, in how they handled things. He explained why God struck out at them by slaying Uzzah. "It was our fault for not following God's protocol." Now, however, they knew better and were prepared to do it as God required. He instructed them, "You are the leaders of the Levitical families. You must purify yourselves and all your fellow Levites, so you can bring the Ark of the Lord, the God of Israel, to the place I have prepared for it."[27] On that day the priests pledged to carry the Ark on their shoulders, with the poles in the rings, just as the Lord had commanded Moses in the beginning.

David stood in his palace, preparing in his mind, how he should posture himself, as King, for this day, when his only desire was to give his best praise to God. He felt that this day was the day, of all the days he'd ever lived, when he must give his best effort to worship. He could not hold anything back. David felt such depth of love and praise that he could even get such an opportunity to bring God to the people in such a way. He realized that Israel was a nation who worshipped God, but he also knew of how secular they had become and how backslidden they were in their daily walk with the Lord.

A LINEN ROBE FELT BETTER TO A HUMBLE MAN, LIKE DAVID, THAN HIS KINGLY ROBES.

The king, on that day looked at his kingly robe and felt put off by its glamorous appeal to the eye. It seemed repugnant to him as he saw himself from different eyes, as he evaluated his own thoughts at the moment. He must not approach God with pompous extravagance; he must not be ostentatious, ornate or overdone, for to do so would be tasteless when reflecting on the glory of a holy God. Today, for David, it must be nothing but joyous humility, extravagant praise, and uproarious celebration. David found himself wanting to prepare for his departure by shedding his Royal Robe. He called for the priests to send to him a linen ephod. This was not the ornate ephod worn by the High Priest, but that worn by the common priest, both for his priestly duties and as his every day clothing of choice. It was simple and made of linen. It was not fancy, but plain and probably had a rope for a belt, but we do not know for sure. We read that the boy Samuel, when serving as an understudy with the High Priest Eli, wore a linen tunic or ephod, like a priest.[28] It was simple and would look to us much like a long nightshirt, most likely some shade of white. This would certainly not be royal or king-like, but it was what David wanted, when he would worship before his God. Today, he determined, I will not be "kingly," but I will be a servant, a worker, a worshipper in the House of the Lord.

The journey to the house of Obed-Edom was only about five kilometers (3 miles) outside of the city of Jerusalem. A throng of Israelites accompanied David to this country home. This time every detail was in order to the required protocol. Every musical instrument they could find was played and all Israel rejoiced, with their new king on his first official duty, after becoming king over unified Israel.

> "After the men who were carrying the Ark of the Lord had gone six steps, David sacrificed a bull and a fattened calf. And David danced before the Lord with all his might, wearing a priestly garment. So, David and all the people of Israel brought up the Ark of the Lord with shouts of joy and the blowing of rams' horns."[29]

David presided over an event, like Israel had never seen before. The Hebrew people have always been a celebratory people, but this day stands apart from any others for its pomp and ceremony. It is worthy of note that this former slave people, were able to see a new picture of God, to which they'd never been exposed. David entered the city as he had done all the way from Obed-Edom's home, dancing and glorifying God. The dance of David has been described in a number of ways:

> "He was dancing for the LORD with all his might...."[30]
>
> "And David was dancing before the LORD with great enthusiasm..."[31]
>
> "Then David danced and spun around with abandon before ADONAI..."[32]
>
> "... King David leaping and dancing before the LORD..."[33]
>
> "... King David leaping and spinning before ADONAI..."[34]
>
> "... King David jumping [leaping] and dancing [whirling]..."[35]
>
> "... King David leaping and whirling before the LORD..."[36]
>
> "... King David leaping and dancing... without thought for how he looked..."[37]

WHEN YOU RECOGNIZE THE POWER AND GLORY OF GOD, YOU CAN'T HELP BUT DANCE!

Because David was able to see things in the Spirit he realized the magnitude of what God wanted to do in the hearts of men and, as a result experienced an overwhelming joy that made him just want to dance with all his might.

Leaders must strike a balance in areas of appetite, passion and culture.

Leaders usually lead according to the body language they feel comfortable with. They get energized by the things that interest them. It is often the case that they feel so connected with the dominant culture that they do not critique their own passion. Passion is often restyled by our appetites, energy and even our fear of others. David could be described as a man who was driven. He was driven by love, by his intuitive nature, by his appetite and by his passion.[38] It does not appear that the opinions of others influenced him very much.

WATCH GOD AND NOT THE PEOPLE ~ IT IS TIME FOR ALL LEADERS EVERYWHERE TO LEAD AS WORSHIPPERS.

Passion can be defined as a "strong and barely controllable emotion;"[39] or as an "extravagant fondness, enthusiasm, or desire for anything."[40] David was filled with a personal dedication and devotion for the one he had fallen in love with, while watching the sheep in the bush.[41] David loved God with all his heart. Nothing in his life seemed to grab him like worship grabbed him.

David is credited with writing many of the Psalms, declaring his inner most emotions of love and appreciation for God and His way of working in the affairs of men. One of my favorite verses says it this way, "A single day in your courts is better than a thousand anywhere else! I would rather be a gatekeeper in the house of my God than live the good life in the homes of the wicked."[42]

If a leader has no unction to worship, then he will be unable to lead people to worship. If you are a leader, it is vital that you strike a balance in all areas of your life, so that you are relevant to your generation. If you are determined to impact the lives of others, then you must have balance between the spiritual and the secular.[43]

The spirit of the age can invade your life, by a side entrance and become a drain on your passion so that you lose vital juices[44] that you need if you are going to change lives. David was Israel's king, but when the spirit of God went searching over the land for a "man after God's own heart" he spotted David. If the Holy Spirit went over the land looking for a worshipper, would He stop and hover over you? If He wanted to spark an awakening to impact the land, could He say, "That is my man… that's my woman… that's my son… she's my daughter? We will all go through the X-Ray, or examination of the Holy Spirit. What does he discover about you and me?

Let this be a revelation to us: Challenge your heart to be a "Heart after God's Heart" and new and powerful things may just come to you.

David was passionate as he entered the city of Jerusalem.

The day this procession entered Jerusalem, was a day to be remembered in infamy. Israel needed a wakeup call and David was just the man to bring it on. He came leaping and dancing, whirling and spinning, as they crossed the threshold of the city. Most of the time when the people of the land observed the king, he was appropriately dressed in regal robes. What they came to realize was that he was now, also appropriately dressed, but by being in the simple long tunic, a priestly garment. It must have been a jaw-dropping moment for the quiet ones. It was a time for personal reevaluation as to each man's body language, when entering the presence of the Lord. If David's aim was to bring God to the main street and to the common man, then he hit the mark and accomplished what he had set out to do. No one would be the same after the Ark was ushered in, by a friendly invasion of joy, happiness and worship; being led by a king who, "without abandon"[45] was fully committed to whatever it took.

Here are the lyrics of "Undignified," a song written by Matt Redman:

"UNDIGNIFIED"

I will dance, I will sing to be mad for my King
Nothing, Lord, is hindering the passion in my soul
I will dance, I will sing to be mad for my King
Nothing, Lord, is hindering the passion in my soul

And I'll become even more undignified than this
Some would say it's foolishness
But I'll become even more undignified than this
Leave my pride by the side

And I'll become even more undignified than this
Some would say it's foolishness
But I'll become even more undignified than this![46]

Dancing is a life experience that is exhilarating!

David had always been a joyful and happy individual, but this day moved him to an even higher level. On the day, David led Israel into the city of Jerusalem, with the Ark in tow, he experienced a heavenly exhilaration.

Dancing takes place because of music in the heart. Without that music then the body movements will lack rhythm. The purpose of "the dance" is to celebrate. Some people celebrate no one, so dancing seems pointless. Unless it is connected to a personal life event, like marriage, graduation, or sports, etc., then they are unable to get into the celebration.

DANCING TAKES THE RHYTHM OF THE HEART AND TRANSFERS IT TO THE FEET.

David, however had the music deep in his heart. That music had been there for much of his life. If you could have stood on the sidelines you might have heard someone say, of David, "He marches to the beat of a different drummer."

On the day of this dance, something very deep within David was dredging up every love emotion he had ever experienced, in dealing with God. He felt as if there was an eruption, as if there were volcanic, or seismic movements, pulling from him all the depth of passion, all the feelings of chaos, as if a waterfall could be found inside a mountain. Like Trümmelbach Falls near Interlaken, Switzerland.[47]

> "Deep calls unto deep at the noise of Your waterfalls; All Your waves and billows have gone over me."[48]

When others didn't hear the music, David heard it rumbling deep within. David lived with the sounds of music always playing in the background. It makes a difference, when you hear the music. David had a skip that others lacked. He had a sway, and a rhythm, when neighbors were sober.

As in the story of the ten virgins,[49] those who had the oil in their hearts, had enough, while others may have been bone dry. Even today, those with the oil have a skip in their step and joy in their hearts. While the others have no oil and nothing to applaud. David had oil in his heart and soul.

The dance did not start for David in I Samuel 16, but back, earlier, while in the bush with the sheep, long before that day of coronation. No one had witnessed David when he was alone in the bush. At that time, it was only David, engaging in his own dance, with God observing from the heavens. But just outside of Jerusalem, everyone watched as the king started with a skip and a sway. Then a leap and the clicking of his heels.

Some thought, that was the day David learned to dance, but David had been dancing for a very long time, even when no one saw him dancing. The blessing for David was that God had seen his dance, and orchestrated life's circumstances, so that he could have a "grand dance," on this day.

David was a benevolent king.

After the festivities of that day, David knew the people would be hungry, so he planned in advance and commissioned for a feast for all who had come, to be fed fresh bread, meat and wine. Every one of the citizens of Israel who had made it a priority to come to join their king in the celebration was invited to join in a common meal on that day. To everyone was given "a cake of bread, and a good piece of flesh, and a flagon of wine. So, all the people departed everyone to his house."[50]

The Bible called this the "Tabernacle of David."

This tent was frequently called a Tabernacle, as the Tabernacle of Moses, was also a tent. The Tabernacle of David lasted for at least 33 years, or until it was moved into the Temple, which Solomon built. "So, they brought the Ark of the Lord, and set it in its place in the midst of the tabernacle that David had erected for it. Then David offered burnt offerings and peace offerings before the Lord."[51]

The prophets wrote of how the Tabernacle of David, which eventually fell into disrepair, will be raised up and restored. In Amos 9:11 it clearly states, "In that day will I raise up the tabernacle of David that is fallen, and close up the breaches thereof; and I will raise up his ruins, and I will build it as in the days of old."[52] Then in Acts 15:13-18 the Apostles reaffirmed the same.

David received a special anointing, on the day he brought the Ark of the Covenant into Jerusalem, and set up a one room tent, in what came to be known as, "The Tabernacle of David." On that day, part of the aura of the event was in how God opened up a portal for him. He saw something, prophetically, which no one else in the Old Testament had seen. It was as if he saw New Testament style worship.

David was a part of the Old Testament Covenant and lived under the culture of that covenant. However, David had "a heart after God's heart." He was hungry for more from God. As much as we see that David lived in a culture of blood sacrifices, we can also see that God was open to receiving those who were hungry for a higher level of relationship with him. For example, Enoch walked with God, Abraham had conversations with God, Moses was a friend of God, Elijah heard the instinctive instructions of God and so did a number of the Old Testament prophets like Samuel, Ahijah, and Elisha. These individuals should open up to us a new reality that God always has wanted to communicate with man. If a heart is open to a personal hunger with God, then God will reveal new and powerful things. Whether under the Law or under grace, then He will reveal His Heart.

In the case of David, the Holy Spirit opened up a portal revealing, in a prophetic sense, the church of the future. He did this to Daniel and others of the Major and Minor Prophets. David was able to see a day when we, who are in New Testament times, could freely worship God, "without abandon." He could see a time when believers would not be bound by rituals, and religion, but would have a personal relationship with God. David was able to take the Holy of Holies, and transfer it, from being only in Shiloh, or Gibeon to the city of David. That one piece of furniture, God's Treasure Chest, found residence for the remaining 33 years of David's reign as King. He established a choir, which sang and danced all through each day worshipping and playing musical instruments and giving glory to God. This was unprecedented. It had never been done like this before and, until New Testament times never existed, except for David's Tabernacle.

IN TYPOLOGY: THE TABERNACLE OF MOSES IS O.T., WHILE THE TABERNACLE OF DAVID IS N.T.!

Something happened in the heavens on that day. It was like heaven responded to what David was sending up to God. Things began to change over Jerusalem and over Israel. All Israel was about to go into unprecedented blessing, divine favor and victories every time their armies went into battle. And all this happened because of the hunger in the heart of one man, David.

Amos picked up on this desire of God to restore what He had revealed to David. Read Amos 9:11 and do your own study.

And then the Apostles picked up on it in the early days of the New Testament Church. Read Acts 15:16 and do your own study.

There were three anointings on David's life.

David was anointed on the day the Ark entered Jerusalem. It is clear that the anointing was strong on David for him to have the passion and the stamina to do all that he did on this day. He was not driven by programming or by agenda, but by passion and a profound love for God.

- **Prophetic Anointing** - The First Anointing came when the Prophet Samuel poured oil from the Ram's Horn upon young David, and he was never the same.[54]
- **Kingly Anointing** - The Second Anointing was when, after Saul's death, the men of Judah crowned him as King over their single tribe.
- **Priestly Anointing** - The Third Anointing was when David offered priestly sacrifices and dressed in a linen ephod, danced his way into the city with the Ark of the Covenant.

That was the day when all of Israel fully realized that David was committed to the dance. The way things transpired on that day are indicative of why God had chosen David. The Holy Spirit had scouted over all of Israel to find a man with a heart hungry after the heart of God. That level of devotion was not found in most lives. But when that shepherd boy, David, was discovered, then the anointing would come, activated by the hand of the Prophet Samuel. That first anointing was a prophetic anointing, and David was still too young to serve the nation. His time to

MICHAL WAS SAUL'S DAUGHTER IN EVERY WAY. SHE DID NOT LEAVE & CLEAVE! SHE KEPT THE CULTURE OF SAUL!

shine would come, but only after some basic and some not so basic training, and conditioning.

Living in the 21st century we are too "others conscious." It would be best if we were not so taken up with our image, or the opinion of others, and how we respond to the Lord in public worship. We should enjoy lifting our hands in worship, in our homes and in a public service.

Your heart will never receive the healing you need, on the inside, if you allow insecurity, self-consciousness and paranoia to rule the day. Keep in mind, that your image concerns should have nothing to do with the sincere expression of worship of God. Still, that is the day we live in and we must find ways to sincerely worship, while keeping the "image police" at bay. We all need the Holy Spirit to apply the "Balm of Gilead" to our souls, so that we remain spiritually healthy enough to engage in spiritual warfare.

David went to his own home to bless it and all who were in it.

The day was nearly over as the festivities were completed and all had found their way back to their homes. David came to the palace, preparing to do one more thing; he wished to bless his own home, for he wanted, not only Israel to be blessed, but also his own family. After all, David wanted desperately to have the blessings upon his house that Obed-Edom had experienced. The Ark had been in the house of Obed-Edom and now it was in a special tabernacle in Jerusalem. David wanted to lay claim to the blessings of the Lord upon his life, his family and over all that he possessed. To David, this had been a personal, as well as a national consecration to the Lord.

The first person David met when arriving at the palace was his wife, Michal.

This was a sensitive moment for the king, because of the high emotion of the day. He had poured himself out in hilarious praise to God and was not prepared for what happened that evening. As David arrived, the first one he met was his wife, Michal, daughter of the former King Saul. She immediately launched into criticism, yelling at him and mocking him[55] on how he had conducted himself in the dance.

In David's heart he was pleased with the national blessing they had received from God. He returned to his home, with the desire to bless his household, and to include them in that national blessing. As he approached, he was abruptly met with strange and antagonistic remarks from his wife, Michal, who is called here, "the daughter of Saul:"

> "How glorious and distinguished was the king of Israel today, who uncovered himself and stripped [off his kingly robes] in the eyes of his servants' maids like one of the riffraff who shamelessly uncovers himself!"

This was like throwing cold water into his face, as she mocked what he had worn and how shamelessly he had danced. She felt that, by exchanging his royal robes for a simple ephod he had distinguished himself only in his own eyes but had dishonored the social dignity of his office. In her mind and because of her pride issues, Michal was furious, because David had not done it the way her father would have done it. The question remains, "did Michal

MICHAL WAS HAUNTED BY IMAGE CONCERNS.

love David, or did she wish to re-make him in her father's image."[56] It seemed that Michal's concerns were all about reputation and issues of pride. In her eyes, it was as inappropriate as if he had gone naked, and the best way she could insult him was to accuse him of going naked before the young girls. Michal did not understand the bigger picture. She did not accept the high praise David was giving to God. Her father had never really taken seriously issues like personal consecration to God, and neither did his daughter, Michal. Rather than seeing Israel and all that this nation represented as needing to be set apart to the Lord, she saw Israel as just one nation among all the nations.

DON'T ALLOW THE IMAGE-POLICE TO LOCK YOU UP ON THE INSIDE!

It is clear that the young Michal loved David with all of her heart. We remember how she had saved David's life, from the hand of her father, King Saul, but that was long ago.[57]

The "Saul spirit" was on display right before David's eyes. It was like having a flashback. Almost as if he could imagine Michal holding a javelin in her hand, preparing to immobilize him against the wall. Could it be that Michal felt the same hatred toward him as her father had? Before David was a clear picture of the dichotomy between the "Saul spirit" and the "David spirit."[58]

Israel had been in a state of secular apathy, but that was changing!

Everything had begun to change, while David had been in "the dance." His entire life had been a struggle involving spiritual warfare. The dance was not about the movement of the body or of the feet, but rather of the heart and soul of a humble worshipper, who was casting himself before God. This had not been a ritual, or a religious act, but a soul searching and heart felt dance of love and devotion to God, the creator of all things, and the God of Israel.

Secular apathy had corrupted the heart of the nation. However, as Israel's king, David had been giving his heart as a worshipper, to combat the decline. While he led the people in the dance, they had together, passed a milestone in their struggle.

As much as David had loved Michal, he was beginning to see her as an agent of the House of Saul. She had a foreign heart and a conflicting agenda. David had a growing suspicion that her loyalties were not in the best interest of his vision to heal the nation. She seemed, because of the personal wounds in her own soul, to be unable to align herself with what God was doing in Israel, on that day. As the seconds passed, David became more and more certain that he must not allow an agent from the former king to undermine and erode what God was doing in the land. Because of the circumstances surrounding her, he felt powerless to draw her in. The nation was bigger than they were, and she was in a state of need that he felt powerless to rescue her from, at the moment. His household and his family must be preserved, and Michal had cast her vote against yielding to God. Not only that, but in the end, she resented David.

David's response was the best he could muster, when considering how deeply she had insulted him, and how strongly he felt about the events of the day. David said these words and he spared no emotion, but gave it back as harshly as she had delivered it:

> "It was before the Lord, who chose me, rather than your father or anyone from his house when he appointed me ruler over the Lord's people Israel—I will celebrate before the Lord."[59]

David was dumbfounded at Michal's comments and felt that they were merciless and uncompromisingly against the heart of God, to which he had now more firmly committed himself. His response was to give Michal a pledge: "In the future, whenever I get a chance to worship God, 'I will be even more undignified than this, and will be humble in my own sight. But as for the maidservants of whom you have spoken, by them I will be held in honor.'"[60] In essence he saw his commitment to God as non-negotiable and was promising that: "whenever I get any chance to worship God, I will dance harder, I will be even more vile;[61] I will even give my flesh to be more humbled and even humiliated[62] than ever before, only let God bless me in every way He chooses."

This story concludes with a statement about the relationship of David and his wife, Michal. It is understood that he felt the rift in their relationship had taken a hit, and consequently he did not visit her again, and so she was, essentially exiled from future contact with him.

That evening something broke within him and he would never recover in his considerations of her. He could not see healing or reconciliation as an option. She had sold out to another alien opinion of him, and he could not go in to her again. She retired to her place within the household and he never again spent time with her, hence, no children would be born between them.

Jonathan and Michal were brother and sister, but that is where their similarities ended.

The spirit of a family will often evolve for good or for bad in the nature or ways of the children. Saul was a man who had profound issues. Those issues fenced him in from so many angles. His children were often defined by the same issues. However, within a single family, the descendants can display totally different natures. Sometimes it is called a "throwback," or atavism.[63] Whatever you may call it, the facts are that all children do not go down the same paths in life. Their values can be totally opposite.

In the case of Jonathan, he became David's best friend,[64] sticking with him,[65] and projecting loyalty to David as Israel's future king, even above himself. He was the heir apparent to his father, King Saul. But from the time of David's successful slaying of Goliath, and then his promotion as a military leader over the armies of Saul, Jonathan recognized that he would never be king, because he was not the Lord's anointed for this role. Instead he deferred to David, because he felt strongly that God's hand was upon David to occupy the place of King. On several occasions he declared to David that God's hand was upon him to be king, renouncing his own right. He truly had the David spirit. There was never any jealousy in this young man's heart. He was a prince, a national hero; he was courageous and he was unselfish.

Michal, however, never felt that level of awareness or value for the anointing upon David's life. She was, in her heart a princess, daughter of Saul. Somehow it was superior in her heart, to be a princess from the house of Saul, rather than to be the queen in the house of David. Michal did not value her role as queen, nor the public opinion that David was the man after God's own heart. Michal did not view David's reign as superior to the reign of Saul. She always felt that Saul's death brought the collapse of a wonderful age. In the heart of Michal, David had not improved the Kingdom of Israel, and she felt "caught in the middle" with a man who never grew up or matured to the classy level of her father's order. When it came to being a royal, she longed for the days of Saul. As a result, she was a walking display of the sour nature of her father. In the context of Bible perspective, Michal is seen as a dismal failure, who had so much to believe in.

How was this a "Heart Revealing Day" in the life of David?

The day of bringing the Ark into Jerusalem was not just to be a holy day of rituals, liturgy and tradition. It was to be a day of joyous celebration and consecration to God. Israel needed to meet God and embrace Him on a higher level than ever before. This extravaganza was not about Israel, David, or the people; it was about God, and how this nation must identify Him as their God. If they responded well, with David, then they could embrace a degree of divine favor, like they needed so desperately.

The thing that set David apart from so many was in his evaluation of what pleased God. The worldview of some is that our credibility as Christians lies in sober piety, and often appears to be a display of "deadpan faces" and polished off in somber moods clothed in religious rites and relics. David did not buy into that thinking but remained ready to acknowledge heart issues instead of bodily soberness.

After all, when God made the earth, he did not go about His creation trying to make boring things. When you stand back and behold all He did, you will be amazed at all the beauty, color, and uniqueness. Nothing is just black and white, except for skunks and perhaps some others.

Flowers do not all smell the same and flower pedals do not all appear the same. It will amaze you when you realize that God did not do His work of creation trying to flat line everything. Even the heart, on the hospital monitor bounces and dances about. The animals of the forest do not just glide along as if they had roller blades, but they move about generally in quite erratic ways. Take a look at the romanticism of the moon. Sometimes it is half, sometimes a quarter and sometimes a full moon.

David did not just talk the psalms, but it seems apparent that he wrote them so that many of them could be sung. This is how God made us and this is how we should respond: with hopeful smiles, jubilant reverence, stated in joyful songs and hilarity, with an occasional skip in our dance. The cry of the victims and the blood of the martyrs, must be met with celebration, so they have the heart to continue their sacrifices, when called upon.

DANCING DOES REVEAL WHAT IS GOING ON IN YOUR HEART!

When David learned to dance, while quite young, it took a while for time and the right moment to bring about an opportunity for him to do this dance with the style necessary to bring God's treasure chest into Jerusalem, but when the time came he did it in grand style, and we're still talking about it three thousand years later. David had a heart like the heart of God and remains one of our best examples today.

Tell me, how could your heart be described? My challenge is that you refashion your heart in such a way, so that you get the right moves in order. After all, dancing can be a lot of fun, and one of the benefits is that it really loosens you up.

Endnotes

1. Jerusalem became Israel's capital city, as soon as David captured it nearly 3000 years ago. From that time until Israel fell, about 2000 years ago, it remained the capital, and then, in the 21st century it has, once again been recognized as the capital of Israel.
2. II Samuel 2 - Ishbosheth, Saul's son, under the military authority of Abner, ruled as king over the northern tribes, while David was made king over the House of Judah. This period lasted for 7.5 years, and ended only with the death of Ishbosheth, II Samuel 4.
3. *Josephus* Book 7, 4:2:78
4. II Samuel 6:1
5. www.distancesfrom.com/map-from-Kiriath-Jearim-to-Jerusalem-Israel/MapHistory - "Distance from Kiriath-Jearim to Jerusalem."
6. *Josephus* Book 7, 4:2:79
7. II Samuel 6:3
8. II Samuel 6:6-7 NKJV
9. Josephus Book 7, 4:2:81 - Uzzah was a Levite, but not a priest, which had been consecrated for service.
10. www.biblehub.com/topical/o/obed-edom.htm - "A Levite, whose special prosperity while keeper of the Ark after the dreadful death of Uzzah encouraged David to carry it up to Jerusalem. Obed-Edom and his sons were made doorkeepers of the tabernacle at Jerusalem, II Samuel 6:10-12; I Chronicles 15:18-24; 16:38; 26:4- 8,15."
11. II Samuel 6:9 NKJV
12. Easton's Bible Dictionary - Obed-Edom - "The Gittite" (probably so called because he was a native of Gath-rimmon), a Levite of the family of the Korahites (I Chronicles 26:1, 4-8)
13. II Samuel 6:9-10 NLT
14. I Chronicles 26:4-5 MSG
15. II Samuel 6:12 NIRV
16. www.idioms.thefreedictionary.com - "Out in the cold" - Excluded from benefits given to others." A sense of felling neglected.
17. *Josephus* Book 7, 4:2:84
18. www.thywordistruth.com/questions/Question-137.html#.WTARwRPyuqA - What is the difference between a priest and a Levite? - The tribe is the tribe of Levi, whereas some are set apart to serve as priests, within the tribe.

19. Matthew 5:48 ESV - "You therefore must be perfect, as your heavenly Father is perfect."
20. Matthew 5:48 AMP - "You, therefore, will be perfect [growing into spiritual maturity both in mind and character, actively integrating godly values into your daily life], as your heavenly Father is perfect."
21. www.quora.com - Why do we leave fingerprints on anything we touch?
22. Exodus 25:12-16 CEV
23. Numbers 4:15-16 NLT
24. I Chronicles 15:24 "And Shebaniah, and Jehoshaphat, and Nethaneel, and Amasai, and Zechariah, and Benaiah, and Eliezer, the priests, did blow with the trumpets before the Ark of God: and Obededom and Jehiah were doorkeepers for the Ark."
25. www.jesuswalk.com/david/08_david_ark.htm - "David Brings the Ark to Jerusalem" - By Dr. Ralph Wilson
26. II Samuel 6:11-15 NLT
27. I Chronicles 15:11-20 NLT
28. I Samuel 2:18
29. II Samuel 6:13-15 NLT
30. II Samuel 6:14 CEV
31. II Samuel 6:14 AMP
32. II Samuel 6:14 CJB
33. II Samuel 6:16 AMP
34. II Samuel 6:16 CJB
35. II Samuel 6:16 EXB
36. II Samuel 6:16 NKJV
37. II Samuel 6:16 VOICE
38. www.google.ie - Driven - operated, moved, or controlled by a specified source of power.
39. www.google.ie - Passion
40. www.dictionary.com - Passion
41. www.google.ie - bush - "(especially in Australia and Africa) wild wilderness or uncultivated country." e.g. "while traveling they had to spend a night camping in the bush."
42. Psalm 84:10 NLT
43. www.google.ie - secular - not connected with religious or spiritual matters.

44. www.dictionary.com - Juices - "essence, strength, or vitality."

45. www.answers.yahoo.com/question - "Without Abandon" - "Without Abandon means that you are going to go for something no matter what the cost and regardless of the obstacles. The term comes from old naval battles when the crew of a ship fought on, without abandoning their ship, even if it was on fire and sinking."

46. Matt Redman, "Undignified," (2005) From the Album Revival Generation: Let Your Glory Fall. For all the lyrics go to the above website.

47. www.myswitzerland.com/ - "Trümmelbach Falls – in the Valley of the 72 Waterfalls. Loud thundering and roaring in the interior of the mountain, gurgling, foaming and churning water: these are the Trümmelbach Falls. They are Europe's largest subterranean waterfalls and are located in the Lauterbrunnen Valley, often called the valley of 72 waterfalls. The Trümmelbach Falls are the world's only glacier waterfalls that are accessible underground by lift, galleries, tunnels, paths and platforms. They alone carry the meltwater of the glaciers from the Jungfrau down to the valley - up to 20,000 liters of water per second." This scene is amazing to visit, while attempting to grasp its grandeur.

48. Psalm 42:7 NKJV and MSG

49. Matthew 25:1-13

50. II Samuel 6:19 KJV

51. II Samuel 6:17 NKJV

52. Amos 9:11 KJV

53. www. christourlife.wordpress.com/2008/04/26/the-tabernacle-of-david-facts-sheet - David placed singers and musicians before the ark to minister to God – 1 Chr. 6:31-33; 9:33; 15: 16-29; 16:4-7, 42; 23:4-6, 30; 25:1-8; 28:10-21; 29: 4-20. 2 Chronicles 5:12-14; 7:1-6; 8: 14-15; 9:11; 20:20-22, 28; 23:13; 29:11-36; 30:21; 35:2, 15; 25. Ezr. 2:69-70; 3:10; 11:22:23; 12:44-47. Singing and instruments in the prophets – Isa. 14:7; 35:2, 10; 38:20; 42:10; 44:23; 48:20; 49:13; 51:11; 54:1; 55:12; Zeph 3:17-19; Ezr. 2:65, 70; 3:10-11; Neh. 12:24, 27-29, 44-47.

54. It states clearly in Acts 2:30 that David was a Prophet. This confirms David, when considering that his first anointing was a "Prophetic Anointing."

55. II Samuel 6:20-23 CEV

56. II Samuel 6:20

57. 1 Samuel 19:11-18 NLT – Michal lied to her father, and assisted David in his escape to protect him from Saul. She even told Saul that David had threatened him with death. Of course, this was not accurate, but her love for her husband was strong enough that she chose David, at least that day, enough to do all she could

58. www.amazon.com - "A Tale of Three Kings: A Study in Brokenness:" Gene Edwards. This best-selling tale is based on the biblical figures of Saul, David and Absalom.
59. II Samuel 6:21 NIV
60. II Samuel 6:22 NKJV
61. II Samuel 6:22 KJV
62. II Samuel 6:22 HCSB
63. www.dictionary.com/browse/atavism - "atavism" - the reappearance in an individual of characteristics of some remote ancestor that have been absent in intervening generations.
64. I Samuel 19:1
65. I Samuel 18:1

The Day God Promised to Build a House for David

II Samuel 9

David was a good man, accomplishing so many things by building and empowering the nation of Israel. Still, it could not be said that he was a man of peace. It is not possible to wage war and peace at the same time. The fact is that the Middle East has always been a volatile place, and Israel has often been in a fight for its very existence. After all the millennia, little has changed.

David had captured Jebus[1] and established Jerusalem, for all time, as Israel's capital city, giving the castle, within it, an additional name, the "City of David." It took some time for David to also establish his residence in this new city, having moved from Hebron.[2]

There came a day after King David had "moved into his new house,"[3] and had a time of repose, where he found himself sitting in his home and reminiscing about the favor of the Lord over his life, and specifically the home in which he lived. It appeared that the extended seasons of war were finished for now, and he was enjoying a break. He looked at his family, he looked at his success in the monarchy, and he appreciated the favor of the Lord in his life.

The house he lived in was beautiful, ornate, and "had the most curious works of architecture."[4] As he reviewed the blessings of the Lord in his life, and the grace of God he had experienced, he drew a comparison and felt guilt in his heart. Why have I enjoyed the benefits of living in a house of cedar, while the God I love and serve dwells in a tent, which has all the appearance of being a temporary structure. I realize that God occupies all the earth and all the heavens, but He also should be honored with a temple where we, who worship him, can come and pay homage.[5] David felt that, perhaps he had been offensive to God, by not being more sensitive to honoring God with a permanent house of worship.[6]

This was David's time of self-evaluation, and he felt as if it was his duty, if not his mandate, to continue honoring God, by building, for Him, a special temple.

This is the Bible account of how God made a covenant promise to David:

> When King David was settled in his palace and the Lord had given him rest from all the surrounding enemies, the king summoned Nathan the prophet. "Look," David said, "I am living in a beautiful cedar palace, but the Ark of God is out there in a tent!"
>
> Nathan replied to the king, "Go ahead and do whatever you have in mind, for the Lord is with you."
>
> But that same night the Lord said to Nathan,

"Go and tell my servant David, 'This is what the Lord has declared: Are you the one to build a house for me to live in? I have never lived in a house, from the day I brought the Israelites out of Egypt until this very day. I have always moved from one place to another with a tent and a Tabernacle as my dwelling. Yet no matter where I have gone with the Israelites, I have never once complained to Israel's tribal leaders, the shepherds of my people Israel. I have never asked them, "Why haven't you built me a beautiful cedar house?"'

"Now go and say to my servant David, 'This is what the Lord of Heaven's Armies has declared: I took you from tending sheep in the pasture and selected you to be the leader of my people Israel. I have been with you wherever you have gone, and I have destroyed all your enemies before your eyes. Now I will make your name as famous as anyone who has ever lived on the earth! And I will provide a homeland for my people Israel, planting them in a secure place where they will never be disturbed. Evil nations won't oppress them as they've done in the past, starting from the time I appointed judges to rule my people Israel. And I will give you rest from all your enemies."

"'Furthermore, the Lord declares that he will make a house for you—a dynasty of kings! For when you die and are buried with your ancestors, I will raise up one of your descendants, your own offspring, and I will make his kingdom strong. He is the one who will build a house—a temple—for my name. And I will secure his royal throne forever. I will be his father, and he will be my son. If he sins, I will correct and discipline him with the rod, like any father would do. But my favor will not be taken from him as I took it from Saul, whom I removed from your sight.'"[7]

Moses was a prophet and spoke of this day, long ago.

Josephus states clearly, that "Moses had prophesied, in Joshua's hearing, of how Israel will build a temple for God, a permanent structure and one of great beauty. He then goes on to say that, if the people transgressed, in the area of their worship, then they could expect to be overrun by enemies, who would bring their weapons of war into their lands." Moses went on to declare that "their cities would be overthrown, and their temple would be burnt; the people would be sold as slaves, to men who would have no pity on them." Finally, he said, "after repentance, you and the temple will be rebuilt and restored." Moses' chilling conclusion was that, "This sad cycle will repeat itself, not once, but often."[8]

David felt such a desire to begin a national project of building a permanent dwelling place for God, and to hold court for those who would come to worship Him. He wanted, so much to build God a temple. He did not know the future, but only the present and the past. He could see that, as a nation, he needed to set a precedent for the nation, so that, even after he passed from this life, the people would continue serving God.

DAVID FELT GUILTY, BECAUSE OF SO MANY DIVINE BLESSINGS. HE WANTED TO GIVE BACK TO GOD.

On that same morning, when David had been deep in thought, he summoned the Prophet Nathan. David began the conversation: "Look, I am living in a beautiful cedar palace, but the Ark of God is out there in a tent." Nathan responded to the king, "Go ahead and do whatever you have in mind, for the Lord is with you."[9]

The prophet had responded to the King, off the top of his head. David's comments sounded like the right thing to do, like a very good thing to do, and so he had affirmed this move as wisdom, without taking it to the Lord, first. It is so easy to proceed in a plan without actually laying it before the Lord. Clearly, the last word must come from God.

On the word of the prophet Nathan, he began planning immediately.

That day, David began dreaming of how he would begin the collection of all the building materials he would need to complete this assignment. He knew the best places to go for all that this task would require. He had spoken with Nathan the prophet, and the prophet had agreed with him. He had said, "Go ahead and do whatever you have in mind, for the Lord is with you." David was excited and ready for whatever would come next.

Through the years, war had taken up so much of his time, as he always saw such need for securing the borders, safeguarding the cities, and making sure that no enemies would defeat Israel. But now, and hopefully, for a long while to come, they would be at peace. God had been good and now this king felt he must do all he could to show his expressions of love and devotion to God.

David was young enough and strong enough and could now give all of his time to build God a temple. Nothing would stand in his way now, as he would solicit all his friends, who were kings from the neighboring nations to supply him with the best of their building materials. He would also negotiate with them to employ the expertise of those artisans and craftsmen, thus, giving to God the very best workmanship this world could supply. David finished out the day excited, because life would now bring to him an even better chapter.

There was one thing that David had overlooked, even in himself. It had become a blind-spot and somehow, he had failed to recognize a growing nature within himself. He had become less committed to worship, and very much committed to the business of making war. As much as his heart of hearts wanted to worship, the "busyness of war" had numbed his ability to be sensitive to the Holy Spirit. War does that to a man. But God was still in control and would not allow David even to do a good thing if he was not the one to do it. A generation later, everything would come together, howbeit, under the next king, his son, Solomon.

DAVID USED MILITARY STRENGTH TO ACHIEVE A LASTING CLIMATE OF PEACE.

Nathan heard the voice of God, which was a message for the king.

Nathan had a short night. The Lord took sleep from the prophet and said: "I have heard David's desire and see the motive of his heart. I realize that no one has ever expressed an interest in building me a temple, but David is not the one to do this.

There are reasons that I cannot allow David to take on this project. "He has shed too much blood in war and has been defiled with the slaughter of his enemies."[10] So, go see the king, and speak to him as I instruct you. When you stand before the king, you are to let him know how history has developed over the centuries. Tell David, "You may not build me a house, but I will build one for you." Nathan returned to the palace and re-approached the king to give God's response on the subject:

> "David, you are my servant, so listen to what I say: Why should you build a temple for me? I didn't live in a temple when I brought my people out of Egypt, and I don't live in one now. A tent has always been my home, wherever I have gone with them. I chose leaders and told them to be like shepherds for my people Israel. But did I ever say anything to even one of them about building a cedar temple for me?"[11]

"GIVE, AND IT WILL BE GIVEN TO YOU: GOOD MEASURE, PRESSED DOWN, SHAKEN TOGETHER, AND RUNNING OVER WILL BE PUT INTO YOUR BOSOM. FOR WITH THE SAME MEASURE THAT YOU USE, IT WILL BE MEASURED BACK TO YOU."
LUKE 6:38 NKJV

We must notice that God is not only masterful at disciplining us, but also at reminding us of how we have grown and done well. Nathan continued being the mouthpiece of God, to David:

> "I took you from the pasture, tagging along after sheep, and made you prince over my people Israel. I was with you everywhere you went and mowed your enemies down before you. Now I'm making you famous, to be ranked with the great names on earth. And I'm going to set aside a place for my people Israel and plant them there so they'll have their own home and not be knocked around anymore. Nor will evil men afflict you as they always have, even during the days I set judges over my people Israel. Finally, I'm going to give you peace from all your enemies.[12]

The Davidic Covenant now comes through the mouth of Nathan.

God changed the focus of the conversation with David. Nathan declared how God was pleased with the heart of David and was now giving to David His pledge in the form of an eternal covenant:

> "The Lord also declares to you that He will make a house (royal dynasty) for you."[13]

This was a total surprise to David. This king was a strong king and able to hold up in the face of intimidating enemies. It is hard for such a man to realize the depth of love, like David was experiencing from God.

> "When your days are fulfilled and you rest with your fathers, I will set up your seed after you, who will come from your body, and I will establish his kingdom. He shall build a house for My name, and I will establish the throne of his kingdom forever. I will be his Father, and he shall be My son. If he commits iniquity, I will chasten him with the rod of men and with the blows of the sons of men. But My mercy shall not depart from him, as I took it from Saul, whom I removed from before you. And your house and your kingdom shall be established forever before you. Your throne shall be established forever."[14]

When Nathan had ended his prophetic word to David, he left the palace, and so did David. David was overwhelmed at the powerful commitment God had just made to him. He was moved to consider His awesome promises. "The Davidic Covenant"[15] was so significant that he was compelled to go to the "Tabernacle of David", which housed the Ark of the Covenant.[16] In this place, he had established singers who were committed to singing and making music to the

Lord around the clock.[17] It was there that David bowed his face to God, to give thanks and to honor God for all that had been said.

The Tabernacle of David had been established in Jerusalem, because, it had already come into David's heart that Jerusalem should not only be the legislative capital of Israel, but also the center of worship for the nation. As a result, "the tabernacle (or tent) housing the Ark of the Covenant actually became a precursor to the temple, that Solomon would build."

For the balance of his time as king, David expended a lot of energy and spared no expense in collecting the materials for building the temple. He was determined to make the job of building the temple easier.

How was this a "Heart Revealing Day" in the life of David?

David was not a perfect man, but his heart was really bent toward serving God. David, as men go, was one of the most proficiently[18] committed to serving God. From the time of his shepherding days, to the days after becoming King, David was fully committed to giving God honor in worship.

David loved God, and clearly God loved David. It could even be said that David's consistent love for God effected the spiritual DNA of whom he had become. God had been looking for a man after His own heart, because His plan was to redeem mankind using him as a channel to work toward redemption. That would only be possible by bringing a Messiah into this world. That Messiah would be Jesus Christ, who would come to earth, be born as an infant, live among men and then be sacrificed for their sins.

When David expressed his desire to build a temple, so that he could continue his plan to make Jerusalem the center of worship for the nation, it was as if the "dye was cast"[19] and God could not resist such a heart of worship. This event shows us how to live our lives, keeping our life priorities in a Godly balance.[20]

The day came when Solomon stood before his failing father, and he would hear the confession of David's heart. David expressed why he had not taken up the cause of building the temple, and why he was passing it off to his son, Israel's new king. David had been transparent most of his reign, and most of his life. Now, in full transparency, he spoke to his son, Israel's new king, exactly how he felt and how pleased he was to pass the scepter of leadership over to Solomon. Here is what the king shared with his son, sparing no details:

> And David said to Solomon: "My son, as for me, it was in my mind to build a house to the name of the Lord my God; but the word of the Lord came to me, saying, 'You have shed much blood and have made great wars; you shall not build a house for My name, because you have shed much blood on the earth in My sight. Behold, a son shall be born to you, who shall be a man of rest; and I will give him rest from all his enemies all around. His name shall be Solomon, for I will give peace and quietness to Israel in his days. He shall build a house for My name, and he shall be My son, and I *will be* his Father; and I will establish the throne of his kingdom over Israel forever.'"[21]

Endnotes

1. I Chronicles 11:4-9
2. Genesis 15:18-21 - When God made a covenant with Abram, he promised the Promised Land to he and his descendants. One of the cities he listed specifically was Jebus (also known as Salem, Jerusalem and "The City of David").
3. II Samuel 7:1 ERV
4. Josephus Book 7, 4:4:90
5. Ibid
6. Ibid
7. II Samuel 7:01-15 NLT
8. Josephus Book 4, 8:46
9. II Samuel 7:2-3
10. Josephus Book 7, 4:4:92
11. II Samuel 7:5-7 CEV
12. II Samuel 7:8-11 MSG
13. II Samuel 7:11 AMP
14. II Samuel 7:12-16 NKJV
15. www.gotquestions.org/Davidic-covenant.html - "The Davidic Covenant refers to God's promises to David through Nathan the prophet and is found in 2 Samuel 7 and later summarized in 1 Chronicles 17:11–14 and 2 Chronicles 6:16. This is an unconditional covenant made between God and David through which God promises David and Israel that the Messiah (Jesus Christ) would come from the lineage of David and the tribe of Judah and would establish a kingdom that would endure forever."
16. Josephus Book 7, 4:4:94-95
17. I Chronicles 16:37 MSG
18. www.thefreedictionary.com/proficiently - Having or showing knowledge, ability, or skill, as in a profession or field of study. Synonyms: proficient, adept, skilled, skillful, accomplished, expert. These adjectives mean having or showing knowledge, ability, or skill, as in a profession or field of study.
19. www.idioms.thefreedictionary.com/die+is+cast - "die is cast - A process is past the point of no return."
20. Ephesians 5:15-20 MSG
21. 1 Chronicles 22:7-10 NKJV

THE DAY DAVID FULFILLED A VOW TO A FRIEND

II SAMUEL 9

Mankind often has good intentions, but is too often a slow learner, and hopelessly forgetful. We overlook the important issues and downplay our responsibilities for bringing hope to others. Those shortfalls in our nature, can be corrected, but it often requires the help of the Holy Spirit to remind us and cajole us to do better.

David had a good heart and excellent intentions. He usually remembered promises he'd made through the years, but time and opportunity did not always work with him to prompt him to urgency. It is easy to get so busy with fulfilling your own assignments and building what you feel you have a mandate to build, that you forget some of those things, which you should have remembered. Time had passed and so many important things slipped by. In an ideal world, we would never allow certain things to escape us, without adjusting and making corrections. And yet it happens to the best of us. On the other hand, lots of people have not listened to their heart of hearts, and consequently, have allowed their core values to deteriorate.

HAVE YOU FORGOTTEN SOME OF THOSE THINGS WHICH YOU SHOULD HAVE REMEMBERED?

This day brought a wakeup call for King David. He had been neglecting old friends and had failed to remember promises he had made nearly twenty years earlier. Keep in mind that people were depending on him to keep his word, yet David, had let so much time pass and the details escaped in the fog of life. Now, the game of life was in overtime and the opportunity to keep this promise could have been lost. It is difficult to lend the ear to the Holy Spirit, to listen to what God may whisper, as He continually speaks in a still small voice. There are some things, which we must "remember."[1] It is good to remember something you forgot to take care of; or remember to take care of a promise, for which you are responsible. These things may mean little to you, but they weigh heavier in the memories of your friends.

When you're asleep, your defenses are not on alert. You're more open to hear the voice of God, speaking in a quiet way. Actually, when you dream, it could be called "night visions."[2] In daylight, you are unconsciously on guard, so perhaps God cannot so easily get to you. However, during the night the Holy Spirit can whisper into your spirit the directions he wants you to follow. After all you are under a sort of "nighttime anesthesia."

The King said, "I summon Mephibosheth to the palace."

One day David remembered a pledge, which he had made many years earlier. More than twenty years had passed and it had totally slipped his mind. Now, as he remembered what he and Jonathan had pledged to each other, he realized he had to act on it immediately.

OPEN UP YOUR HEART DURING THE DAY, TO RECEIVE DIRECTIONS FROM THE HOLY SPIRIT!

David called in one of his staff and asked him a serious question: "Is there anyone left from the lineage of Jonathan, to whom I can show kindness?"[3] David had waited, perhaps, too long. Even the way he asked the question shows he was concerned of his timing. Could it be that all who were the loved ones from the family of Prince Jonathan, had already died? David had committed himself that he would honor Jonathan's descendants. And yet, until now, he had neglected to take care of business.

David was advised that nearby there was a servant of Saul's household named, Ziba. The king summoned Ziba to the palace and asked him the same question. Ziba responded by telling him of how Jonathan had a son, who was still alive and by the name of Mephibosheth, but he was lame on both feet. This was like a knife in David's heart. He was now hearing that his dear friend, Jonathan had a son who would now be in his early twenties, but they had never met? Why had the king waited so long, and almost missed his opportunity to show kindness and a caring heart to this young man?

The Story of Mephibosheth is one of Redemption.

Ziba informed David of how Mephibosheth had been injured on the very day his father and grandfather had been slain. He told the story of what was going on in Jonathan's home on the day of his death on the battlefield.

In the culture of the Middle East, great fear often causes panic for the family of an outgoing king. Saul had even appealed to David, when they were in one of their greatest conflicts, that he not wipe out his descendants from the earth. It was common for the incoming king to order the slaughter of every member of the preceding royal family. This had been done by some, and now Saul's constituency had been afraid for the life of young Mephibosheth. Saul realized that David would later become the King:

> "And now I realize that you are surely going to be king, and that the kingdom of Israel will flourish under your rule. Now swear to me by the Lord that when that happens you will not kill my family and destroy my line of descendants! So, David promised this to Saul with an oath."[4]

On the day of the death of Saul and Jonathan, news came from the battlefield, to the house of Jonathan. The nurse who was caring for five-year old Mephibosheth, panicked, snatched up the child and fled. Unfortunately, the little boy fell from her shoulders and he was seriously injured, so that he could not walk again.[5] The family members who were nearby whisked Mephibosheth away to a remote part of the Trans-Jordan region, not far from Mahanaim, in the ghetto town of Lōdēbär. This area is, what is today known as the Golan Heights.[6]

The area where Mephibosheth was taken was a hotbed of support for King Saul, which meant that it was not necessarily friendly to David. David had little contact with this area, because of its remoteness to Jerusalem. The Jordan was not easily crossed, and so the frequency of contact was limited. Mephibosheth's host guardian was Mākir, son of Ammiel and his adoptive hometown was Lōdēbär. There was an air of quiet hostility against the new regime, even though it had been in power, for nearly two decades.

MEPHIBOSHETH HAD BEEN HIDDEN AS FAR FROM JERUSALEM AS POSSIBLE!

David was about to enter a region, which needed redemption, but he was totally unaware of the bigger picture. Neither did he know that that day's actions would cause him to be "redeemed" in the hearts of locals, and would bring home to him new friendships, which he would need much later, but that is a story for another day.[7] Because of the events of this day, Mākir began his move from a place of distrust of David, to a place of warmth and camaraderie. This transition was not an easy one to make, but because of the heart of David, something was deposited in Mākir on the day when the soldiers arrived to escort Mephibosheth away.

"Go to Lōdēbär, and bring Mephibosheth to my palace."

David instructed his men to go, prepared to bring this young man "home."[8] David said to Ziba, "I will send my soldiers to move Mephibosheth from his home to my home."[8] This must have been a shocking moment for this loyal servant of Saul.

David's body guards came on horseback, with all the competence and prestige that horses could bring, bearing men of strength. These were not "David's Mighty Men,"[9] but were certainly men who took care of whatever assignment given to them with a regal comportment. They did not shy away from doing the king's business, nor minimize the image of their office. In a sense, these men were not unlike "The first Musketeers," even though muskets had not yet been invented. They certainly carried themselves well as they entered the ghetto village of Lōdēbär, stopping only to ask for directions to the house of Mākir, son of Ammiel. The village was abuzz. No runner had announced their coming, and no one had a clue what the King's men were here to do. Horses were not a common sight, resulting in the phenomenon, that no one could take their eyes off of them. Even the men who rode on the backs of these stately beasts were not dressed like the locals. These were, quite simply, the King's men, causing all who viewed them to be in shock and awe.

SOME FEARED AS THE KING'S MEN ENTERED LODEBAR, ON A SEARCH.

Questions, rumors and speculation swarmed from one end of the village to the other; from the time they entered to well after they departed, with Mephibosheth in tow. Almost none of their questions were answered, even after they were gone. All anyone knew was that King David wanted this young man to come to Jerusalem.

Mephibosheth's true identity had been kept secret throughout all these years, for security reasons. This could best be described as an early version of a "witness protection program."[10] Few besides, Mākir knew of the true identity of this member of the Royal family who was hiding living in plain sight, from those who could mean him harm. Certainly, a small circle of loyalists from the former house of Saul knew, as did Ziba, but very few others had any idea who was living down the road.

Mephibosheth had grown up in Lōdēbär, without ever going very far down the road in any direction. After all, he could not walk, and so he was just one of the kids who played on the road, albeit on the sidelines; a quiet member of the community. Recently he had gotten married and had appreciated the fact that he was now a dad himself to a healthy son, Micha.[11]

MEPHIBOSHETH WAS ON AN EARLY VERSION OF "THE WITNESS PROTECTION PROGRAM."

Mephibosheth's house parents had told him everything he knew of his family connection but had urged him to keep quiet about it for obvious reasons. However, the events of this day were as much a surprise to him as anyone else. No one had seen this coming and would now face the challenges of dealing with realities outside their community. The future was all a question, and waiting was all anyone could do, even for Mephibosheth.

The men who had transported Mephibosheth back across the Jordan River and to Jerusalem did not give him any more details, because, even these men knew nothing about what was about to happen. The reality, in the minds of all, was that he could either be traveling to his execution, or he could receive extraordinary favor. The concern was that the first was most likely, because, only Ziba really had any idea of what was in David's heart and he was still back in Jerusalem.

Into the Palace he was ushered, and into the court of the king.

The story goes that when Mephibosheth came into the hall of King David, his body language was that of humility and of one giving total honor and respect to his king. We have to assume that he could walk, but not very well. It is not stated how severely his legs had been damaged in the fall. It may very well be that he was just visually injured so that he struggled with walking, perhaps with the use of makeshift crutches. At any rate, scripture states that "he bowed deeply, abasing himself, honoring David."[12]

David explained why he had been brought to Jerusalem.

The conversation began: "Are you Mephibosheth?" to which he responded, "Yes my lord."

As David looked at this young man, his heart went out to him, because of their common history, and yet Mephibosheth knew nothing of these things.

> Mephibosheth felt uncomfortable and began shuffling and stammering, not looking David in the eye. Mephibosheth said, "Who am I that you pay attention to a stray dog like me?"[13]

It was obvious to David that he must explain some things, so that Mephibosheth would realize the reasoning for bringing him to Jerusalem at this time. The conversation went something like this:

> "Mephibosheth, please do not be frightened, but understand that you are too young to know what I am about to tell you. You need to know more about your father, and that is the reason I have

brought you here. The things I want to tell you about, happened before you were born and I am so glad to finally meet you."

"I had trouble with your grandfather, King Saul. But your father became my closest friend. He warned me that the king wanted to kill me. But our friendship was so close that, on the day he warned me, we made a covenant[14] together that, if I outlived him, I would protect his descendants; and if he lived longer, then he would do the same for me."

"I'm sorry that it has taken me so long to fulfill this promise to you. I have not known you existed, and only found out a few days ago, but God knew all about you, and I believe God put it in my heart to search you out."

"Right now, because of my strong commitment to your father, I want to make some promises to you."

"I'd like to do something special for you in memory of your father, Jonathan. To begin with, I'm returning to you all the properties of your grandfather, Saul. Furthermore, from now on you'll take all your meals at my table with my sons."

David then called in Ziba, Saul's steward, and gave this command:

"Everything that belonged to Saul and his family, I've handed over to your master's grandson. You and your sons and your servants will work his land and bring in the produce, and provisions for your master's grandson. Mephibosheth himself, your master's grandson, from now on will take all his meals at my table."[15]

King Saul was a member of the tribe of Benjamin and had his home and likely all of his property in the region of Gibeah. Consequently, his estate was in that area of the country and only about 11 kilometers away (about 7 miles). David gave a royal decree that all the properties of Mephibosheth's grandfather would be passed on to his grandson, effective immediately. Furthermore, the man who had been the steward of Saul's possessions would now become the same for Mephibosheth. In addition, Ziba would surrender his sons and all of his servants to serve Mephibosheth, the son of Jonathan, and grandson of Saul.

Ziba accepted this assignment and set about getting all of Mephibosheth's affairs in order.

In the meantime, it was now time for Mephibosheth to join David and all the Royal family for his very first meal as the newest resident of the palace. Although he would not actually live in the palace, he would live comfortably nearby. He was given a choice seat at the table and was assigned to take his place as an equal participant with the rightful heirs of David's estate and kingdom.

Mephibosheth must have thought, "I really need to get word back to Lōdēbär that things have turned out really well for me and I am quite happy in my new home and with my new family. My inheritance has been fully restored to me, so, in effect, my grandfather, King Saul, is now paying my bills and I have no fear, and absolutely no complaints."

How was this a "Heart Revealing Day" in the life of David?

This day revealed how David kept covenants and considered them sacred. He had a heart that was full of generosity, benevolence, and was given to "acts of kindness."[16] He did not only seek to benefit himself as king, but also used his position to bless others.

David was a loyal man. He never forgot the kindnesses and favor, which came to him through his friends. Jonathan had been a close friend and ally who had stood up for David when it seemed no one else cared. In the course of their friendship, Prince Jonathan recognized that God had made a choice for Israel's next king and, although he was heir apparent, the crown would and should land on David. He made that plain to his father and all those around him, including David. As a result, they'd made a covenant of friendship, which bound them to each other as brothers. This covenant had basically two ingredients: we will guard each other's backs and we will honor each other, even in death.

DAVID KNEW THE BENEFITS OF KEEPING COVENANTS!

David had outlived Jonathan and must ultimately remember the factors he had committed himself to in that vow. Now it was time to remember Jonathan and he certainly did, in celebrating Mephibosheth. The last years had been busy, but David was good for his word.

David's heart really was like the heart of God in many ways, just as the scriptures foretold. God remembers covenants and honors those who honor Him.[17] We must not be self-focused and self-centered. We must look to the right and left as well as to those who are behind us, and those who have not achieved their life dream because of misfortune. If it is within our power to give honor to those who have honored us, then it is imperative to do so. This should become a lifestyle decision. To be benevolent, kind, considerate, charitable and tender hearted can enhance your life and all you hope to achieve.

Endnotes

1. www.macmillandictionary.com/dictionary/british/remember - Remember - "to have an image in your mind of a person, a place, or something that happened or was said in the past"
2. http://www1.cbn.com/biblestudy/dreams-and-visions - Article entitled: "Dreams and Visions: God Uncensored," by Hannah Goodwyn - "Dreams are the perfect way to hear from God. When you are dreaming, you are quiet, so you can't ignore Him. Plus, you are not easily distracted. You're basically all ears for about 7 hours every night."
3. Josephus Book 7, 5:5:112
4. I Samuel 24:20-22 NLT
5. Josephus Book 7, 5:5:113
6. www.en.wikipedia.org/wiki/Lo-debar - Lo-debar was a very remote part of the land and not easily accessible unless you planned to go there. This provided a safe place for the royal prince, Mephibosheth.
7. II Samuel 17:27-29
8. II Samuel 9:11-13
9. II Samuel 23
10. mentalfloss.com/article/77695/12-secrets-witness-protection-program - "Developed by Justice Department employee Gerald Shur and beginning in 1971, the Federal Witness Protection Program or Witness Security Program (WITSEC)—has provided safe harbor for over 18,000 federal witnesses and their families in exchange for damning testimony." Born of the Organized Crime Control Act of 1970, and the brainchild of longtime Department of Justice attorney, Gerald Shur, the U.S. Marshall Service Witness Security Program (WITSEC) has successfully protected more than 18,000 people since it first began operations in 1971. Membership in the witness protection program is typically for life, and usually begins with a visit from U.S. marshals, whether anticipated or not. While many of the witnesses and their family members have time to make the decision and prepare for their new lives, others are forced to choose rather quickly. Even occasionally having to leave within moments of the marshals arriving." The US Marshalls will provide these with a new life, and a new identity. Contact is never to be made again with friends or family, because their life is at serious risk.
11. II Samuel 9:12 KJV
12. II Samuel 9:6 MSG
13. II Samuel 9:8-10 MSG
14. I Samuel 18:3

15. II Samuel 9:7-10 MSG

16. www.randomactsofkindness.org/kindness-quotes - "The best index to a person's character is how he treats people who can't do him any good, and how he treats people who can't fight back. - By Abigail van Buren" Also known as "Dear Abby," a syndicated advice columnist.

17. 1 Samuel 2:30 TLB - Eli, the high priest, dishonored God, and so he was removed from office, and his family after him. Here is what the Lord said of this event: "Therefore, I, the Lord God of Israel, declare that although I promised that your branch of the tribe of Levi could always be my priests, it is ridiculous to think that what you are doing can continue. I will honor only those who honor me, and I will despise those who despise me."

THE DAY DAVID REPENTED OF HIS SIN WITH BATHSHEBA

II SAMUEL 12

The day began as normal for David the King. However, the night had not gone so well with Nathan, the prophet. While the king slept, the prophet was bereft of sleep. After a while the prophet had rolled out of bed to face the rest of the night in audience to the voice of God. God was displeased with the head of state, and the gauntlet had fallen squarely at the feet of this prophet, who must pass it on.

David had become convinced that he was above the law and able to live his life without penalty, even when he had violated at least three of the "Ten Commandments"[1] handed down by God to Moses on Mount Sinai.

Nathan heard God loud and clear and was in prayer as to how he should handle the king's transgressions.

Not everyone was privy to the misdeeds of the king. The inner workings of the government, the military and of the Royal household were not things known by the people of Israel. There was no technology, no public news outlets, no means of obtaining reliable coverage of what anyone in high levels of the government was doing.

In the 21st century lots of people identify as "news junkies,"[2] wishing to keep up with events, to some limited degree. However, things were different three thousand years ago, in the Middle East. Few people knew much about David, his family, his wives, or his business dealings. It was, therefore, easy for someone like David to, quite literally, get away with murder; unless, of course there was a prophet in the land. It must be noted that: "Whatever the Lord God plans to do, he tells his servants, the prophets."[3] This was a fact in the days of both the Old and New Testament times. Contrary to popular opinion, it is still true in the 21st century. God is still God and still able to communicate with men and women who are sensitive to the Holy Spirit.

"NO ONE KNOWS WHAT GOES ON BEHIND CLOSED DOORS."

Prophets, like Nathan, were rare, unique and, at the same time foreboding. Largely, the reason for this is the perception that they had been in touch with the unseen God of the universe, and as a result, because their words were final, they were unpredictable. They existed for the pleasure of being a mouthpiece for God himself. Not much was known about men like Nathan. They seemed to rise out of the ashes and rant about things no one else knew much about. Men like Nathan had an audience with God and then came in, sometimes like mad men to point fingers and make declarations. Nathan was a lot like this, but was highly respected by men who loved God, like David. Add to this a loss of sleep and the fact that God was not just displeased, but angry[4] at the king, and you have a "mood changer" in the making for the king and his entire staff.

David was happy that day and unguarded for he felt that the worst was over, the potential scandal had dissipated, and anyone who could accuse him had likely forgotten and moved on. Little did David realize that dark clouds over his life, his household and the Kingdom were just beginning to gather. His thoughts were that this day, like yesterday, would be just fine. But, keep in mind the day was just beginning. He had not even had his breakfast.

"THERE'S AN ALL-SEEING EYE WATCHING YOU!"

The birds were singing, a slight breeze was blowing, the flowers were glorious and the new yet unnamed baby boy, another prince, had just been born to the king and his lovely wife, Bathsheba. What is not to love about a day like this?

There came an intrusive bang at the palace gate.[5] Take note that palaces do not have doors but gates. Big gates, made of heavy wood makes a lot of noise when the staff or rod[6] of a prophet begins banging and thumping on them. To David, this gate was a means of separating he and his family from the general public. It gave them privacy, and yet they were all surrounded by non-family members of the staff, as well as an occasional soldier who was there to ensure that safety. But to the prophet it was an affront to his access to all things government. Nathan wanted to enter the palace and someone was taking their time to swing open the gate. When finally, the shattered quiet had settled down and the prophet took to his stride to enter, all the king's household was at rapt attention to know what had moved Nathan to be there. After all, it was still early and the sun was just barely risen.

Prophets didn't visit often. They were reclusive types who didn't dally for small talk and social interaction. You just don't call a prophet up and invite him for tea, or coffee and crumpets. Nathan was not given to chatter or being patronized by whoever was sanguine and wanted some fellowship. This man was strictly business. No one knew for sure, but it was the suspicion of almost everyone that God had prophets as His friends and kept them close, so no one else got to spend much time with them. Nathan, for having had little rest last night, seemed, really, to be in a descent mood. He didn't say much at first, but for his quest to see the king.

In king's palaces, it is not the king or one of his wives, or even a butler, who would meet you at the gate. There was likely no welcoming mat, and certainly not any of the young princes or princesses to just swing the gate opėn unreservedly. It would most likely be, some sober individual with little or no personality. In fact, the palace was more than a place of residence, but the seat of government in some respects.

And so, the prophet Nathan glided into the lounge hall of King David. There were no doors to separate one room from the living quarters, but rather openings with hanging curtains, or linen draping, which would allow the breeze to pass through in this hot and desert climate.

THE FINGER OF A PROPHET WILL POINT AT SIN AND POINT THE WAY!

Almost as quickly as Nathan arrived into the hall, so did the King. The disposition of the King was friendly and almost lighthearted. His mood was tempered by his feelings that "congratulations are in order," as our family is happy and growing larger. The new addition to his family had him feeling quite chipper.

The prophet, however was sober, casting looks of inquisitiveness all around. David had no idea of what was setting Nathan's tone, but he felt he could cheer him up if given time. However, it was not to be for the prophet owned this moment and not this king.

"So, how is my king today?" The prophet enquired.

"Happy," were David's first words.

"Perhaps my king will not be so happy when he hears the problem I have come to speak to him about." It was then that Nathan presented a parable, for which he was seeking the wisdom of the king to help him solve. This did not seem so bad to David and would likely hold some key to lightening up the atmosphere he could feel in the hall. David was blind-sighted by what came next.

Nathan began: "King, please tell me what you think of the story I shall tell you now?"

"There were two men in the same city—one rich, the other poor. The rich man had huge flocks of sheep, and herds of cattle. The poor man had nothing but one little female lamb, which he had bought and raised. It grew up with him and his children as a member of the family. It ate off his plate and drank from his cup and slept on his bed. It was like a daughter to him.

"One day a traveler dropped in on the rich man. He was too stingy to take an animal from his own herds or flocks to make a meal for his visitor, so he took the poor man's lamb and prepared a meal to set before his guest."[7]

Nathan's discourse troubled the king.

The king denounced the rich man, saying, "this man is a wicked man. Who could dare to do such a thing?"[8]

In true kingly fashion, and with authority, David declared, with an oath:

"As surely as the Lord lives," he vowed, "any man who would do such a thing deserves to die! He must repay four lambs to the poor man for the one he stole and for having no pity."[9]

The conversation now turned from the King to the prophet Nathan, who gave a stinging indictment, first stating that "you are judged by your own words."[10]

Then Nathan said to David, "You are the man! Thus, says the LORD God of Israel: 'I anointed you king over Israel, and I delivered you from the hand of Saul. I gave you your master's house and your master's wives into your keeping and gave you the house of Israel and Judah. And if that had been too little, I also would have given you much more! Why have you despised the commandment of the LORD, to do evil in His sight? You have killed Uriah the Hittite with the sword; you have taken his wife to be your wife and have killed him with the sword of the people of Ammon. Now therefore, the sword shall never depart from your house, because you have despised Me, and have taken the wife of Uriah the Hittite to be your wife.' Thus says the LORD: 'Behold, I will raise up adversity against you from your own house; and I will take your wives before your eyes and give them to your neighbor, and he shall lie with your wives in the sight of this sun. For you did it secretly, but I will do this thing before all Israel, before the sun.'"[11]

"The King was troubled at Nathan's words and sufficiently confounded, so much so, that he repented with tears and sorrow for his great sin."[12] In turn, God was moved at the depth and sincerity of David's repentance. With great authority Nathan responded with this pronouncement:

> "God has had compassion on you, and will be reconciled to you, and will preserve both your life and your kingdom."[13] "He has put away your sin, you shall not die."[14] "I am no longer displeased with you."[15]

How could God forgive so quickly after David had done so much wrong?

Forgiveness is a gift of God, as well as an element, which can only be grasped by those who have taken on board the heart of a loving God. This is not a natural human trait. In other words, it does not come easily. Looking at what was going on in that royal hall, between David and Nathan, we must find it hard to understand how instantly, God forgave and accepted David, as a bona fide son, who was forgiven.

GOD WANTS TO FORGIVE & REDEEM YOU ~ MORE THAN YOU THINK!

At this point, we must take a look at our benevolent God. These are the words about God's commitment to forgive:

"As far as the east is from the west, so far has He removed our transgressions from us."[16]

You are forgiven, but still there are natural laws, for "Sowing and Reaping."

Although David was forgiven for his transgressions, the natural laws of sowing and reaping[17] were still in play, because of the gravity of David's sin and the levels, to which he had sank, so the prophet concluded with this proclamation:

> "The Lord also has put away your sin; you shall not die.[14] However, because by this deed you have given great occasion to the enemies of the Lord to blaspheme, the child also, who is born to you shall surely die."[18]

The prophet Nathan had spoken all that the Lord had prompted him to say, and now he was finished. His last words had been spoken, and no further comments should be made. The prophet moved from the center of the hall and exited the palace, as quickly as he had entered. The mood of the room was sad, final and sober. No words were appropriate for this moment, so none were given.

That day ended differently than it began.

Everyone in the palace could see that David was unable to respond to words of comfort from anyone. The day had begun with the birth of a child, hence profound joy; but it would end differently, because the clouds held nothing but death and sorrow. Yes, God had judged, and so He must; but He had also shown mercy and forgiveness, so they were consoled that the world would not end that day. There is no word that describes perfectly, how the royal family felt on that day. Life would change and hope would return, but perhaps these words best describe the brokenness of this home on that day and, at that moment:

- Catastrophic sorrow
- Trauma of soul
- Extreme disappointment
- Speech without words, because words don't work today
- Grief unfathomed
- Eternal bereavement
- Inconsolable weeping
- Despair, which refuses to go away
- A day, which will never end

How do you tell a new mother, that her son will die?

Bathsheba had been with the baby boy. The king had faced the prophet alone, as it was only fitting. Perhaps this new mother had not even known that a visitor had come. After all, their home was more than a house, it was more like a huge state house; it was a palace. Now David, had to get a handle on his emotions, as he realized that he must deliver the damning and personally injurious message to his wife. This king, was forgiven, and that was good. But little comfort this would be for he and Bathsheba, as the next few days would be days of mourning, and grief; leaving them aware of a finality, whose pain was so severe that medicine could not alleviate.

We do not know the exchange or conversation, which occurred between David and Bathsheba, but we do know how they felt, and we do understand the depth of personal trauma they both were experiencing. We have not walked in their shoes, but we can imagine the horrific sorrow, which they must have experienced over the next few days with the death of that son and the reality of why any of this had happened.

The Lord sent a deadly illness to the child, who became very sick.

That day melted into the next and then the next, until one week had passed. David tried to rest but could not. He tried to pray but could not. He tried to lay upon his bed but did not feel worthy of the comfort it afforded him… and so he selected the floor, and then he found a spot on the bare ground. The king was beside himself in grief.[19] He refused food or drink, or anything that could give him physical comfort or relief.

David knew his sin had been a profound disappointment to God, and now was so deep in despair that he was determined to yield to the dealings of God, which he felt on the inside. Yes, the prophet said he was forgiven, but now David wanted further assurance, and he hoped that would come in the form of redemption for his newborn, and yet unnamed son. He faced several fronts and was dealing with them all simultaneously. This broken man was dealing with personal remorse. He had lived out his life so strongly connected to God and now he had failed in ways he could never have believed possible. He now realized that he had been walking in the lifestyle of a backslider, and that he had violated three of the ten commandments. He had coveted his neighbor's wife, and that had led to adultery and finally murder. As this king lay upon the bare ground he felt as if he should be the one to die, but this would not be how this story would end.

What bothered David most was how easily and almost naturally, he had fallen into sin. These failings had not been second nature to him, and yet, now he could look back upon his last few months and felt like his actions were a miscarriage of righteous living. For a while he had focused on not being like Saul, and yet, he could see that he had fallen into that same trap.

> DAVID LAID UPON THE HARD FLOOR. HE HOPED FOR A REPRIEVE. HE FELT THAT HE DID NOT DESERVE COMFORT!

David heard, loud and clear, the decree by Nathan. His response was to withdraw to his private quarters, and to lay upon the ground for days, experiencing torment and concern over his own failure, knowing that this innocent child was suffering and would die, because of his actions. David rehearsed it all in his mind, and how he had allowed power to corrupt him. This poem speaks to the nature of man:

"There is so much good in the worst of us,
And so much bad in the best of us,
That it hardly behooves any of us
To talk about the rest of us."[20]

How was this a "Heart Revealing Day" in the life of David?

This day was one of the most difficult kinds of days any leader could ever face. On the day of David's sin, we must conclude that it was clearly not a day which reflected that David, was manifesting the heart of God. Nor had it been for upward of eighteen months. He had to admit to himself that, for these months he had been selfish, self-absorbed, and backslidden. As a matter of fact, Nathan had summed it up well, by denouncing David and his actions with these words, "you did things that made the Lord's enemies lose their respect for him,"[21] and furthermore, "by this deed you have given great occasion to the enemies of the Lord to blaspheme."[22]

The summation of this matter is that it is difficult to find a redeeming day in this entire affair,[23] until you find it on the very day when David was confronted and stopped in his tracks, and then challenged by the Prophet Nathan. The prophet Nathan was remarkable. First of all, God removed any semblance of rest for Nathan so that he would get his ire up enough to decisively move out of his home and in the direction of the palace and all before anyone could have their breakfast, to throw the gauntlet down to the highest and most powerful leader in the land. You have to love this man, for his skills in drama.

The first flicker of the spark of redemption, came only after the prophet had spoken and laid out his case. David had been wide-eyed and totally silent, but he found a window of opportunity, when he could say something. David realized, at the crescendo of Nathan's dramatic discourse, that he was in trouble: At that moment he cried out, "I am sorry, I have sinned. May God forgive me, for I have done wrong." We must be aware of the scripture "The sacrifice you desire is a broken spirit. You will not reject a broken and repentant heart, O God."[24]

It was David's broken contrition, his admission of guilt, without any attempt to defend himself, or give excuses, that reveals the true heart of David and how it was quite responsive to God. Listen to the Apostle Paul, as he spoke in a synagogue in Antioch in Pisidia, these words about King Saul and then King David:

> "The people of Israel begged for a king, so God gave them Saul, who ruled for forty years. Then God "put King David in his place, with this commendation: 'I've searched the land and found this

David, son of Jesse. He's a man whose heart beats to my heart, a man who will do what I tell him."[25]

David had done so many powerful things and accomplished so much for God and his nation. Again, this story of David with Bathsheba was a difficult one. He had failed God, his family and those who trusted him to live a life of integrity and righteousness. The prophet Nathan had come to call at the most unexpected time, the morning after the "love child" was born. David was not prepared for the events of that day, or for the next few days.

When Nathan challenged him with his declaration of, "You are the man," and spoke of the displeasure of the Lord against him, David's knees buckled. He fell on his face and repented immediately, because he realized the great offence he had committed against God. David did not justify himself, his actions or his intentions. He did not give excuses or explain his actions. David repented by throwing himself on the mercy seat of God. David cried out for forgiveness, acknowledging everything he had done, and repenting totally and fully.

Because of this immediate and total act of full repentance, God forgave him and restored him. However, the child would die, because, although we may be forgiven of our infidelity, there is also a law of "sowing and reaping." Nathan did not call out Bathsheba; the guilt did not rest on her. It seems that she truly was "the one ewe lamb."

No righteous leader would attempt to justify David and his transgression, but we must all acknowledge that David laid out a pattern of heart repentance, which we all hope to pattern after. Although we must not imitate David's transgression, we do all hope to emulate his repentance.

Endnotes

1. Exodus 20:1-17
2. www.brushfiresfoundation.org - News Junkie - "Are you one of those people who always need to know? Do you watch or listen to the news religiously, convinced that what you hear will give you an edge? You might be surprised, then, to learn that the news is bad for you and that giving it up might make you healthier and happier. So, argues author Rolf Dobelli."
3. Amos 3:17 CEV
4. Josephus Book 7, 7:3:147
5. II Samuel 12:1-15 - The full story of Nathan's visit to the Palace is given here.
6. www.patheos.com/blogs/christiancrier/2015/07/24 - Question: What is the difference between a rod and a staff? "Rods were sometimes used as weapons of defense or offense and sometimes simply as a walking stick (Gen 32:10) but a few times the rod and the staff were referred to as the same thing since the Hebrew word for rod (shebet) means both a rod or a staff but it can also mean "a club" but most of the time the rod was a symbol of correction and discipline like when Solomon wrote Proverbs 13:24 'Whoever spares the rod hates his son, but he who loves him is diligent to discipline him.'"
7. II Samuel 12:1-4 MSG
8. Josephus Book 7, 7:3:150
9. II Samuel 12:5-15 NLT
10. Josephus Book 7, 7:3:150
11. II Samuel 12:7-12 NKJV
12. Josephus Book 7, 7:3:153
13. Ibid
14. II Samuel 12:13-14
15. Josephus Book 7, 7:3:153
16. Psalm 103:12 NKJV
17. Galatians 6:7 NKJV - "Do not be deceived, God is not mocked; for whatever a man sows, that he will also reap."
18. II Samuel 12:13-14 NKJV
19. Josephus Book 7, 7:3:154
20. www.quotationspage.com/quote/27756.html -By: Edward Wallis Hoch, of Marion, Kansas

21. (1849-1925)
22. II Samuel 12:14 ERV
23. II Samuel 12:14 NKJV
24. II Samuel 11 – The entire chapter is about David and his acts of: Lust, adultery, deceptive behavior, treachery, order to have Uriah murdered, and finally stealing another man's wife.
25. Psalm 51:17 NLT "The sacrifice you desire is a broken spirit. You will not reject a broken and repentant heart, O God."
26. Acts 13:22 MSG

The Day A Man Threw Dirt in David's Face

II Samuel 16

Absalom's root of bitterness had led to his determination to usurp the throne from his father. He led a military detachment of 200 men, from Jerusalem to Hebron, where he activated his treasonous plan of Coup d'état.[1] Absalom's root of bitterness had taken hold of his life from nearly a decade ago when his sister, Tamar, had been raped by his half-brother, Amnon.[2]

Panic permeated the minds of everyone in the Land.

The day after Absalom declared himself king, in Hebron, had just begun, and a runner had delivered this message:

"'All Israel has joined Absalom in a conspiracy against you!' 'Then we must flee at once, or it will be too late!' David urged his men. 'Hurry! If we get out of the city before Absalom arrives, both we and the city of Jerusalem will be spared from disaster.'"[3]

The King was put on alert by those loyal to him. This news had been expected for days. They knew it would come soon but were not sure just how it would arrive and what the report would contain. Now it was definitive and haste must be taken to exit, or all of their lives could be at risk.

The bad news had been filling the minds of every official in Jerusalem and growing more intense by the day. Absalom had moved into Hebron several days earlier and had shamelessly worked to undermine his father, the King, currying favor and swaying the people to join him to topple David from the throne.

David loved his son, Absalom, but had finally made the hard decision to exit the city and to place his kingdom, his rule and his own life into God's hands. He fully trusted that God would be a righteous judge and would do the right thing for all concerned.

Stay in Jerusalem and fight, or flee to safety?

All this had plunged David into a state of soul searching to understand just what he should do and how he should react. This day would be a long day for him, because of his decision to vacate the city. There had been a number of his advisors who strongly favored standing to fight against Absalom and his army. They certainly had a good argument, but David had already suffered fall-out from other recent events and did not wish to stand up against his own son, whom he distrusted, but still loved very deeply.

Absalom was wrong to have embraced such disdain for his father. Bitterness is never really justified. Certainly, things can go wrong for you, but we all must proceed with grace, and forgiveness, reflecting the integrity of the Lord as we determine to respond and not to react. After all, we will be the losers when we allow bitterness to enter our hearts.

David felt hugely responsible for how he had mishandled the family affairs of recent years. The rape of Tamar (Absalom's sister) by her half-brother, Amnon, had all but destroyed Absalom's confidence in his father's ability to be just and fair. That had planted deeply the seeds of hatred and David realized that he had failed his son terribly. Now, nearly a decade later, there was nothing he could do to rebuild the relationship. It had become a toxic situation and was about to solidify the downward spiral.

David was very concerned about the dark clouds, which were gathering overhead. Absalom was in full attack mode, leaving the king insecure as to who would live and who would die. Things had gotten very serious, so quickly. Absalom would not listen to reason and had not responded to any attempt to negotiate. The dye was caste and getting worse with each incoming message.

Absalom's criticism had not fallen on deaf ears, as far as David was concerned. In his heart, he felt he must plead guilty, throwing himself at God's feet to pray for mercy. Perhaps God would be merciful and come to his aid. He was even concerned that his failings might neutralize or disqualify him, not just before the nation, but in the mind of God. It was very clear to David that the judgment of God had come upon the king and his household, because of his sin with Bathsheba.[4] There was one comforting reality in David's heart of

GOD MUST DECIDE.

hearts, and that was that God loved him, whether he would continue as king or not. Therefore, his trust of God could carry him out of Jerusalem and down a road, which would take him out of this city, and possibly across the River Jordan. In David's mind, God would decide the future and not him,[5] and certainly not his armies. The King decided that any fighting by his army must take place far away from Jerusalem.

David had made his decision and now must alert his family and whomever should exit with him. "We are leaving the city so that Absalom can enter it unchallenged. We are removing our hands from the scale, so that God will have freedom to decide my fate in whatever way He chooses. I will not even pray for my return, unless I see God's hand at work in it. I will not demand loyalty of anyone, unless it is freely given. Everyone is free to decide between the choice of David or Absalom, as Israel's king. This is not my kingdom, but God's kingdom."[6]

Their personal items were hastily packed and the route southward was chosen. There was not much time before they had to rush out of the palace. David had embraced a principle that, "I want God's help, and will not fight for my continued role as king, but my prayer is that God will fight for me. Perhaps God is finished with me and will now pass the crown to Absalom. God will decide; our fate is in His hands."

Those were treacherous times

Treachery has always existed throughout history. It has existed in families, business, marriage relationships, politics and in religion. The form of treachery varies from case to case. The fallout can be that you stop trusting. Our tendency is to "trust no one", and yet trust, you must. Swirling around King David, as he exited Jerusalem was treachery on every side. The good thing was that not everyone was guilty; some were loyal to a fault and to the end.

Treachery[6] was coming at David from Absalom's side. He even met up with it on the road from Jerusalem southward. Ziba, came out to meet David to give him gifts as he fled the city. Ziba brought donkeys to ride, food to sustain, and wine to revive, when the journey gets exhausting. When David inquired as to the purpose of these gifts, Ziba maligned Mephibosheth and deceived David. Later it would be proven that Ziba was lying; but for now, he was taking advantage of the king's misfortune, seizing a chance that he could profit by Mephibosheth's demotion.[7] David was too hasty to give Ziba all that belonged to Mephibosheth, but later would sort out the issues.[8]

By that time, David and his entourage were passing through the tribal areas of Benjamin and the town of Bahurim. A man, named Shimei, who was related to Saul's family and disloyal to David came out cursing him, and throwing stones erratically at both the king and all who traveled with him. These are the words Shimei screamed at the king:

> "Get out of here, you murderer, you scoundrel! The Lord is paying you back for all the bloodshed in Saul's clan. You stole his throne, and now the Lord has given it to your son, Absalom. At last you will taste some of your own medicine, for you are a murderer! Look at you now—ruined! And good riddance, you're a pathetic old man!"[9]

Immediately, one of David's body guard, Abishai,[10] arose and prepared to strike Shimei down. He appealed to David for permission to take off the head of Shimei, saying, "why should this dead dog curse my lord the King? Please, let me go over and take off his head!"[11] As he drew his sword, David ordered him to put down his weapon. Then all those around David heard him say this to Abishai:

> THE SWORD CANNOT SOLVE EVERY PROBLEM! PERHAPS YOU SHOULD STAND DOWN AND "LET GOD."

"Who asked your opinion, Abishai, son of Zeruiah! If the Lord has told him to curse me, who are you to stop him?"

Then David said to Abishai and to all his servants, "My own son is trying to kill me. Doesn't this relative of Saul have even more reason to do so? Leave him alone and let him curse, for the Lord has told him to do it. And perhaps the Lord will see that I am being wronged and will bless me because of these curses, today."[12]

So, David and those traveling with him, continued down the road. Shimei made a nuisance of himself, by throwing dust and stones at David, as well as bellowing curses at the king.

Although the intention was to press onward and to cross the Jordan River, so many of David's family and friends were exhausted in the journey with all the emotional drama, so that, by this time it was decided that they make camp and refresh themselves.

How was this a "Heart Revealing Day" in the life of David?

David appreciated the gift God had given him to serve Israel as their king. Initially, it was not the crown that he had thought of pursuing, as much as it was, as a young shepherd, to bask in the afterglow of worshipping his God. However, when the crown was promised to him, of course, he seized upon it as a gift to be accepted, and treasured, as his destiny. The Crown had been God's idea and plan for David.

It was not easy to respond to the dark clouds and cold winds, which were facing the Kingdom on this day. The family was being torn apart by treachery and betrayal; and the king's government was being ripped into shreds by this military coup d'état. However, David had renewed his commitment to God, and had diminished his own attachment to his kingdom. In other words, David was willing to let God rule the day. He had now decided that God was the center of the world, and not himself.

It is worthy of note that, following David's moral failure, came his repentance, and then redemption. Yes, he must reap a harvest for some of the seeds he'd sown, but he was personally redeemed, and that meant more to David than anything. It could be said that, after God had taken David to the "woodshed"[4], he was able to think more clearly. He was no longer driven by the human passion of lust but had allowed the Holy Spirit to refresh his heart so that he could return to God.

This world does not generally see leaders who occupy high positions like kings, emperors, presidents, governors, or prime ministers who are so willing to give up their expectations to God. Most of them hold on as long as possible and pay no attention to what God thinks. David was a different kind of man. Yes, he was flesh; but he also recognized, his need for God to be involved in his life and his life plan. These comments reflect David's heart of hearts:

- David was determined not to steal God's glory.
- David did not want to covet the throne, that God might want to give to another.

- David did not want to judge a man like Shimei, when he did not know how God felt about this drama.
- In David's "heart of hearts", he wanted what God wanted for Israel.

David could have stayed in Jerusalem, to fight Absalom and his forces, just because he had that right. However, he decided that he needed a word from God on the question of "who should be the king?" He did not assume that God still wanted him to remain as king. Of course, David could see that God was not through with him, but the humility in his heart took nothing for granted. God needed to give David insight and he felt that this was the best way. David felt like his own failures had left him in a weak place, when it came to negotiating with God. As a result, he was yielding his crown to God, to allow God to reaffirm him, or pass it on to Absalom.

Often leaders just assume that God wants them to maintain their position, when it may be time for change. Transition must be seen as a positive response from the hearts of all concerned, but God should remain the one with the "Trump card."[14] Another misunderstanding, which leaders often have is that because of their long history, they have tenure, or seniority, but remember this, there is no seniority in the Lord's work. David understood the answer to the question of, "does seniority equal entitlement?" It is a fact that, "when you begin to talk about seniority, the waters can get muddy, really fast." Most of us would agree that "hard work, commitment, and loyalty should be rewarded, but longevity in a position is not necessarily proof of that."[15]

When we all began, we understood that the world would be a competitive world, and even the ministry would face some of this. In the place of kings, it is no less competitive, although the politics of things also often play into the mix. In David's case, he really wanted to remain king, but he was clear on one thing. This role, as Israel's king, was an appointed position and should go to the one God favored and anointed for the role. It is always good when the appointed can have enough humility not to call foul, when God sees it is time to move on. David had that clearly in focus, which qualified him for being a part of the future.

Endnotes

1. II Samuel 15:1-12
2. II Samuel 13:32 KJV
3. II Samuel 15:13 NLT
4. II Samuel 12:11
5. Daniel 2:21 NKJV - "He changes the times and the seasons; He removes kings and raises up kings; He gives wisdom to the wise and knowledge to those who have understanding."
6. I Samuel 19:24-30 - Later David learned of Ziba's lies and deception.
7. www.merriam-webster.com/dictionary/treachery - violation of allegiance or of faith and confidence; Treason
8. II Samuel 16:1-4 - David gave everything over to Ziba, because he believed the lies against Mephibosheth. Later he learned of Ziba's lies (II Samuel 19:24-30).
9. II Samuel 16:7-8 MSG
10. II Samuel 16:9 - Abishai was the oldest son of David's sister, Zeruiah. He was also listed in II Samuel 23:18, as one of the top three of David's Mightiest Men. On one occasion, Abishai had used his sword to slay three hundred men who had come against him in battle.
11. II Samuel 16:9 NKJV
12. II Samuel 16:10-12 NLT
13. www.thefreedictionary.com - An idiom: "woodshed" - "An instance of being reprimanded or punished." David had been reprimanded by God.
14. www.vocabulary.com/dictionary/trump%20card - "Trump Card" - The trump card is the winning card. If you play a trump card during a game of Spades, it means that you take the whole trick — in other words, you'll pick up every card on the table.
15. www.techrepublic.com/blog/tech-decision-maker - "Does Seniority Equal Entitlement?" - "Having said all of the above, in a perfect world, the most qualified person for a position would fill a position when it becomes available. However, we don't live in that perfect world nor is determining who is best qualified anything close to an exact science. In fact, it's closer to an art than a science."

The Day David Purchased Araunah's Land, on Mount Moriah

II Samuel 24

The people of the nation of Israel were sliding into a lifestyle of pride. It seems that all of Israel had grown comfortable and were filled with a level of pride that incensed the Lord. This attitude was engulfing all of Israel from the youngest to the greatest, which meant that even David was showing the effects of arrogance.

It was at that time that David felt within his own heart a desire to know Israel's strength in battle. It should have been enough to know that God was on his side. He had won every battle he had ever faced on the battlefield, but still, out of shear curiosity, David was tempted, to know the numbers. He would not have conducted this particular census, had he remained consistently full of faith.

Whereas, we can see that not only the people of Israel, but their king was faltering in their trust of God's faithfulness. This got them into lots of trouble. This was one of those flesh moments, when the flesh got the better over sound judgment.

> SAMSON, WITH DIVINE STRENGTH DEFEATED AN ARMY!
> JUDGES 15:14-17

Logically, when going to war, a leader should know his capability before engaging the enemy. This is the way man thinks, when functioning in the pride of his heart. However, God does not think in this way. With God, all things are possible. With God, you can go into war with shortages of every kind, and still accomplish great victories, because God goes with you. With God, even one man can go up against an entire army and, with divine empowerment, defeat those who oppose him. David was specifically interested in knowing how many men of war he had. So, this is the basis of the ensuing dilemma.

David had neglected to do his research about the command of Moses, on the subject of taking a census. Moses did not say that Israel's leaders must avoid taking a census, but if they do find need to conduct a census, then that occasion should be used as an essential time to redeem the people, in the form of an offering. This offering would be a half shekel per person, twenty years of age and above, whether rich or poor. This was a flat-tax or poll-tax, that recognized each person and was to be a way of acknowledging how they were redeemed before God. This had become a principle for the Hebrew nation. Israel could not be a God-fearing people unless they acknowledged their need for redemption, and this was one way for that redemption to take place. After receiving that offering, in this case a flat-tax or poll-tax, then it was to be placed in the memorial fund for the Tent of Meeting, in honor of God, to make atonement for their lives.

It was fine to know how many citizens the king had in all the land, but that census, in the law of Moses, was tied to a method of funding the operational expenses of the Tabernacle of Moses.

FACT:
GOD DOES NOT HAVE POWER
~
GOD IS POWER!

> The Atonement-Tax ~ God spoke to Moses: "When you take a head count of the Israelites to keep track of them, all must pay an atonement-tax to God for their life at the time of being registered so that nothing bad will happen because of the registration. Everyone who gets counted is to give a half-shekel (using the standard Sanctuary shekel of a fifth of an ounce to the shekel)—a half-shekel offering to God. Everyone counted, age twenty and up, is to make the offering to God. The rich are not to pay more nor, the poor less than the half-shekel offering to God, the atonement-tax for your lives. Take the atonement-tax money from the Israelites and put it to the maintenance of the Tent of Meeting. It will be a memorial fund for the Israelites in honor of God, making atonement for your lives."[1]

On this occasion, David's primary interest was to know how many men of war he had in his army. Joab reacted, quite critically, but respectfully, "May the Lord your God give you 100 times as many people, no matter how many there are! And may your eyes see this thing happen."[2] Then Joab continued, "but why on earth would you do a thing like this?"[3] Joab was aware of the trouble they could get into, but David seemed, for the moment, to be too concerned with "issues of numbers." David was himself a prophet.[4] He respected, very much, the prophets whom God sent to him[5] on a number of occasions. He listened carefully to their messages; he obeyed the instructions that God gave him, by means of them, but this time he was not paying attention to the still small voice giving him warning. Joab tried to help, but David was not listening. If we are open to the voice of God, He will often give us someone in our lives who will whisper words of wisdom. If, however, we refuse to adhere to that counsel, then trouble may soon await us.

ISRAEL'S NATIONAL SIN WAS THE FIRST PROBLEM ~ GOD USED DAVID'S SIN TO DEAL WITH EVERYONE.

Joab left the palace and went about the task, over the next nine months and twenty days, of taking a census of the men of battle age. All through the nation Joab and his officers traveled, carefully tabulating the numbers in every tribe and village. At the very end, before including the figures for the tribes of Levi and Benjamin, Joab brought the figures of 1.3 million men of battle age to fight in the army. Keep in mind that Joab did not want to do this in the first place.

On the following morning, David awoke to a stirring, which alerted him, deep within his soul. Actually, scripture says that "David's heart smote him."[6] What had escaped him before, only now moved him to sincere concern. He realized that God had been speaking, but he had not been listening, when Joab had warned him nearly ten months earlier that he must not number the nation.[7]

David had sinned, but so had the entire nation. In this story, we see that God saw Israel as having sin issues of pride. They were not devoted to God as much as they were to their own lusts. This had to be dealt with, and yet they were unaware of their own failures. Because of this, David was drawn into taking them down a road to enable God to hold up a mirror, after which He could deal with everyone.

David had been blinded by the sin of pride. The scripture, at the beginning of this story, tells that the anger of the Lord was kindled against Israel. It seems that all of Israel had grown comfortable and were prideful, losing the closeness of their loyalty to God. This census had brought it to light, by David's demand to number all the men of war.

THE ANGER OF THE LORD HAD BEEN KINDLED AGAINST ISRAEL.

It seems that, the nation's sin was not public knowledge enough for God to route-out and deal with. Because of David's sin, God had a legal authority to deal with the entire nation.

The reason pride issues can be such a problem for an individual or a society, is that they grow like a weed instead of like an organic plant. If we do not function with self-discipline and humility, then we may also find ourselves in trouble with God.

In other words, the sins of pride were rampant from the palace to the smallest home. Sometimes, mankind gets pompous and arrogant, but it is not so easily visible, until those attitudes show up as a public symptom.

David's error was in thinking that the size and number of military age men had anything to do with God's ability to win wars. God was his source for victory, and the king needed to be reminded that, the favor he received on the day he was anointed by Samuel was his source of strength, and not the size of his army. Keep in mind, that, "some trust in chariots and some in horses, but we will remember the name of the Lord our God."

Read the first five verses of the "Song of Moses," which all of Israel sung, while standing on the east side of the Red Sea, after leaving their slave years in Egypt:

The Song of Moses

"I will sing to the Lord, for He has triumphed gloriously!
The horse and its rider He has thrown into the sea!
The Lord *is* my strength and song,
And He has become my salvation;
He *is* my God, and I will praise Him;
My father's God, and I will exalt Him.
The Lord *is* a man of war;
The Lord *is* His name.
Pharaoh's chariots and his army He has cast into the sea;
His chosen captains also are drowned in the Red Sea.
The depths have covered them;
They sank to the bottom like a stone."[8]

David repented immediately, when his sin was pointed out to him. He yielded by going into full and humble repentance for his sin. The problem was that David was only the visible part of the problem; all Israel was in their own variation of sin, and now was the time for the prophets to call the entire nation to repentance. A nation, which has made vows and commitments to God cannot just carry on when issues arise and those vows are violated. If that nation wants to continue on with divine favor, then it must bend the knee and repent of its errant ways. This event was not just about David's sin, but about an entire nation that had stumbled and needed to follow their king in repentance.

"If My people who are called by My name will humble themselves,
and pray and seek My face,
and turn from their wicked ways,
then I will hear from heaven,
and will forgive their sin and heal their land."[9]

The Story

The sun had not been up long. Usually, when the Holy Spirit chooses to deal with a problem, is when the prophets have begun to lose sleep. Their rest is withdrawn and they can more easily feel the darkness of the hour and the seriousness of the gloomy situation. So, the prophets were moved to come to the palace for a session with the king. The prominent prophets of the day, and close to the heart of David, were both Gad and Nathan.[10]

In the scripture, it says that Gad took the dominant roll, as he approached the king. In Josephus it states that, also present, was the prophet Nathan. These men were generals in God's work force. Now, to deal with the king's desire to know the number of his military strength, God called out heaven's generals to deal with an earthly problem.

PROPHETS DON'T JUST DROP IN FOR SOCIAL CALLS.

These men of prophecy did not mince words. They got right to the point, because, it was clear to them, as soon as they arrived, that David was smitten by the Lord and was fully aware of his error. David began by saying, "please entreat the Lord, on my behalf that He forgive me of my sin, and that He will be merciful to me, for I have greatly sinned against God."[11]

They began with Gad speaking directly and in a fatherly manner, to the king: "Today, God will give you three choices, so that you, as king of Israel, will determine the manner in, which God deals with the problems He sees. This nation needed redemption. You did not choose to go down the road of redemption by charging a tariff to give as a temple tax, according to the words of Moses, so now you must deal with the heart of the problem, by choosing the method of discipline." According to your election, this shall be the way God routes-out the problem, which is in my people:

- "Shall seven years of famine come to you in your land?
- Or, shall you flee three months before your enemies, while they pursue you?
- Or, shall there be three days' plague in your land?

Now consider and see what answer I should take back to Him who sent me."[13]

David admitted to the prophet that he was in consternation regarding his decision, and so he must consider the ramifications as closely as possible. The king realized that either choice would be a fatal choice for some. The collateral damage was very high and yet the prophet was demanding that the decision must be made, today. David reviewed the options:

- If I choose **seven years of famine**, it will surely last longer than the huge storage of corn, which I have stored up against such possibilities. David felt that if he chose famine, he would possibly not be touched personally, and thus would be delegating to the rest of the nation the punishment, which he felt was because of his own bad decisions.[14] And seven years is a long time for prolonged agony, and for Israel.[15]
- And then there is the option to flee three months before my enemies, while they pursue us? David felt that this would not be a wise choice, because he did have so many strong

and capable soldiers, on whom he depended. If he chose this option it would appear that he trusted in his own strength and preferred to have his hand on the scale, by reason of his valiant men and strongholds. David was concerned that, if he chose this option it would appear that he was personally confident of his own ability to weather the storm.[16]

- And then the final option is to choose, **three days' plague in the land**? David recognized this as the best option because, by this choice he would be placing himself and the people directly into the hand of a merciful God, rather than in the hands of a merciless enemy. Also, by this option, he was electing to go the way of a normal affliction so common to kings and the nations.[17]

David was really frightened and said, "It's a terrible choice to make! But the LORD is kind, and I'd rather have him punish us than for anyone else to do it."[18] Therefore, David took the third choice, knowing that the nation must endure three days of plagues. Even so, David realized he must intercede for the people, if perhaps God would shorten the time.

When the prophet heard David's choice, right there in front of the king and those officials who were present, he turned his face upward and declared the decision to God. In moments, a kind of distemper[19] filled the land and touched the people.[20] There was no warning and no preparation was made or even possible. The best way to describe this pestilence and mortality, is that it was an infection and characterized by fever, vomiting, diarrhea, and leading to dehydration. It was contagious and finally, this left many of the people with weaknesses, which became life threatening.[21] Whole families became casualties, often interrupting funeral services with the deaths of several who fell down on the spot, with no warning.

The people were not aware of what was going on in Jerusalem and in the palace. In three long days, the plague was gone, leaving in its wake the passing of seventy thousand souls."[22] Even in the twenty-first century, because we as citizens of a nation, cannot know what is happening in the government, then it is advisable that we pray for those in government, for their decisions and even transgressions, may affect us.[23]

We do not always know what is going on in the halls of governmental power. As a result, we could be subject to dangers in unpredictable ways. So, we must pray for them that they will have wisdom, insight and good judgment, on their part, so that our lives may be without fallout, disease and calamity.

The plague, over the three days, took casualties from Dan to Beersheba, in every tribe, in every village, and some in nearly every family. No one was untouched in some way.

David went out to the roof of his palace and donned himself in sackcloth and ashes, and lay prostrate on the ground, as he prayed, wept and interceded for the people. He looked at the people of Israel through his shepherd eyes. He cried out to God for the lives of all the people of Israel. He entreated God that the distemper would be stopped and that judgment would be satisfied with the taking of those who had already passed. David appealed to God in this prayer, "I have sinned, I have done wickedly; but these sheep, what have they done? Let thine hand be upon me and against my father's house."

While David looked up to God he could see the angel of God with his hand outstretched toward Jerusalem. It was at that moment, that God looked favorably upon David's repentance and intercession for the people. The Lord called back the Angel of Death and said, "That is enough! Put down your arm and stop the plague."[24]

The angel came to a total stop, when positioned over the threshing floor of Araunah,[25] the Jebusite.[26] Immediately, the prophet came to the King and said, "Go up to the threshing floor of Araunah, to build an altar."[27]

David, lived in the City of David, which was a part of Jerusalem. From where he was praying, he could tilt his head upward and, within a few hundred meters (or yards), see the place where the Angel had stopped, at a higher elevation over the city of Jerusalem, and well known as Mt. Moriah.[28]

Araunah offered all, but David graciously declined the gift.

It is a fact that David had spent time traveling all over the land of Israel, both as a military leader for Saul, and all during the years when he was running from him. During those years, he had made friends with foreign kings, like the king of Moab,[29] Nahash, the king of Ammon,[30] and locals in every area of the nation of Israel, such as in the region of Jebus. Araunah was one of those friends, even though he was both a Jebusite and a Canaanite. At the time when David captured Jebus, he saw no reason to include Araunah in this assault. This man was a peaceful man and quite frankly a business man who had become a loyal friend. This occasion of making friends everywhere he went, served David well, as it did on that day, when he needed the kindness and favor of a friend.[31]

Just outside of Jerusalem and overlooking it, was a separate area, which we know as Mount Moriah, and also as the threshing floor of Araunah.[32]

David left immediately and came to the summit of what is today called, "The Temple Mount," or Mount Moriah.[33] This is where Araunah lived and had his threshing floor. The king, his servants, and the family of Araunah all could see the Angel of the Lord positioned above them. When the four sons of Araunah saw the angel, they ran away to hide, for they were frightened.[34]

David walked up the hill of Mt. Moriah, and Araunah came down to meet him. When they met, he bowed his face to the ground giving honor to the king. It must have been a sacred moment, for their meeting to be coming together with an angel positioned overhead.

David said to Araunah, "Sell me your threshing floor. I will pay you the full market price. Then I can use the area to build an altar to worship the Lord. Then, this terrible sickness will be stopped."[35]

Araunah first looked at David, and then above their meeting place and watched the Angel of the Lord. It struck awe and reverence into his heart. He felt compelled by his own spirit that he must give all to such a powerful and awesome God. It was then that Araunah, declared "I will give you whatever you need as Israel's leader. Please take my offerings and use them to please the Lord. He said, "Take this threshing floor. You are my lord and king, so do whatever you want. Look, I will also give you oxen and my ploughs, for the burnt offering. You can have the wooden threshing tools to burn for the fire on the altar. And I will give the wheat for the grain offering. I will give all this to you."[36] So Araunah offered all to the king, as a gift. David graciously listened to his offer of generosity, but declined to accept it, stating that he must pay a full price, in order for his offering to have credibility with God.

ARAUNAH TALKED WITH DAVID, ALL THE WHILE WATCHING THE ANGEL OVER THEIR HEADS!

It is worth mentioning that Araunah's enterprise was harvesting and then threshing wheat. By giving all of this to David, he would be giving away his business and all the assets necessary for him to make a living for his family. Araunah offered all, even down to the threshing equipment needed to do the threshing. He suggested that this equipment could be broken up and used as firewood, to make the sacrifice to God. This man Araunah was, not only a true friend, but was a humble and sacrificial man. His heart was right and what he offered to David was quite honorable. Araunah concluded his offer to David, with "and I pray that God will accept your sacrifice."[37]

David responded to Araunah that he accepted his kindness and generosity as an act of good will, but today was not a day for him to receive gifts when he wanted, so much to offer a sacrifice to God. "If I obtain this threshing floor from you it can only be, because I have paid you the fair market value for everything." "I will not take anything that is yours and give it to the Lord. I will not give offerings that cost me nothing."[38] "I'm not going to offer God sacrifices that are no sacrifice."[39]

David paid Araunah, that day, 15 pounds of gold,[40] for the summit of Mt. Moriah, where Abraham had gone to offer up Isaac to the Lord, as a sacrifice. This was the same place where Solomon built "Solomon's Temple" and later Herod rebuilt the temple. It is today the site of the "Dome of the Rock," in the heart of Jerusalem.

On this site, David built an altar for worshipping the Lord. "He offered burnt offerings and fellowship offerings. He prayed to the Lord. The Lord answered David by sending fire down from heaven. The fire came down on the altar of burnt offering.

Then the Lord commanded the angel to put his sword back into its sheath."[41]

It is worthy of consideration that, on this occasion David purchased the Temple Mount, or Mt. Moriah, to be under the legal ownership of the Hebrew nation of Israel, so those who have advanced the claim that they have a right to Araunah's land, are gravely mistaken, as this legal ownership has never been revoked.

The High Place was in Gibeah, but God redirected things.

It is worthy of note that David could have gone to Gibeah, the official high place at that time, but the prophet Gad instructed David, to go instead to Mt. Moriah to build an altar and make sacrifices.[42]

God always has hidden blessings for us in the needlework of His tapestries.[43] Sometimes we have to look closely, but Father God loves us and wants to coax us toward a place of restoration. Regardless of our failures and even our sins, Creator God is our friend.

This had been a very dark time in Israel's history; it had been beset with failure, missteps, deaths, and all as a result of sin. But, God had a plan and wanted to open up a way to the healing of the nation. He was poised to open to David a portal through, which he could get a glimpse of better days, and see the nation come to a full redemption.

When first looking over this event, I was initially disappointed with the challenges it posed in the bigger picture of things. I was concerned that this "numbering of Israel" and the deaths of seventy thousand people had to be the last day of David's heart revealing days. I scoured David's entire story to see if, perhaps it could be moved back to earlier times, but discovered that it was one of David's last days, and before he turned it all over to his son, Solomon. I finally began to research this event to see how it had a redemptive quality, besides what I could plainly see were the "passing of the test, heart issues" displayed by David. This was the last chapter and rightly should be examined lastly.

Well into this story, I began to discover some moving nuggets, which opened me up to see that, in order for David to finish well, he needed to have all sin in his life and that of Israel to be fully disclosed, and all so that redemption could have its perfect work of grace. It is a sad thing when a life comes to a close and yet there are hidden flaws, which could have been redeemed, but were never addressed during that lifetime. This is no way to face eternity.

As challenging as this story is, we find it finally culminating, with a focus on Mt. Moriah, where sacrifice should be made. This holy mountain had been the focus of Abraham's greatest battle, when he had led Isaac to the top with plans to obey God and sacrifice his son. This mountain was also to become the building site for Solomon to construct the Temple in a few short years after David's passing. Near the base of Mt. Moriah, was the site of the "Tabernacle of David," which had been established as the first step of moving the Tabernacle of Moses from Gibeah to Jerusalem.

Scripture does not give us any idea of where David had hoped to build the Temple of Solomon. We only know of the exchange between David and the Lord, about how God did not want him to build a temple, but that God volunteered to build, for David, a house, or a dynasty, through the Davidic Covenant."[44] We would only assume that the temple would be in Jerusalem, but no indication is made as to the actual site, until David's repentance for numbering Israel. It was then that the prophet instructed him to

IT IS AMAZING HOW GOD CAN REDEEM THINGS. ARUNAH'S THRESHING FLOOR BECAME THE SITE FOR THE TEMPLE!

watch where the Angel had stopped his assault; i.e. directly adjacent to the summit of Mt. Moriah, at the threshing floor of Araunah. It was, at that point that Araunah and his family were at immediate risk, if the angel continued.

David laid on the ground, with sack cloth and ashes to plead with God, that these three days be wrapped up and the attack halted. God saw David's heart and commanded, "Stop, enough is enough! Go no further." Then he moved on the prophet Gad, to come to the palace and give instructions to the king. "Go up immediately to the threshing floor of Araunah, the Jebusite, and build an altar there to God, and offer sacrifices."[45]

David and Araunah did not on this occasion, exchange the normal pleasantries of friends.[46] This was an official visit, with David coming as the head of state, in repentance to satisfy the requirements of God. This was a serious business meeting, leaving no time for small talk.

After David negotiated with Araunah, and paid him for the purchase, he immediately prepared to build the altar and then to offer sacrifices. David could see Jerusalem better from Mt. Moriah than from any other place. Although past historical events on this mountain, were significant to all of Israel, the events of this day, confirmed many other things in the mind of David. God had sent him to this place and he saw this mountain in a new light.

Years earlier David had chosen to bring the ark of the covenant to Jerusalem rather than to Gibeah,[47] and so he had carried it to this city, so that special focus could be placed on Israel's need to be aggressive worshippers of their God. It had become a progression, perhaps without David even realizing it. The ark of the covenant, was established in a "one room tent,"[48] at the base of Mt. Moriah, in the vicinity of what is known today as the "Wailing Wall," and now he was in the business of choosing the site for the future Temple. This had become a summit for David to meet with God. Decisions were made, as the fire struck the sacrifice from heaven. This was a moment to remember.

How was this a "Heart Revealing Day" in the life of David?

That day was coming to an end. So much had happened. David had strayed into forbidden territory, with his having numbered the men of war, then by not redeeming them in obedience to the law of Moses on the subject of census. That had led to a confrontation by God and his prophets. Now the nation, through correct responses, had repented and were being redeemed on top of Mt. Moriah. The king and the nation had stooped to pride issues, but hopefully that had been resolved. As a nation, they were only strong as long as their hearts were compliant with honoring God and walking in righteousness.

In David's heart of hearts, he felt relieved, when he realized that he was now, once again walking in the approval of God. He had loved God from his youth, had failed a few times, had repented every time; but now, in his final years, was refreshed in his relationship with God. His heart confirmed his repentance, by requiring of his knees, the buckling and bending to the floor. He was always ready to surrender to God and bend his knees in submission; and always ready to comply with whatever God required. His heart may stand up and flagrantly violate God's laws, but in the end, he would always, and most willingly seek God's favor and forgiveness.

David had spent the three days on the ground in sackcloth and ashes, repenting, without eating and drinking, in his humblest posture, because, in his heart of hearts, he loved God from the depths of his heart.

This day, as much as any other of the days of his life, reveal a genuine, sincere heart bent on serving and obeying God. Nothing else was ultimately significant for him. David had been chosen and carefully selected by God to be Israel's second king, and that had been a good call by God and his prophet, Samuel. Now, in his later years, he had won victories in war, turned a fledgling nation into a powerhouse to be reckoned with by all who opposed them, and showed that, regardless of how high you get, you still must bend low before the God of the universe. You may go high, but God is higher still.

Araunah's gift was a wonderful and generous gesture, but David could not accept a shortcut to his sacrifice to God. There was too much at stake. To define the word sacrifice meant, that it must not come easy. David's heart was sincere and he placed such value on the word sacrifice that he refused to give, without sacrifice. If he is to give to God, then he must find that it bites into his personal economy. There would never be a compromise in David's heart to his gift of response or generosity to God. God had given David so much that he was determined to remain a giver, in every area of his life. This fact is the primary sign of how this day revealed the heart of David, as a man after the Lord's own heart.

Besides the obvious, we must admit that anytime you start counting your strength with the idea that your success does not require God's help, thinking that you can do it on your own, you must realize that you are in trouble.

I realize that you must prepare for life, by educating and equipping yourself, but this only works so far. You will then discover that the biggest battles in life can only be won by having the hand of God doing miraculous things for you. God is your reconnaissance force, in the heavens above you and without His "eyes in the sky," then you will come up short.

Keep in mind that there is the "cherry on top of the cake" issue that you can always do better if the favor of God tips the scale to your advantage.

Some people live in a dream world where no one suffers the consequences of their actions. Therefore, they believe there is no judgment of God. This could be labeled, selective atheism.[49] There is a Supreme Being, he is Jehovah God and his way of dealing with transgression leaves you with two choices:

- Repentance, and humility, which leads to redemption. Build your house on the Rock, Christ Jesus.[50]
- Rejection of His authority in your life, which will bring you to destruction. If you build your house on the sand, it will collapse when the trials come.[51]

Endnotes

1. Exodus 30:12-16 MSG - "The Atonement-Tax"
2. II Samuel 24:3 ERV
3. II Samuel 24:3 MSG
4. Acts 2:29-30
5. 1 Chronicles 29:29 - tells us that the prophets Samuel, Gad and Nathan wrote the records of David's life. That is, Samuel wrote the first part of the records. Then Gad wrote the next part. Finally, Nathan wrote the last part; Nathan continued to serve as a prophet during the beginning of Solomon's rule.
6. II Samuel 24:10 KJV - This gives the impression that the king's eyes opened wide, that morning as a result of God smacking him into an attitude adjustment. God really got David's attention, so that he could realize he had sinned.
7. II Samuel 24:1
8. Exodus 15:1-5 NKJV - The Song of Moses
9. II Chronicles 7:14 NKJV
10. Josephus Book 7, 13:2:321
11. Ibid
12. Exodus 30:12 NLT - "Whenever you take a census of the people of Israel, each man who is counted must pay a ransom for himself to the LORD. Then no plague will strike the people as you count them."
13. II Samuel 24:13-14 NKJV
14. Josephus Book 7, 13:2:322
15. Seven years of famine was the length of famine, during the days of Joseph in Genesis 41.
16. Josephus Book 7, 13:2:323
17. Josephus Book 7, 13:2:323
18. II Samuel 24:14 CEV
19. www.merriam-webster.com/dictionary/distemper - distemper - Several choices of definitions, but one of the most likely is this one: "a highly contagious virus disease especially of dogs that is marked by fever, leukopenia, and respiratory, gastrointestinal, and neurological symptoms and that is caused by a paramyxovirus of the genus Morbillivirus (species Canine distemper virus)"
20. Josephus Book 7, 13:2:327

21. www.dictionary.com/browse/distemper - "Distemper" It appears that the closest thing to what came upon the people was a distemper often seen in dogs and cats.

22. Josephus Book 7, 13:2:324-326

23. I Timothy 2:1-3 ERV

24. II Samuel 24:16 ERV

25. It is noteworthy that Araunah (or Arunah) was also called by the name of Ornan in I Chronicles 21:15, "And the angel of the LORD stood by the threshing floor of Ornan the Jebusite."

26. Ibid

27. II Samuel 24:18

28. www.generationword.com/jerusalem101/3a-map-of-modern-jerusalem.html - Map of modern day Jerusalem. Compare where David lived in the City of David, against the Temple Mount.

29. I Samuel 22:3

30. II Samuel 10:2- Then David said, "'I will show kindness to Hanun the son of Nahash, just as his father showed kindness to me.' So, David sent some of his servants to console him concerning his father…"

31. I Samuel 30:26-31

32. www.generationword.com/jerusalem101/13-mount-moriah.html - Mount Moriah is the mount on which Abraham offered Isaac in Genesis 22. In 1 Chronicles 21 it is identified as the location of Arunah (Araunah or, Ornan) the Jebusite threshing floor that David bought for 600 shekels of gold. This purchase is an important fact since it demonstrates that the Jews received this area through a legal transaction. They have never sold the rights to Mount Moriah. King David said to Ornan (Araunah), "No, but I will buy them for the full price. I will not take for the Lord what is yours, nor offer burnt offerings that cost me nothing." So, David paid Ornan 600 shekels of gold by weight for the site. And David built there an altar to the Lord and presented burnt offerings. - 1 Chronicles 21:24, 25

33. www.google.ie - Where is the threshing floor of Araunah? "Araunah was a Jebusite who … owned the threshing floor, on the summit of Mount Moriah, that David purchased and used as the site for assembling an altar to God."

34. II Samuel 24:20 ERV

35. I Chronicles 21:24 MSG

36. II Samuel 24:18-23

37. Josephus Book 7, 13:2:331

38. II Samuel 24:24 ERV

39. 1 Chronicles 21:24 MSG

40. All translations agree, for the most part, but use different measures. Some say, 600 shekels of gold, others 600 gold coins, others 15 pounds of gold, and one says $4,300 in gold. This was the price for the summit of Mt. Moriah.

41. II Samuel 24:26-27 ERV

42. 1 Chronicles 21:29-30 NKJV

43. www.challies.com/articles/gods-tapestry - tapestry's needlework - "Have you ever compared the front and back of a tapestry? The front of a tapestry is art. In the hands of a skilled weaver it displays incredible artistry and fine detail. The back of a tapestry is a mess. A tapestry is made by weaving together different-colored threads, and the images and designs are created by the interplay between the different colors and textures. What is clear on the front is opaque on the back. The back shows something of the image, but it looks more like a child's attempt than a master's: it lacks nuance and clarity and detail. Where the front is smooth, the back is covered in knots and loose ends."

44. www.gotquestions.org/Davidic-covenant - The Davidic Covenant refers to God's promises to David through Nathan the prophet and is found in II Samuel 7 and later summarized in I Chronicles 17:11-14, and II Chronicles 6:16."

45. Josephus Book 7, 13:4:329

46. Josephus Book 7, 13:4:329 - "Araunah was, by his lineage a Jebusite, but a particular friend of David's: and for that cause, it was that, when he overthrew the city of Jebus, he did him no harm."

47. I Chronicles 15:3

48. Amazon.com - "Living the Presence of the Spirit," by Jack Haberer. Page 57. I Chronicles 16:1

49. Selective Atheism - A state of denial, where, although you say you believe in God, you deny Him the right to be "your judge" and to call you into accountability.

50. Matthew 7:24-25

51. Matthew 7:26-27

EPILOGUE

David was a man with many facets to his nature. We can agree that he was a worshipper, and that he was a noble leader, among leaders. Even 3000 years later and in such modern times, we can see him as having attributes worthy of embracing and modeling.

It is my hope that by reading, The Mentor King, you get a better picture of King David. I hope you can find in him a hero to challenge you to live a life of courage, aggressive faith, and total commitment to God's plan for your life. We all need strong parents, heroes, mentors and teachers. David can be such a man for you, and for those you wish to influence. Don't misread David's heart because you are critical of his failures. In your study of his life, discern his "heart of hearts" as that of a man who was often dealing with treacherous individuals and primitive societal challenges. Every culture and every era brings its own tolerances and intolerances, so hopefully you can come out of this read with strong and positive lessons to help you and all those around you.

David truly loved God from his youth, saw giving place to God as necessary to his very life, and determined to reach out to all those around him to include them into his idea of worship. David was kind, unselfish and redemptive in his embrace of those whom he respected. He had a clear picture of justice, fair play and redemption.

THERE IS A DIFFERENCE IN "THE HEART" AND "THE HEART OF HEARTS." THE REAL YOU, IS BEST SEEN IN "THE HEART OF HEARTS."

Even today, there are those who cannot see David's good points, for focusing on his failures. Please keep in mind that life is not easy to live, in the best of times, whether in past millennia or in our day. This book was not written to give a breakdown of David's life in total. No attempt was made to give a total evaluation of the man who set out to live his life, amidst the good, the bad and the ugly, which would come his way. What I have tried to do is to challenge you, the reader, with how you can live your life in a divinely principled way, in spite of uncomfortable situations, and embrace God's plan so that you do not fail in your quest to have a strong legacy.

It is not good to live in the flesh only, when you could have the still small voice of God giving you wisdom. Lots of leaders are wrapped up in "busyness", but fail to allow God to have a bigger say in what they do.

Failure is a possibility to us all, but don't make room for such failures. Ask the Holy Spirit to help you pass the tests of life; yield to that still small voice, which comes more often than you may remember, and then stand up like a warrior and launch into the battle, with a determination to win for the Kingdom of God.

Bonus Addendum A

THE SWEET PSALMIST OF ISRAEL

In II Samuel 23:1 David is called, "The Sweet Psalmist of Israel".

What was it about David that kept such a vigilant pursuit of God, that he wrote psalm after psalm celebrating God, extolling His greatness, applauding Him for every victory he ever experienced and petitioning Him to fight against his enemies?

David was not ego driven. He did not boast of how he would, in his own strength, stomp his enemy into the ground; but time and again, he boasted of the Divine strength of his God who could and would bring about victories. There are 150 Psalms, which are so beautiful, with 73 of them, and possibly more, having been credited as written by David.[1]

Leaders are too often not worshippers, but so self-focused as to demand allegiance to their reign and cooperation with their plans and purposes; therefore, never focusing on a "higher power," because somehow, they feel it would detract from their place in the spotlight. It is a wonderful attribute to give honor to Almighty God; to acknowledge that, without help from God, you may not have successfully come to this present victory.

It has become abundantly clear that David surrendered all of the glory for his every accomplishment to God. He never asked for the accolades and never sought for a place, which was not volunteered by God. The Sweet Psalmist sang so much in his generation, that if he had lived today he would occupy the stage worldwide on a higher plane than most of the rock stars. He loved God and "served his generation well."[2]

DAVID RECOGNIZED THAT GOD WAS THE INITIATOR OF LIFE, THEREFORE HE MUST ACKNOWLEDGE HIM IN ALL HIS WAYS.

The New Testament writer, the Apostle Paul, traveled through Asia Minor visiting the cities, and occasionally, even speaking in synagogues. While in Pisidia Antioch, he was invited to speak words of encouragement to the Jewish people who were present. In his talk, he essentially outlined the history of Israel, with emphasis reaching all the way back from their years of slavery in Egypt, and up to the wilderness wanderings. He spoke of how God overthrew seven Canaanite nations to give to Israel their own nation in what is generally called Palestine. He tells how all this took about 450 years. Then Paul told Israel's story, taking them through the period of the judges, and how he gave them their first king, Saul, choosing him, based on the ideals of that generation, and what they wanted in a king. Then God, after 40 years removed Saul, because he was not walking in obedience to God. Notice that he did not say that Saul lived a long time, and then after a long reign of 40 years, came to the end of his reign. Instead, it states clearly that God removed Saul. It is obvious that Saul did not pursue a covenant with God, but ruled in his own strength, and according to his own world-view. Paul then gave insight on how David was God's choice to become king, in his comment, "I have found David son of Jesse, a man after my own heart; he will do everything I want him to do."[3]

MAN'S IDEAL IN A KING TO RULE WAS SAUL.

~

GOD'S IDEAL IN A KING WAS DAVID.

Paul continued, saying that Jesus came to their current generation introduced as a descendant of David, and was announced and introduced by the famed John the Baptist, who came baptizing and prophesying of the Messiah, who would shortly come. John was that "voice crying in the wilderness."[4] When John met Jesus, during one of his services on the banks of the Jordan River, he made a public pronouncement that Jesus was the Christ, hence the Messiah.

In Paul's conclusion, he stated how David served his generation well, was a good man, but when he passed from this life was buried in a grave with his fathers and his body decayed. However, Jesus was more than a good man. When, by crucifixion, he died, and was buried, his body did not see the same decay, but he arose again on the third day, and is our savior. The law of Moses helped us a lot, but only through believing in Jesus Christ can we be justified and forgiven of our sins.[5]

David was declared by the writer of II Samuel to be the "sweet Psalmist of Israel" and became the line through, which came the Messiah, and savior for all of mankind.

Paul declared that David, was a prophet, and served his generation ell.[6] As a prophet, David could see, the different nature of worship, which was to develop in New Testament times. It is amazing how David was able to embrace more of a New Testament style of worship, because of his prophetic insight. Even though David lived under the Old Testament covenant, he could discern what God was really after, in the arena of worship. This is dealt with more completely in the addendum "Why is the The Tabernacle of David Mentioned in the New Testament?" It is necessary to note, at this time, that the Davidic Covenant was fulfilled because of Jesus. For a time, the dynasty of David was suspended; however, the Davidic Covenant was fulfilled by the coming of Jesus Christ, the son of David. He ascended from the tomb and sits today and forever upon the throne of David. There were four Old Testament Covenants between God and Man:

- **Noah:** "Noah found grace in the eyes of the Lord… was a just man and perfect in his generations."[7] "The Lord made an everlasting covenant with Noah and his descendants, establishing the rainbow as the sign of His promise."[8]
- **Abraham, Isaac and Jacob:** God made covenants with the three patriarchs: Abraham, Isaac and Jacob.[9]
- **Moses:** God made a covenant with the children of Israel, beginning with the ten commandments, which were given to Moses. This is not the full covenant, but the beginning of it. The Gentiles were not a part of this covenant, so it was a temporary covenant, to be replaced in the New Testament with Jesus Christ.[10] This is why the Old Testament is considered the "Old Covenant" or Old Testament; while the New Testament is considered the "New Covenant" or New Testament.

- **David:** A covenant was given by God to David. This was to speak of the passing of the throne from David down through the centuries to his descendants, to include Jesus, "the son of David," as he would come from his lineage and sit upon the throne forever.[11]

The Covenant of Moses was a temporary covenant. It gave the Law of Moses, but it would pass away in due time, and when the Messiah would come then a new covenant would be given, to include all of mankind.

David was a prophet and could see further down the road of history, to view what the nature of worship would become, during the times of the New Testament. The time ahead would be a worshipping time, unlimited by Old Testament paradigms, rituals and even Levitical order. David could see a time when men and women could gather and worship unencumbered. In the Old Testament, much would be made of buildings, clerical clothing and rituals, whereas, in the times of the New Testament, these things would not be a part of New Testament worship. Men would approach God directly, with only Jesus Christ as their mediator. The Holy Spirit would come to the church as a comforter, making available wisdom and understanding by impartation and infusion.

The Sweet Psalmist of Israel was one of the most passionate and colorful of personalities we see in the Bible. He was intriguing, very human and full of intuitive expression. He loved God and gave from his heart daily, drawing all of mankind throughout the generations to share in his love. "Shepherd, warrior, musician, outlaw, first of a dynasty of kings, statesman, exile: these are some descriptive facets of the man we know and admire, but as the sweet psalmist of Israel he left for his people and for the godly of every age, a rich treasury of poetry and song which, under God, has enriched their thoughts and meditations. Few of us can adequately express our innermost thoughts or put words to the deep longings of our spirits towards our God like David could. But we can find our own experiences reflected in the psalms of David and can draw from them comfort in our deepest trials, expression for our secret longings and inspiration for our highest worship.

Why would David have received such a title, as Sweet Psalmist of Israel, unless:

- David always had a song in his heart.
- Was always humming the tunes that had awakened him each morning?
- Was known as a musician.
- And played his instruments incessantly.
- As well as constantly searching for some way to document what he had written that day.

When he was in the field, he'd often lay on his back and appreciate the clouds, the stars and all of God's creation. When with his people, David would mentor and influence them to embrace a greater relationship with his God. This man was good for refocusing the nation and for pointing men toward heaven. David was a master at taking heaven's perspective and using it to manage earth matters. God said, "I have found David son of Jesse, a man after my own heart. He will do everything I want him to do."[12] Clearly, God saw in David a different nature than can be found in many men.

Take a look at the writings of the "Sweet Psalmist of Israel" by reading Psalm 27 from the New Living Translation:

A Psalm of David

1 The Lord is my light and my salvation—
so why should I be afraid?
The Lord is my fortress, protecting me from danger,
so why should I tremble?
2 When evil people come to devour me,
when my enemies and foes attack me,
they will stumble and fall.
3 Though a mighty army surrounds me,
my heart will not be afraid.
Even if I am attacked,
I will remain confident.
4 The one thing I ask of the Lord—
the thing I seek most—
is to live in the house of the Lord all the days of my life,
delighting in the Lord's perfections
and meditating in his Temple.
5 For he will conceal me there when troubles come;
he will hide me in his sanctuary
He will place me out of reach on a high rock.
6 Then I will hold my head high
above my enemies who surround me.
At his sanctuary I will offer sacrifices with shouts of joy,
singing and praising the Lord with music.

7 Hear me as I pray, O Lord.
Be merciful and answer me!
8 My heart has heard you say, “Come and talk with me.”
And my heart responds, “Lord, I am coming.”
9 Do not turn your back on me.
Do not reject your servant in anger.
You have always been my helper.
Don’t leave me now; don’t abandon me,
O God of my salvation!
10 Even if my father and mother abandon me,
the Lord will hold me close.
11 Teach me how to live, O Lord.
Lead me along the right path,
for my enemies are waiting for me.
12 Do not let me fall into their hands.
For they accuse me of things I’ve never done;
with every breath they threaten me with violence.
13 Yet I am confident I will see the Lord’s goodness,
while I am here in the land of the living.
14 Wait patiently for the Lord.
Be brave and courageous.
Yes, wait patiently for the Lord.

David cried out from the depths of his soul,[13] and he sang from the heights of hope and happiness.[14] He praised God for being his

Rock, his fortress and his deliverer,[15] and always made room, in his thought life, to glorify God.[16]

He was constantly aware of God's love and of his desire to deliver him out of every temptation, trial or battle. David held up God as the all caring and all-powerful God. He challenged all of Israel to come to the feet of his God to worship. It worked and they loved him for it.

Endnotes

1. www.gotquestions.org/Psalms-David.html - David's psalms express a heart devoted to God. His music comforted King Saul, influenced the nation of Israel, and continues to change lives today.
2. Acts 13:36
3. Acts 13:22 NIV
4. Isaiah 40:3
5. Acts 13:13-40
6. Acts 13:36
7. Genesis 6:8-9
8. www.padfield.com/2004/covenants.html - Genesis 9:1-17
9. Exodus 2:24 ERV - "God heard their painful cries and remembered the agreement he made with Abraham, Isaac, and Jacob." - Genesis 12:1-3 Shows us the Abrahamic Covenant.
10. Jeremiah 31:31-34 - God made a covenant between himself and the people of Israel. It was not a permanent covenant, but temporary. He promised a lasting covenant, but it would be made later, and would be to all mankind.
11. II Samuel 7:12-13 ERV - "'When your life is finished, you will die and be buried with your ancestors. But then I will make one of your own children become the king. He will build a house for my name, and I will make his kingdom strong forever."
12. Acts 13:22 NLT
13. Psalm 42:7
14. II Samuel 22:17 NLT - "He reached down from heaven and rescued me; he drew me out of deep waters."
15. II Samuel 22:1-4
16. Psalm 8

Bonus Addendum B

MICHAL AND THE SAUL SPIRIT

King Saul had pledged to give, to the man who slew Goliath, the hand of one of his daughters in marriage. The oldest daughter of Saul was Merab. After David had slain Goliath, Merab had been promised to David, as a reward for his feat of bravery. However, apparently on the eve of their marriage, after Saul's heart began to change toward David, he withdrew the offer and gave Merab, instead, to Adriel the Meholathite.[1]

Michal was the second daughter of King Saul, and his youngest. She was quite the high-spirited girl. She fell in love with this young musician and national hero, David.[2] It became known that she had a personal chemistry for David. Her feelings were relayed to her father, who recognized it as a means to entrap David.[3] He had become jealous of David but did not want blood on his hands. "Saul thought to make David fall by the hand of the Philistines."[4] He required David to bring a bride-price of 100 Philistine foreskins;

David complied with double the requirement, and "brought their evidence back in a sack, and counted it out before the king—mission completed!"[5]

Saul could not renege from his commitment, since David's response to his demands had been played out in such a demonstrative and public way. The wedding went forward, and the marriage became a reality. However, shortly after their union, Saul lapsed into dark moods and continued his pursuit of David, with even stronger determination. Since the Philistines had failed to bring David down, Saul became determined to do it himself. He sent soldiers to the home of David and Michal with intent to bring him back to the palace for death. Recognizing the danger her husband was in, Michal warned David that her father was about to capture him.[6]

Clearly Michal loved David, and even proved it by saving his life. She was not a bad girl, and throughout the early years, sincerely loved her husband. We see nothing but good in Michal, in the beginning, because she appreciated who David was and saw her husband's worth. However, after his escape, David saw the risk of re-entering Gibeah, to reach out to Michal. After all, she lived in Saul's house until she moved to her new home with Palti. It was a sticky issue for many years.

Michal was not a bad girl. It is certainly to her credit that she did help David escape from her father's threat.[7] However, she could have gone with him. She could have said:

> "Please, my love, take me with you. God is with you and I must also be with you. My home is with you and I will only be happy if I leave as well. I have nothing here to hold me, given the fact that my father, as the king, wants to destroy you."

If David had felt that she would have gone away with him, he would surely have sent one of his trusted men to Gibeah to appeal to her to escape with him in cover of darkness, so that she could live with him as his wife, in Adullam.

There is another reason David probably never came back for her. He may have suspected that Michal would not have adjusted to being on the run, and specifically to be transformed into a "cave dweller". After all, there is a huge difference between living in a palace and living in a hole in the ground, or for that matter, a whole trail of caves and caverns scattered throughout the land. This, also facing the fact that they might be on the run for year after year. It is my opinion that this would have been a stretch for the princess, or daughter of King Saul.

The story continues that Michal aided David in his escape and then remained behind hopeful that her father would mellow toward her husband. That was not to be, as Saul only declined in his moral compass thereby threatening everything the marriage and relationship of David and Michal represented.

During that time, Saul, did a great indiscretion and, during David's absence, gave Michal to another man in marriage. Saul resented the fact that Michal chose David over him, as her king and father, by saving his life. Therefore, he dishonored the relationship she had with David and commanded a new course for her. Because of this, she was given in marriage to Palti.[8]

It is a fact that Saul committed a serious indiscretion against his daughter, which resulted in a "father wound" deep inside. A wound that would never heal, thus breaking or sabotaging his own daughter's heart. Michal's marriage to David was legal and legitimate. This second marriage was not legal, but a sham, forced by an angry father.

Michal and David were still married; there had been no divorce.

David was not a part of Michal's life for quite some time. There is no record that David had any contact with Michal for possibly as long as fourteen years. In defense of David, we must realize that it was hostile territory for him to return to Gibeah until after Saul's death. It was his intention to contest the marriage of Michal to Palti, and to reclaim her as his wife, but unsafe to do so, until the appropriate time. About the only way he could have done that would be if he had slipped in and kidnapped her. Otherwise, she was totally under the authority of her father, the king. Still, it is understandable that she must have felt abandoned by her husband, and then misunderstood by her father, and now forced to cohabit with a different husband. This stoked her feelings of helplessness and disillusionment.

Initially, she felt frustration, but as the years passed, she likely developed anger toward the men in her life. In the early part of her life, it is especially easy to empathize with Michal, and feel compassion toward her.

Michal was Saul's youngest daughter, or baby girl, and yet he appears insensitive and unable to draw her close to his heart. She was used as a pawn to serve his purpose in political matters. As a result, he dealt to her a "father wound" and destroyed her emotionally. Michal lost her tenderness and the innocence, which would normally help her respond to the men in her life.

When finally, David re-entered her life, it may seem unkind and selfish for him to snatch her away from her *illegitimate* husband, Palti. However, we must recognize the fact that Michal's and David's marriage had never been legally dissolved; and there is no mention of King Saul's officially annulling the marriage.

There were issues that must be resolved before David could assume the place as King over the unified tribes. Until the issue of David's marriage was addressed, then the nation was really in a quandary, because Michal was both the daughter of the previous king and the wife of the incoming king. It was not acceptable for David to even consider being King, as long as his lawful wife was living with a man to whom she was truthfully not legally married. In this story, Palti would be considered an interloper, and not a legitimate husband. The marriage to Palti was, in reality, against the law of the land, and stood as a scandal ready to de-legitimize the new king. All this, and not to mention the fact that it was against the Law of Moses. Therefore, David rightfully, brought this issue up to Abner, who was the broker to bring David to the throne. Unfortunately for Michal, protocol was not in place for her feelings to be diplomatically heard. She was, once again, victim to the circumstances.

Realize that the issue at hand was not based on selfishness, or self-centeredness on David's part, but on the legal standing of his position. Michal was of the tribe of Benjamin. If David became king over all the tribes, inclusive of the tribe of Benjamin, then this issue had to be resolved ahead of his coronation.

Also, note that David appealed to Saul's son, King Ishbosheth, (Michal's brother) for the marriage to be restored.[9] It was surely complicated and that, in itself made Michal's cause challenging. It is amazing that Ishbosheth responded favorably to David's request, given the fact that his compliance would give legitimacy to David. It is, however, also a fact that Ishbosheth was a weak king, propped up by Abner, and sinking in the popularity of the people. Time was about over for this king of the northern kingdom.

David made arrangements with Abner to reclaim her as his own, without notifying either Michal or Palti.[10] It is a very sad picture, which played out near their home as Abner and the soldiers snatched her and took her toward Bahurim. Finally, Abner turned and chased Palti away,[11] commanding him to return alone to his own home.[12]

Michal's "Father Wound" robbed her of love.

David returned home, after bringing the Ark of God to Jerusalem. At days end, he wanted to invoke the blessings of God upon his home. The writer of II Samuel 6:20 wrote the passage as he saw it, choosing to refer to Michal as the "daughter of Saul," rather than as "the wife of David," because this is the direction of her mental state. She did not see herself as David's wife, but as Saul's daughter. This posed a problem, because of the mental paradigm, which she had within her heart. How could she be loyal to David when she was still so loyal to the previous king.

Now that she was David's wife, and he continued in the process of legitimizing and stabilizing his position as king of Israel, she just could not make the leap of loyalty to David, over her father. The father wound, placed there by Saul, and the resentment she had against David, which had never been resolved, brought her down to a personal defeat.

It is necessary to also recognize that Michal became who she was because of the family culture of Saul, which had been a part of her since birth. She was, after all considered royalty, and thus in a social class above the common man in the streets. The reason was because of the mere fact her father was the king of Israel. Still, that did not exempt her of the same litmus test we all must face when we stand before Almighty God. We all stand equal when facing God. We can polish ourselves up any way we wish, but without God's grace applied to our lives, we are nothing but flesh, and flesh is always inadequate.

In recapping Michal's story, it can be said that, after all that took place in Michal's personal history, she resented David and developed a stubborn resistance to whatever he valued or desired. In short, Michal became obstinate. She felt superior and expected David, who was the current king to act like he was above the people he served.

It is clear that Saul used Michal as a pawn, taking her away from her husband, and giving her to Palti.[13] David and Michal had lost contact with each other. Michal's home city of Gibeon, was a hostile place to David. It was dangerous, so he never went back. As a result, on the first occasion of their reunion, it was in an awkward setting, where she was being reclaimed by David as his wife. The reason it had happened this way was simply because of her relation to King Saul. Because of her father, she was repeatedly being thrust right into the middle of national politics. Naturally, her worldview became skewed and distasteful, at best. She was caught in the middle. Even though Saul was dead, David felt that Michal was his wife. He had paid the bride price and she had been his first love. In the final analysis of things, it was unthinkable, within the culture of the day, and in the middle east that his crown would be legitimately his, if he did not have Michal by his side.

Endnotes

1. I Samuel 18:19 NKJV - But it happened at the time when Merab, Saul's daughter, should have been given to David, that she was given to Adriel the Meholathite as a wife.
2. I Samuel 18:20 - Michal loved David and it was told to the king.
3. Josephus Book 6, 10:2:197 - Saul used Michal's love for a snare against David.
4. I Samuel 18:25 NKJV
5. I Samuel 18:27 MSG
6. 1 Samuel 19:11-14 MSG
7. 1 Samuel 19:11-14
8. 1 Samuel 25:44
9. II Samuel 3:14-15 NKJV - So David sent messengers to Ishbosheth, Saul's son, saying, "Give me my wife Michal, whom I betrothed to myself for a hundred foreskins of the Philistines." And Ishbosheth sent and took her from her husband, from Paltiel the son of Laish.
10. II Samuel 3:12-14 NKJV - "Then Abner sent messengers on his behalf to David, saying, 'Whose is the land? saying also, 'Make your covenant with me, and indeed my hand shall be with you to bring all Israel to you. And David said, 'Good, I will make a covenant with you. But one thing I require of you: you shall not see my face unless you first bring Michal, Saul's daughter, when you come to see my face.' So, David sent messengers to Ishbosheth, Saul's son, saying, 'Give me my wife Michal, whom I betrothed to myself for a hundred foreskins of the Philistines.'"
11. 2 Samuel 3:16
12. II Samuel 3:16
13. I Samuel 25:44 NLT - Saul, meanwhile, had given his daughter Michal, David's wife, to a man from Gallim named Palti son of Laish.

Bonus Addendum C

DAVID'S STRONGHOLD

Please allow me to define a stronghold.[1] First of all, there are several kinds of strongholds to consider. Two of these immediately come to mind:

A Stronghold can be a negative thing.

This is a force, a vice, a weakness. A kind of monkey on the brain, a kind of diversionary power, which defeats, weakens and prevents an individual from finishing strong.

Saul had a stronghold and it kept him from ever getting close to God. In the end, his stronghold was his own "selfish will", which he never yielded to God. To put it simply, it would appear that Saul was never able to take God as seriously as he should.

"For though we walk in the flesh, we do not war according to the flesh. For the weapons of our warfare *are* not carnal but mighty in God for pulling down strongholds, casting down arguments and every high thing that exalts itself against the knowledge of God, bringing every thought into captivity to the obedience of Christ."[2]

A Stronghold can also be a positive in your life.

This is a destination to which you can go when the pressures build, the clouds become dark, and the storm gets out of control. It can become your "War Room", a place of Refuge and a domain of peace where you can meet with God. The Lord is also a destination to which David would run. It doesn't matter where you are, you can stand still and enter into the presence of the Lord, and that will always make all the difference for you. So, there are places you can run to, but stand where you are and you can enter into the presence of the Lord and find strength and solution.

David had at least four positive strongholds to which he could run without a lot of effort.

- The first was the grazing land where he led his sheep, as a very young shepherd boy. In his youth, he discovered that when no one really wanted to hear what he had to say, God was always ready to listen, and so, he would slip away early in the morning leading his sheep, so that they could have nourishment, and he could revive his own soul in song, in prayer, in prose and in the dance. It may have looked fool-hearty to his critics, but God was assisting David in the building of his life into a strong place.

- The second stronghold in David's life was discovered right after he left Nob, where he obtained, from Ahimelech, the sword of Goliath.[3] When he discovered the cave of Adullam, he often referred to it as his stronghold. This cave was the stronghold to which David and those who would eventually join him came to hide.

SOMEONE SAID: "ROBIN HOOD HAD HIS NOTTINGHAM FOREST, AND DAVID HAD HIS CAVE OF ADULLAM."

- The third stronghold in David's life was the City of David, a castle, a fortress, which was right inside of the famed city of Jerusalem.[4] Occasionally, it was said that David went to his stronghold, and that was the fortress within the city of Jerusalem.
- The main stronghold for David, was the Lord Himself.

"The Lord is my rock and my fortress and my deliverer; My God, my strength, in whom I will trust; My shield and the horn of my salvation, my stronghold."[3]

In our growing into maturity we have to seek out a destination, but as we mature in our relationship and trust of the Lord, we will eventually discover that we don't have to run far, but can just stand still, pray and see the salvation of the Lord as we appeal for his help.

You can have a stronghold too.

Men and women, all over the world, both inside and outside of Christianity have their own strongholds. So many of them, too many of them, have the negative strongholds, which defeat them, rob them, and drive them to a destructive end. Some of those strongholds are:

- Hatred
- Bitterness
- Anxiety
- Unforgiveness
- Pride
- Fleshly or sexual desires
- Jealousy
- Gambling
- Loneliness

But then there are others, so many powerful men and women, as well as young people who have none of these vices, or failures at work in their lives. The primary reason is because they have a stronghold to which they can go so that they can get alone with God in prayer.

- When the storm-clouds gathered around David he often retired to his stronghold to meet God and seek his counsel.
- David would become aware that the Philistines were advancing from some direction, so he would rush to his stronghold or his strategy center, so that his spirit could become empowered by spiritual warfare, and prayer.

- David realized when he was only a shepherd boy that the greatest power of the universe could reside in his heart and soul. This especially helped when the giants were bigger than he was, when his army around him was outnumbered by the opposition, and when he had been counted out because he was too small, or too young for men to believe in.

You can have a stronghold too. However, let it be a destination, a place of Refuge, where you can be topped off, if your joy has drained out. There, you can experience a redefining moment:

- Redefine your identity.
- Realign your commitment to Christ.
- Refit where you are outdated and need an upgrade.
- Refresh because you've become stale or discouraged.
- Revive your faith.
- Restore your hope, to combat the feeling of failure.

Endnotes

1. www.google.ie - a place that has been fortified so as to protect it against attack.
2. II Corinthians 10:3-5 NKJV
3. I Samuel 21:8-9
4. www.bibleplaces.com/areag - "The city of Jerusalem was originally built around the Gihon Spring, on the southeastern hill to the south (left) of the Temple Mount, which is today crowned with the gold-domed Dome of the Rock. Jerusalem has been continuously inhabited since at least 3000 BC, but it was only in the time of Solomon that the city limits expanded beyond the southeastern spur, known today as the 'City of David.'"
5. Psalm 18:2 NKJV

WHAT MADE THE DIFFERENCE IN DAVID'S MIGHTY MEN?

David's men learned that faith in God would make all the difference in the world. Just the mere fact that David could call his men "Mighty Men, reveals that he was spiritually, physically, culturally and "in faith" very strong.

We must never give Satan top billing in our lives. It always shows wisdom to give top billing to the Lord. A good practice is this: "Turn every negative wind to be an instrument of God for you." There is a key to David's life; the prophets called it, "The key to the house of David."

"When he opens doors, no one will be able to close them; when he closes doors, no one will be able to open them" (Isaiah 22:22, Revelation 3:7 NLT).

David was branded as an outlaw.

When thinking of the men who gathered around their leader, in David's story, I do not think of weak men, or physically challenged men, but of men who were strong, rough and sometimes rowdy. They had no doubts of their masculinity, but they did lack in some other qualities. Many of these men had struggles with life issues. Many were in some kind of trouble, lots were in debt, essentially because life is not easy, and generally, so many of them were just not satisfied with the way their lives had gone.[1] To put it clearly, those who gathered to follow after David were in three categories: those who were in distress, in debt and discontented.[2] In school these could be labeled as "D students." Not "A students," but "D," so we would agree that they were getting a poor grade.[3]

So many men were drawn to David by the stories of his bravery and leadership style. They saw him in his role, either as he went up against Goliath, or as their military commander, after he'd been appointed by King Saul. The common belief was that David would be willing to make any sacrifice for the sake of his men, or the people of Israel.

Let it be duly noted, however, David sorted them out, mentored them and showed them how to be "real men." When these men brought their families, and rallied around David, they found in him a leader who was branded as an outlaw against the status quo, a good guy at heart, and a giant killer through faith. With David, everything either began or ended based on his grasp of faith. David was a man who was totally secure in who he was. Abigail, the wise wife of Nabal, challenged David to do the right thing when he almost went down the low road in retaliating against Nabal. David passed the test and did as she suggested.[4]

David's men had joined him, bringing their own baggage, and personal quandaries. They were all in various levels of brokenness. Each of them was socially unacceptable in an imperfect world. Some would reject them outright, labeling their condition as grievous,[5] while giving them no path to redemption, but not David. David did not hang up a counsellor's shingle, nor did he attempt to analyze them. He continued doing what he did best, always setting an example. David was a giant killer and a victorious man to his core. Therefore, he continued living his victorious life, facing every day with the optimism, which is becoming of a leader. Keep in mind that leaders reproduce after their own kind, and David was that kind of leader.

These men likely had their own ideas of what made David tick. At first, they were taken aback by his focus, but after they were up close and personal, they began to see David as a man who, not only displayed strength, but who could impart strength and courage.

The nation of Israel was still in its developing stages, with their ancient history of slavery, and then having come through a rocky and tumultuous 3-4 centuries, with the erratic leadership styles of impromptu judges responding to troubles and disagreements; and then a king who did not follow after God in any way. It is no wonder that their society was a mess. No one had the answers, because society was yet to really make peace with God. Those who gathered around David, were reflective of the lot who came to Ellis Island, and to the Statue of Liberty in the United States. In 1903, this poem was engraved on a bronze plaque and mounted inside the pedestal's lower level. Following is the portion of the poem you will find there:

"Give me your tired, your poor,
Your huddled masses yearning to breathe free,
The wretched refuse of your teeming shore.
Send these, the homeless, tempest-tost to me,
I lift my lamp beside the golden door!"[6]

David's challenge was to turn the lives of this crowd around?

David's life assignment was to live for God, be a worshipper before the nation; and then to establish Israel as Godly followers of the Lord. He would begin with this initial crowd of 400 men, and their families. If he can pass the test with this bunch of broken souls, then he could build the nation in the same way.

The first step he took was to make sure his prayer life and worship focus were in order. Then he would make sure that God was at the center of his decision-making skills. Before he would go into battle he would consistently pray and make sure that he was pursuing the will of God. Nothing else mattered. Finally, he would continue to practice his musical skills daily, so he could make music to God. David concluded that keeping God happy with him was his primary task. If God was pleased with him, then he would continue to do well, and the nation would prosper.

Watching David, became a military pass time, for these men and their families. At first it was like a puzzling challenge of attempting to force a square peg into a round hole. They found David different, unrealistic and mind challenging. But, it did not take long before they realized that something about him had drawn them to align themselves with him, and for good reason. Some of them had served with him in Saul's army, while others had just dropped in out of curiosity. Whoever they were, and whatever had brought them to David, did not matter, because soon, their lives began to change. Now that they were here, these men decided their best bet was to stay the course and see where it would take them.

As time passed they found themselves feeling good about the changes they could see in themselves. They discovered that their energy for battle had increased, their perspectives on life were vastly improved, and their skills for winning were taking them to new levels. Whenever, they came in from a battle they felt genuinely good about how their lives were going. David gave them affirmation when they needed it. These families discovered that listening to him as he worshipped each night was enriching.

The space in the caves and caverns of Israel were tight at times, especially as their numbers swelled to over 600 men, plus their families. It was difficult for David to pull aside for those desperately needed, times of worship. Quite often, he was worshipping with a built-in audience of people who were just going on with their lives. This meant that there were frequent times when David's worship seemed like "surround sound" background music, permeating into the inner souls of his men, their wives and their children. This created a "life giving culture" for David and his Mighty Men.

It was a slow transformation, but a continuing metamorphosis.

No one saw it coming, until it had arrived. What with David's continuous worship, singing and playing of his harp, the men and their families were becoming healed, whole, fun-loving and ready for whatever conflict could come their way. No battle was too challenging and no enemy big enough to win against them. The phrase they could have easily used, would sound something like this: "The bigger they come, the harder they fall." This would have been a takeoff on the famous David and Goliath story. These men were not intimidated by size, numbers, or boasting. They had seen David go up "against all odds," and they were quickly discovering that there was a divine favor within them that drove them, against all odds, to their own successes.

Each man began to discover that whenever they faced conflict they were going to be empowered beyond their wildest dreams. They had heard David's account of the Prophet Samuel's words so often, it had become their own testimony, and their own confession. Each man had embraced as their own, great faith and courage. It could be said that "David's faith rubbed off on every man."

TRANSFORMED MEN ARE HAPPY MEN.

These men, all of them, received those words as truth for David, and now, slowly, they were absorbing it, to a limited degree, for themselves. If it was their battle and they were under David's authority, then they would surely win this one and the next one. No, they would not be king, but they would uphold, support and stand like a wall with Israel's next king, their fearless leader, David. This helped them every time they went into battle. They did not accept the language of defeat, but only that of "over the top victory." These men had been so transformed that their idea of victory, was not simply, achieving a win,[7] but achieving an extremely or excessively flamboyant or outrageous victory.[8] David, by his example had brought strong influences into the lives of these men. They had come to him with issues, many of them debilitating issues, but a few months later, they were in the process of being virtually transformed. They no longer were the "D Troop," but they were the "A plus Army."[9]

A principle, which described David's men: "Transformed men are happy men." When you move from brokenness to wholeness, your world changes and you, unconsciously develop a sparkle in your eyes, and a spring in your step, because you have lost your fear of failure. It is a wonderful thing when your mood becomes excited, you feel confident and energetic, and you exude a carefree way when you walk.[10] Thirty-seven[11] of these men achieved such historical successes that they were revered almost as "super heroes." They have been described as extraordinarily strong, courageous, unflinchingly brave, and completely committed to David."[12]

> "They were a combination of combat commandos, stealth rangers, navy seals, green beret, special ops and Delta forces, who had acquired the skills of battle demanded to survive and conquer in hand-to-hand warfare. They engaged in clandestine operations and were often outnumbered by staggering odds, pitted against them, yet they stood their ground. Time after time, on fields of battle, they were the last men standing."[13]

Examples of the exploits of these men are found most graphically in the stories of the three mightiest of David's Mighty Men:

- Adino - an amazing man who lifted up his weapon and slew eight hundred men in one battle.[8]
- Eleazar - On one occasion David and Eleazar met up with the Philistine army on the same site where David had, years earlier, slain Goliath. The setting was a simple field of barley. A group of Philistine soldiers grew excited, when they found two Hebrew men in a barley field, alone. They assumed their sheer numbers would overwhelm them and give them an edge. What they did not take into account, was who these men were. These men were David and Eleazar. Note: the score

had already been settled, before the first weapon had been drawn. Eleazar stood beside David, and the two of them arose and attacked the Philistines who had gathered to do battle against them. No others of David's men were around, so it was left up to these two men. God did not allow them to be defeated, even against such profound odds. When the battle was over and they had soundly defeated their enemy, David turned to Eleazar and saw that Eleazar's hand had so much dried blood on it that, along with being weary from a hard battle, he had difficulty releasing his sword.[15] Notice that it states: "and the Lord rescued them by a great victory."[16] God was there to make sure the prophetic word of Samuel would, once again, be honored. And notice that all this occurred on the same site where David had slain Goliath. That battlefield was anointed and David and Eleazar enjoyed God's enabling presence.

- Shammah – There was an occasion when Shammah was out in the countryside and came upon a piece of ground full of lentils. He recognized that the Philistines were determined to take this field, but he decided that he would not allow them the pleasure of this success. He positioned himself in the middle of the field and defended it. He slew the enemy, because he did not want them to take even one more piece of ground. Note: it states that God was there and "wrought a great victory."[17]

God was there every time David or his men faced their enemies. It must be considered that, when we have the promises of God in our hearts, whether by His Word, or when we have felt an unction, which has come to us from the Holy Spirit, we can be assured of a greater level of victory. In the case of David and his men, the prophetic words of Samuel had remained so forcefully in their minds. When Israel's enemies became aggressive, God always showed up to help David or his men, win the battle.

GOD ALWAYS SHOWED UP TO HELP DAVID.

It is interesting, as we read of the accounts by Josephus that these three mighty men of David were only the front-runners to the winning team. Their virtues help us to recognize similar experiences were going on with the other soldiers who were with him in battle. They may not have had such illustrious victories, but they were victories, nonetheless, as they were operating under the umbrella of David's anointing. David's men were powerful enough to subdue countries and conquer great nations.[18]

- Sheba - Another of David's mighty men was Sheba, the son of Ilus. David's army of men were formidable and this man Sheba was equal to the challenge. The people of Israel, were often caught in difficulty, and fled from the presence of enemy forces, such as the Philistines. Once, in a place called Lehi, Sheba did an amazing feat. Although he was alone, the aura of victory was all over him, and he had the same results as if he had been a large body of men, or an army. Sheba overthrew many of them, and many fled in fear. So, Sheba took off after them and pursued them, taking the battle to them.[19]
- Abishai - Joab's brother, and nephew to David, by the name of Abishai, slew six hundred Philistines.

Benaiah, the Sixth of David's Mighty Men.

The last of David's mighty men whom I will list was Benaiah, who was a priest by lineage, and a general. Benaiah's father was Jehoiada, a leader among the priests. This means that Benaiah was from the tribe of Levi, and a descendant of Aaron, Moses' brother. It is worthy of note that Benaiah's grandfather was a valiant man from Kabzeel, who had done many feats.[20]

Although Joab was the General and commander of the Hebrew army, Benaiah was a lesser General and the commander of the Cherethites and Pelethites: alien mercenary forces who were David's personal body guard. However, for one month each year, Joab was relieved of duty, leaving Benaiah to serve over all Israel's forces.[21]

Some of the feats of valor credited to Benaiah.

There were many unique incidents, when Benaiah was challenged by Israel's enemies. On one occasion, two Moabite princes, came against him in a battle. They were described as being so ferocious that they were almost lion-like. They were renowned, and seasoned in battle, but Benaiah took them on and slew them both, on the same day and in the same fight.[22]

On another occasion Benaiah slew a huge Egyptian, even though he had no sword. One day, Benaiah was on the battlefield, without a weapon. All he had was a club. Unexpectedly, before him loomed a massive 7.5 feet tall Egyptian,[23] "who was of vast bulk."[24] This man was carrying a spear the same size of the one Goliath carried, and was only slightly shorter than Goliath, the Philistine.[25] He challenged Benaiah and came at him with his weapons. Benaiah did not hesitate, but launched into a full attack, even though he himself had no sword. Benaiah wrestled the spear from the Egyptian, then, slew this man, who was fighting with all his might. The story of what happened on that day was noised abroad, almost taking the form of a legend, because of the inspiring profile of this man, Benaiah.[26]

Then on another day, during a snowfall, the ground was slippery and thus, difficult to navigate confidently. Benaiah heard the roar of a lion in distress, coming from a pit. When he went to inspect the situation, he could see that the lion had fallen into the pit, by accident. He could see no possible means of rescue for the lion, so it was "evident that he would perish, being trapped by the snow; so, when he saw no way to get out and save himself, he roared." In mercy, as much as anything, Benaiah decided he must take care of the situation, being alone and responsible for what he was seeing, he dropped down into the pit to confront the lion in close quarters. Benaiah had entered the pit with no weapon at all. During the struggle, he spotted a stake, laying near the lion. He picked it up and slew the lion.[27]

Benaiah was loyal to the very end. On the very day when David lay dying, he waited patiently to hear the wishes of his dying king, to know who should sit on the throne after him.

When he heard David state clearly that the one to sit on his throne would be Solomon, he rallied the mercenary armies to stand as a determined force to bring about the coronation of the new king. The Cherethites and the Pelethites had been under the command of Benaiah for many years, and now remained loyal, even as the king was about to pass. Led by Zadok, the priest and Nathan the prophet, they proceeded to escort Solomon to his coronation, making him king over the land.[28]

After Solomon became king, he recognized Benaiah's faithful service and appointed him to replace Joab as the Commander General over all of the military. He had been a lesser general, over only the mercenary forces. Now, this man from Levi, was the highest-ranking officer in the Hebrew military.[29]

The Mighty Men were not only formidable, but unstoppable.

The remaining thirty or so mighty men were like the six men named above.[30] They performed great feats of strength and accomplished myriads of military successes.[31] It is a well-known and documented fact that nearly forty men made up the special forces of David. These men were unpredictable and ready to take on any assignment, whenever the need presented itself. Each of them came under David's command, or Joab's authority, or Benaiah's directives. They were also ready, and that without notice, to be a "one-man war machine." Just about any job description could have been assigned to them at any point. Sometimes they were special forces, while at other times they were commandos,[32] while on other occasions they were ready to take on surprise attacks behind enemy lines.

These Mighty Men of David felt that they were almost invincible, so there seemed to be no limits in their minds. When they stood with David against the enemy, whomever that enemy might be, they would be victorious, as God always went with them into the conflict. Remember this, "If God is for you, then who can be against you?"[33] One translation says: "If God is for you, what does it matter who is against you?" I like that translation, because it sends a signal that you will win, if God is on your side, period. It really doesn't matter if others stand against the plan and purpose of God in your life. You must calculate that they are doomed to failure. A very good prayer would be, "I rebuke every enemy who raises its weapon against the people of God, and if they do, then God will not allow them to prosper." It must also be remembered that, if you want God on your side, then you must, without hesitation, be on His side.

David was not only King, but he was also a Mentor.

The Mighty Men of David, became just that, because of the mentoring of their leader. Many men serve under the authority of a leader, whether in ancient days, or in the 21st century, but do not get life changing mentoring like these men received from David. The anointing of David was a force to be reckoned with, by all those who attempted to stand against him. The anointing was also something to be embraced by all those who stood with him.

When facing David's enemies, these men were transformed into something they could never have hoped to become. They could not be normal, when facing David's enemy; because God was with David, and now they had God with them. So, by association these men became empowered by the same anointing David was anointed with. No, it was not the anointing to be "king," but it was the anointing to be a winner. When you become a winner, by having God's anointing, then you cannot fail. David was, by default a servant of God who was going to win, in every battle, regardless of the size of the enemy. Samuel had prophesied this to young David, and life had brought it to David in a defendable reality.

Whenever these men were on David's battlefield, then God was with them, just as He would be with David. For example, when David stood with Eleazar on that "barley field," Eleazar was invincible. David had fought on that same field many years earlier and had slain Goliath. Now, he was Eleazar's mentor and the two of them became a winning team, to defeat the Philistines. So, the drama continued year after year, skirmish after skirmish, and battlefield after battlefield. "If God is with you, then it really does not matter how big or how well-equipped your enemy is." Your enemy can have it in the bag, he can have all the polls in his favor, but "God remains the final arbiter of history." God always has the veto power as the universal judge.

What made the difference in "The Mighty Men of David"?

Two additions to the lives of these men made the difference, namely, the favor of God and the "anointing." Nothing else could make them reorder their thinking, and their lives like aligning with David. Until meeting David, these men had never been exposed to the anointing. They had experienced days, which seemed a lot like accidental good fortune, but never had they experienced divine favor, like they felt when they joined forces with David. God was a force in their lives, but arguably in limited degrees. The history of these men had never revealed much about God. It seemed that they were essentially unaware of the anointing of the God of Israel. He wanted to work in their lives, but they did not know that for certain.

It was through David and his openness to God that they began to look through a small window at the Lord. In the history of Israel, very few had drawn close enough to God to receive from Him. But this man, David, approached God regularly, and even frequently throughout each day. The prophet Daniel said it best: "the people that know their God shall be strong and do exploits."[28] The defining difference in David's life was distinctly, the anointing of the Lord. This eventually began to be absorbed into the subliminal lives of each of these men. The anointing had come into David's life as an impartation from God, through the Prophet Samuel.

The mighty men of David were, by association, infused with the anointing. Their successes, and their exploits should be credited to them secondly; but firstly, their accomplishments came to them, because of how they lived and functioned under the divine authority, which had been given to David. Theirs was a case of "overspill."[29] Without David in their lives nothing would have changed, but with this relationship, everything had surged to a higher level. They discovered that if they stood close enough to David, then whatever God poured into David's cup would spill over into theirs. So, these men stood very close to their leader.

It is common to live in a worldview where all things must be viewed as normal, and nothing is exceptional; but when the anointing comes into your life, it puts a shine on how you think and on your perception of everything. Life is good, if you have God and if you have the unction of the Holy Spirit, then the sun shines and happiness prevails. However, without the presence of God in your life, there are overcast skies and dark shadows.

Endnotes

1. www.yourdictionary.com/victory - Victory is a win, such as beating an opponent or achieving success in something.
2. www.merriam-webster.com/dictionary/over-the-top - extremely or excessively flamboyant or outrageous; *an over–the–top performance.*
3. www.google.ie - "Passing grade" - "The typical grades awarded for participation in a course are (from highest to lowest) A, B, C, D, and F. Variations on the traditional five-grade system allow for awarding A+, A, & A-; B+, B, & B-; C+, C, & C-; D+, D, & D-; and F. In primary and secondary schools, a D is usually the lowest passing grade."
4. www.idioms.thefreedictionary.com/spring+in+your+step - "A spring in your step."
5. Josephus Book 7:12:4:307 - "Those that were most illustrious and famous of them for their actions were thirty-eight."
6. www.tifwe.org - "David's Mighty Men: Stewardship in Action"

7. *David's Mighty Men*, by C. David Jones. Copyright 2009. ISBN: 978-1-4415-2645-8

8. II Samuel 23:8

9. II Samuel 23:9-10

10. Ibid - AMP

11. II Samuel 23:12 KJV

12. Josephus Book 7, 12:4:307

13. Josephus Book 7, 12:4:309-310

14. II Samuel 23:20; I Chronicles 11:22

15. 1 Chronicles 27:5-6 TLB

16. Josephus Book 7,12:4:315

17. I Chronicles 11:23 ERV

18. Josephus Book 7,12:4:315

19. I Samuel 17:4-7

20. Josephus Book 7,12:4:315

21. Josephus Book 7,12:4:316-317

22. I Kings 1:36-40

23. 1 Kings 2:35 AMP - "The king appointed Benaiah, the son of Jehoiada over the army in Joab's place, and appointed Zadok the priest in place of Abiathar." Also, confirmed by I Kings 4:4

24. The six men who were the most formidable of David's Mighty Men were: Adino, Eleazar, Shammah, Sheba, Abishai and Benaiah.

25. It is difficult to confirm the exact number of men who were known as David's Mighty Men: as they vary from a total of 36-38, depending on how you would monitor the lists found in II Samuel 23:8-39; I Chronicles 11:10-47; and Josephus Book 7, 12:4:307-317. It would suffice to say that nearly forty men made up the special forces of David.

26. www.google.ie/search?q=define+commando - "Commando" - "a soldier specially trained for carrying out raids."

27. Romans 8:31 KJV

28. Daniel 11:32 ASV

29. www.google.ie - "Overspill" - "the action or result of spilling over or spreading into another area." When there is more of something than will easily fit into a container. In the case of David, the anointing was so great that it spilled over, and into all of those people in his life.

Only the Philistines Had Swords of Iron

The picture of David, as he took up the challenge against the threats of Goliath is riveting. Since that story was acted out in the Valley of Elah, it has found its way into the conversation, if not the pop-culture, of many societies. David was considered the underdog against an overwhelming opponent. Therefore, when an underdog emerges on the scene, and he is likable, the audience cheers him onward to victory.

The Philistines were not originally from Palestine.

The Philistines were either from Crete, or from Egypt according to a number of sources. According to the most reliable sources, they are thought to have originated from the island of Crete, and migrated first to Egypt, and then to the area near to where Israel settled.

"They were known to be a seafaring culture, and accustomed to living near to the Mediterranean Sea. Dagon was the god of fertility and crops, and their principal deity."[1]

We do know that the Egyptians had smelting iron, and most likely obtained that secret from the Philistines, or possibly it was the Philistines who obtained it from the Egyptians. One confirmation of that fact is heard in the prayer of Solomon, as he was dedicating the new Temple, which he had built. One of the main portions of his prayer was a reference to God's people who had been rescued from Egyptian slavery. That bondage was aided by the very fact that Egypt possessed "iron-smelting furnaces."[2]

The Philistines were in a strong position, while Israel's was weak

It is an amazing comparison to realize that Israel was in a difficult place when facing the Philistines in battle. Israel would raise their swords of bronze and the Philistines their swords of iron. This was the beginning of the Iron Age[3] and, although often Israel would defeat their enemy, it was usually because of a divine intervention.[4] Otherwise, Israel was usually in a similar situation, as was David when facing Goliath. Note that Israel was fighting with outdated weapons, while the Philistines had the latest and the greatest. The Philistines were already in the Iron Age, while Israel was lagging behind in the Bronze Age.[5]

The Philistines were masters of iron technology. The Bible confirms this fact:

> "There were no blacksmiths in the land of Israel in those days. The Philistines wouldn't allow them for fear they would make swords and spears for the Hebrews. So, whenever the Israelites

> needed to sharpen their plowshares, picks, axes, or sickles, they had to take them to a Philistine blacksmith. The charges were as follows: a quarter of an ounce of silver for sharpening a plowshare or a pick, and an eighth of an ounce for sharpening an ax or making the point of an ox goad. So, on the day of the battle none of the people of Israel had a sword or spear, except for Saul and Jonathan."[6]

"Today, archaeologists find iron artifacts at most Philistine-Israelite sites from this period, but weapons are found only at Philistine sites."[7]

Israel had no advantage when it came to dealing with the Philistines. They had as many soldiers but remained out-gunned and overwhelmed. The only thing Israel had going for them was their God.

It is an accepted strategy that, in every victory, the weapons available to each opposing force must be up to date and of the highest technological quality, if they expect to win. In the end, the hope remains that every leader and every soldier must agree on the best strategy and steward the best use of those weapons, if he is to achieve that victory.

> "Before 1200 BC, bronze was the metal in the Near East. Scholars believe that the technology of the ancient world was not advanced enough to heat metal to the temperatures needed to melt iron and work it. The melting point of iron is 1,550 degrees Celsius, whereas copper melts at only 1,100 degrees Celsius. So, for more than 2,000 years, bronze was the metal of choice. Bronze was a significant step beyond the stone tools and weapons of earlier times, but because it was composed of

> copper and tin, it was soft and didn't hold an edge well. There was plenty of iron ore around, but the technology needed to smelt it didn't exist. It is not certain if the Philistines invented iron technology, but they did make the most effective use of it (e.g., they developed a process that included leaving iron in the fire long enough to absorb the carbon from firewood to form another, more malleable form of iron/steel). This superior metal so revolutionized life that it gave its name to the next 600 years: The Iron Age."
>
> Whoever had this metal could produce superior tools and weapons, leaving other societies behind in the "dark ages" of stone and bronze. Iron was to the biblical world what nuclear energy or the computer is to ours. It determined who would dominate and who would be relegated to the fringes of world events. Iron revolutionized how people lived: how much land they could plow, how much stone they could shape, how much wood they could cut. And it changed warfare to the same degree gunpowder did centuries later."[8]

God was always on the side of his people Israel. However, often Israel was not on God's side. As a result, we can learn many lessons from reading the stories of struggles, situations and the solutions, which came to them in their challenges. Often victories came to Israel because of prayer and humility, not because of the superiority of their weapons. Later on, in their history, when they had the superior weapons, victory was illusive, simply because their relationship with God was not thriving.

This remains a challenge in the 21st century, to keep your heart right before God. If you succeed in areas of honesty before

God, humility and repentance, as well as walking in righteous wisdom, then you will also thrive and discover that:

> "No weapon formed against you shall prosper, And every tongue, which rises against you in judgment you shall condemn. This is the heritage of the servants of the LORD, And their righteousness is from Me,"[9]

Endnotes

1. www.thoughtco.com/dagon-chief-god-of-the-philistines-118505 - Dagon, the Chief god of the Philistines.
2. 1 Kings 8:46-51 NKJV
3. www.en.wikipedia.org/wiki/List_of_archaeological_periods -

    Stone Age (2,000,000 - 3300 BCE)

    Bronze Age (3300 - 1200 BCE)

    Iron Age (1200-586 BCE)
4. Judges 1:19
5. www.study.com/academy/lesson/iron-vs-bronze-history-of-metallurgy.html - "Differences Between Iron and Bronze - While wrought iron was not much stronger than bronze, a small addition of carbon (about 2%) could turn iron into steel. This discovery was probably accidental. Fires generate a great deal of carbon. Each time they put the iron back into the fire to work, they added a bit more carbon to the metal. Steel is one of the hardest substances on the planet. It is certainly much stronger than bronze. This added strength meant that less steel had to be used to make effective tools, weapons or armor, making steel a lighter alternative. This strength also allows steel to hold an edge better than bronze. By 1100 B.C.E., iron had replaced bronze as the metal of choice in the Near East. Another three centuries would see it spread across Europe."
6. 1 Samuel 13:19-22 NLT
7. www.thattheworldmayknow.com/the-latest-technology - Ray Vander Laan
8. ibid.
9. Isaiah 54:17 NKJV

THE REAL CITY OF DAVID

The leaders of the twelve tribes of Israel came to Hebron to crown David king over all the nation. They had a coronation ceremony and celebrated him as their king.

> "Then all the tribes of Israel came to David at Hebron and spoke, saying, 'Indeed we are your bone and your flesh. Also, in time past, when Saul was king over us, you were the one who led Israel out and brought them in; and the Lord said to you, "You shall shepherd My people Israel, and be ruler over Israel." Therefore, all the elders of Israel came to the king at Hebron, and King David made a covenant with them at Hebron before the Lord. And they anointed David king over Israel.'"[1]

After just a few days, David led Israel's army to the walls of the city of Jerusalem, with determination to capture it. The inhabitants of the city, were called, Jebusites, but, in fact were just another faction of Canaanites. A rumor spread throughout the land that Israel's new king was mounting an assault by leading his army against them.

The leaders of Jerusalem were of the opinion that David would absolutely fail in his attempt to capture their city. And so, they rallied the people to mock and observe his inadequate assault. They realized they were in imminent danger, but determined to taunt their enemy, doing everything they could to insult and intimidate them. The people rallied on top of the city walls, and in every place where they could gain a vantage point to view the scene below them and rant their mockery. As far as they were concerned, the walls were both thick enough, and high enough to prevent this invasion, and therefore virtually impossible to penetrate.

David and his army gathered outside of the walls, and watched them, as their self-confident arrogance grew more defiant and boisterous, by the minute. The Jebusites rounded up the physically handicapped and positioned them on the top of the walls. The blind, the maimed and the lame were placed in plain sight of David and his army. The leaders and the citizens of the city mocked the invaders, saying, "'You might as well go home. Even the blind and the lame could keep you out. You can't get in here!' They had convinced themselves that David couldn't break through."[2] He was not intimidated by their antics. David did not attempt to hide his contempt for their mockery and jeering. He was enraged and began the siege of the city.[3] All of their antics only fueled his determination to bring them down to defeat.

David and his army were successful and took the larger part of Jerusalem. It was then that they discovered that, within the city there was a citadel[4], which towered adamant and foreboding. The citadel was also called the castle and was proven to be a stronghold against enemy invasions. It was an inner city, much like a "safe room" to protect the heart of operations. This citadel was the most refined and fortified part of Jerusalem and proved to be the big prize for David. It was the first time, David or any of his men had been inside Jerusalem,[5] so this was an entry they would long remember and appreciate.

The part of Jerusalem that was the most difficult, was the "fortress of Mount Zion."[6] So, they began searching for a creative way to invade. David and his men realized that a city like Jerusalem required a water source and, in their search discovered an underground water system. They had found that the perfect way to deal with these Jebusites, was to slip in through this shaft, or tunnel, one man at a time.[7]

David strategized that his men needed motivation. He felt that they had only one opportunity to gain access to the citadel. So, he gave them a directive, stating: "the man who navigates the underground water system, and makes it to the top of the citadel first, will become the commander of the entire army. It became the opinion of every man that, "no pain, or sacrifice would be too great to exercise that day. There could be no higher honor than to be the chief commander of David's army. The man who achieved this was Joab, the son of Zeruiah, David's sister. As soon as he made it to the top of the citadel, Joab cried out to the king, and claimed the chief command."[8]

> "David went right ahead and captured the fortress of Zion, known ever since as the City of David. That day David said, "To

> get the best of these Jebusites, one must target the water system, not to mention this so-called lame and blind bunch that David hates." (In fact, he was so sick and tired of it, people coined the expression, "No lame and blind allowed in the palace.") David made the fortress city his home and named it the "City of David." He developed the city from the outside terraces inward. David proceeded with a longer stride, a larger embrace since the GOD-OF-THE-ANGEL-ARMIES WAS WITH HIM."[9]

Upon capturing Jerusalem, David took the fort or fortress of Jebus, and made it his home. At the point of capture, it was called, the "Fortress of Mount Zion. This fortress, became David's residence, so it consequently, came to be known as "The City of David". Although many have not been aware of the existence of this castle, the fact remains that the real "City of David" was this inner city, and not the entire city of Jerusalem.

Here are some of the names given to this small part of Jerusalem:

- Fortress of Mount Zion
- The Castle of Jerusalem
- The Royal palace of Mount Zion
- The Citadel of David
- City of David

Endnotes

1. II Samuel 5:1-3 NKJV
2. II Samuel 5:6 MSG
3. Josephus Book 7, Chapter 3:1:61
4. www.merriam-webster.com/dictionary/citadel - CITADEL - "a castle or fort that in past times was used to protect the people of a city, if the city was attacked."
5. www.generationword.com/jerusalem101/16-salem-jebus.html
6. www.christiananswers.net/dictionary/david.html - David took from the Jebusites the fortress of Mount Zion. He "dwelt in the fort and called it the city of David" I Chronicles 11:7. This was the name afterwards given to the castle and royal palace on Mount Zion, as distinguished from Jerusalem, generally. (I Kings 3:1; 8:1) It was on the southwest side of Jerusalem, opposite the temple mount, with which it was connected by a bridge over the Tyropoeon valley.
7. www.chronicle.augusta.com/stories/1999/01/23/ent_251040.shtml - "Much hangs on the obscure Hebrew word "tsinnor" in this verse. Most modern Jewish and Christian translations interpret it as water shaft, channel, tunnel or gutter… So, Joab (identified as commander in the 1 Chronicles 11 parallel) seems to have sneaked his men into town through a water system. That interpretation was supported in 1867 when British explorer Charles Warren discovered a 40-foot vertical opening through solid rock, which came to be called Warren's Shaft. The shaft was near a system of tunnels around the Gihon Spring, Jerusalem's only natural source of water located outside the city walls to the south. The tunnels must have provided access to the spring when the city was under siege and, so the theory went, also provided Joab's point of entry."
8. Josephus Book 7, Chapter 3:1:63-64
9. II Samuel 5:7-10 MSG

Bonus Addendum G

Significance of David's Being Anointed Three Times

The transforming experience of being anointed of the Lord makes all the difference for those who are called to serve. Those times in David's life qualified him and brought him to a higher level.

- He was ceremonially and prophetically anointed the first time by the Prophet Samuel in the city of Bethlehem.[1]
- Then again, immediately after the death of Saul, David was in the city of Hebron, and was anointed as King of Judah, by the elders of his own tribe of Judah.[2]
- Then, a third time by the elders of all the joint tribes of Israel, inside the city of Hebron, before Jerusalem became the national capital.[3]

David was anointed Prophetically by Samuel. This acknowledged his prophetic insight

All of Bethlehem, as well as Jesse and all his family were surprised when Samuel had come to visit. The events of that day had made an indelible impression on David's life. He found that everything changed for him immediately. As Samuel poured the oil upon David the anointing also descended upon him. An unction from the Holy Spirit ushered in the presence of God. From that moment every instinct in David's life increased to new levels. He moved more quickly into manhood and his love for God intensified, as he began to receive prophetic insights, and a powerful courage.

Although David was a young boy, he received an added layer of anointing, as a prophet from that day onward.[4] Over half of the Book of Psalms gives us the writing, the songs and the thoughts of David, regarding life, spiritual challenges and of the Messiah. One writer even said, "The psalms of David are the gospel of Jesus Christ in song, in transports of affection, in thanksgiving, and in holy desires."[5]

This transformation took the heart he already had and carried him into a place where he was seen as being "a man with a heart like the heart of God."[6] To confirm this prophetic unction in David we read,

> "Being a prophet and knowing that God had sworn with an oath to him that of the fruit of his body, according to the flesh, He would raise up the Christ to sit on his throne."[7]

Further, we read the words of Jesus, when they asked, "How can David call his descendant, Lord?" Jesus answered and said, while he taught in the temple,

> "How is it that the scribes say that the Christ is the Son of David? For David himself said by the Holy Spirit: 'The Lord said to my Lord, Sit at My right hand, Till I make Your enemies Your footstool.' Therefore, David himself calls Him 'Lord'; how is He then his Son?"

The writer of Mark goes on to say, "And the common people heard Him gladly."[8]

The Kingly Anointing by David's home tribe authorized him as the rightful Monarch.

When David was anointed the second time, it was just after Saul's death in battle on top of Mount Gilboa. David had just turned thirty years of age, which was, in the middle eastern culture, the legal age of a man. This ceremony, was carried on in Hebron, by the leaders of his tribe of Judah.

The elders of Judah knew that "the scepter would not depart from Judah."[9] It seems to be public knowledge, throughout all Hebrews, that Jacob had declared this on the day of his prophetic words over Judah, near the time of his death. Some of them had likely been surprised when a king was chosen over Israel from Benjamin (Saul) rather than from Judah. Now as the chapters of this nation had progressed they felt that they had to be true to divine inclination and go with one of their own, namely, David, a son of Judah.

This coronation and anointing gave him the crown but did not replace anything that had been given to David in the first anointing, by Samuel. This ceremony added a new layer of authority onto his life, as he appropriately was recognized as a legitimate king, howbeit over only one tribe, Judah. It added a new dimension to the unction and anointing that had enhanced the life of David. He was no longer a fugitive at large and constantly looking over his shoulder. King Saul was no longer his sworn enemy and David could choose Hebron as his home to legally and safely live there. This was the first time in at least a decade that he could relax and not be constantly on the move.

The Priestly Anointing to lead the unified nation gave David the spiritual authority to lead for God.

After seven and a half years of serving the lone tribe of Judah as King, now Saul's son, Ishbosheth, was dead and all of Israel's leaders made the journey to Hebron to appeal to David.

The leaders of the other tribes, had done what they thought was right by standing with Saul's son, after the King had died at the hand of the Philistines. However, when treachery was committed by two of the prominent men of that realm, resulting in the assassination of Ishbosheth, the entire nation began to re-evaluate the place in which they now found themselves.

They had long memories of how David had been loyal to Saul, and how he had served as a military leader for his forces. They were all aware of how he had then been cast aside by the king for more than a decade. They had all watched as David had never spoken ill of the king, and had just kept out of his way, even when he was consistently an object of Saul's hatred.

Now the national wisdom pointed in David's direction. They needed a leader, and no one could give any just reason why that leader should not be David. From every direction, the people began to step forward to admit to themselves and to remind others of the rumors, which had been so commonplace, that "David was the anointed of the Lord."[10]

As all the tribes of Israel gathered by the hundreds of thousands, they came to proclaim, in a public forum, these heartfelt words:

> "We are your own flesh and blood. In the past, when Saul was our king, you were the one who really led the forces of Israel. And the LORD told you, 'You will be the shepherd of my people Israel. You will be Israel's leader.'
>
> So, there at Hebron, King David made a covenant before the Lord with all the elders of Israel. And they anointed him king of Israel.
>
> David was thirty years old when he began to reign, and he reigned forty years in all. He had reigned over Judah from Hebron for seven years and six months, and from Jerusalem he reigned over all Israel and Judah for thirty-three years."[11]

At the time of David's third anointing, Israel was in a difficult state of mind. As a nation they really were a blank page. Although they were a nation committed to God, it was largely because of the Patriarchs and all that had transpired in the beginning. From Abraham, to the other patriarchs and finally to Joshua, we see that Israel's head had been turning slowly to the Great I Am.

Conventional thinking is often that Israel backslid during the reign of Saul. However, the fact is that the Hebrews had never personally embraced a vibrant faith in God until David.

David became their king, but even more than that he became their Shepherd, their mentor and their example. His faith was deep, it was passionate and it was life challenging to all who came near to or who served under him.

God's plan to empower David was three unique coronations.

As we look in on David and his third coronation, we discover a new aspect, which developed, and was different to the previous times. After capturing Jerusalem, and making it his Legislative Capital, he turned his sights toward spiritual matters. The years had enabled him to accomplish great and mighty things, but King David, found it was not enough to satisfy his deep longing, in his quest to bring the nation to a close relationship with God. He wanted to establish a house of the Lord in Jerusalem. This would require bringing the Ark of God from Gibeah and the house of Abinadab[12], to the City of David.

Reordering the mindset of the nation to make God more central to their lives proved to be a bigger undertaking than he had anticipated. At first David transported the Ark, following the protocol used by the Philistines,[13] but discovered that this was in error, as they had failed to choose the protocol established by Moses.[14] This resulted in a major delay, with the death of Uzzah, prompting a three month stay for the Ark of God, in the house of Obed-Edom.

Finally, David required the scribes to research God's word and their history, to discover the instructions God had left with regards to the Ark of the Covenant. It was then that David followed the instructions given to Moses, in an exacting manner.[15] The nation regathered just a short distance outside of Jerusalem to the house of Obed-Edom to properly, judiciously and respectfully carry the Ark to the one-room tent David had prepared for it.

If you will notice, David's actions and body language, was more like a priest than that of a king.[16] Certainly, Michal, who was David's wife and also Saul's daughter, would have agreed.[17] David was overwhelmingly exuberant in his joy, his devotion and in his uproariously happy mood of worship. David led the priests in offering sacrifices to the Lord. He danced, he played so aggressively that all of Israel had to agree that he was "beside himself" in worship. David was "dancing in front of the Lord with all of his strength, while wearing a linen ephod."[18]

David was more than a king, he was also a Prophet and a Priest.

One important aspect to being God's chosen leader is to lead as a whole person. David's nature and character reflected that of a multi-faceted man. There were aspects of David and his leadership assignment, which could not be fulfilled by merely being the king of the nation. Choosing David as the king was God's idea, and God saw into the heart of his chosen leader. God could see that, in order for David to be an effective and imposing king, and to do so with divine unction, then he must do so embodying all the aspects of Prophet, King and Priest. So, it was that God oversaw these three coronations in a God ordained sequence, while all the time responding to the needs of the nation, as they were to move forward in establishing their relationship with their God.

This divine attention was certainly not to puff David up as a man. These three anointings, or coronations occurred so that David would have the authority and the tools he needed to break down the fleshly and pagan barriers, which had developed over the centuries of Israel's being human centered, rather than God focused.

David was a man in authority and so would move forward as a humble, but empowered man to bring into being God's plan and purpose in that nation. Father God was building up His people, and David was his best instrument.

Endnotes

1. I Samuel 16:13
2. II Samuel 2:4
3. II Samuel 5:1-3
4. Acts 2:30
5. https://catholicexchange.com/jesus-prophecy-david
6. Acts 13:22
7. Acts 2:30 NKJV
8. Mark 12:35-37 NKJV
9. Genesis 49:10
10. Psalm 89:3-4 "I have made a covenant with my chosen, I have sworn unto David my servant, Thy seed will I establish forever, and build up thy throne to all generations. Selah."
11. II Samuel 5:1-5 NLT
12. II Samuel 6:4
13. I Samuel 6:7-8 and II Samuel 6:3-4
14. Numbers 4:15-16
15. Ibid
16. www.bereanwife.net/2009/10/did-david-dance-before-the-lord-naked - "An ephod was a priestly garment, worn over a simple robe; there was nothing immodest about it. David just had simple (humble) clothing, not his kingly garb that would have designated him as above the others, he was dressed as the rest of Levites bearing the ark… Michal accused David of dancing like a common man and beneath his station in life, no robe or crown to set him off as more important than others… Wearing a linen ephod was symbolic of serving before the Lord, it was the attire of the priests. David was serving just as if he was a priest."
17. II Samuel 6:20-23
18. II Samuel 6:14 ISV

Why is the Tabernacle of David Mentioned in the N.T.?

The Tabernacle of David, quite simply was the one room special tent, set up by David to receive the Ark of the Covenant in Jerusalem. The Ark had been separated from the Tabernacle of Moses for over 90 years, and now David felt it must be brought back into the culture of Israel, so that Jerusalem could become a spiritual home for the nation. He had transported the Ark from the house of Abinadab, in Gibeah, to the capital city, designating Jerusalem as the center of worship for the nation (II Samuel 6:4).

> "They brought the Ark of the Lord and set it in its place, inside the special tent David had prepared for it. And David sacrificed burnt offerings and peace offerings to the Lord."

There is a special designation for what David brought together on that day about the time he was crowned king over Israel, when at the age of 37. The reason goes back to the anointing and to how he interpreted what God wanted in His relationship with mankind.

Prophetic word: "I will restore the Tabernacle of David."

The prophet Amos, made several comments that are intriguing and, which give us insight on what will happen in the future. In giving special attention to the Tabernacle of David, we are left with a reality that it had been a significant symbol of worship in the heart of God. Amos actually said that the Tabernacle of David would be restored.

- Amos said, "When the Lord God decides to do something, he will first tell his servants, the prophets."
- He then went on to say, "On that day I will raise up the tabernacle of David, which has fallen down, and repair its damages; I will raise up its ruins and rebuild it as in the days of old."
- Then he continues by inferring that the tabernacle of David will not only be restored, but that there are "gentiles who are called by my name," leaving us with the idea that the gentiles and their being seen as having the name of the Lord emblazoned upon their lives, is in some way connected to the restoring of the tabernacle of David. Therefore, and most assuredly, to take place in New Testament times.

The very statement, "the Tabernacle of David, shall be restored," suggests that the core concept of redemption of the New Covenant, was not just a New Testament thing, but had already held a strong place in the heart of God, from much earlier days. In other words, God always wanted to have fellowship with mankind. But because of the reluctance of man to draw close to an all-powerful God, it launched him into a long process, which would eventually give mankind the opportunity to desire it as well.

David was a dreamer, was constantly worshipping and also was clearly musical. But he was also a prophet, who conducted himself at times, as a priest, and certainly a king.

Then in Acts 15 we see how the question before the leadership of the New Testament church in Jerusalem, was discussing requirements for the new gentile converts. There had been a real debate between the traditional believers and those who were actually expanding the church throughout the Middle East, Asia and into Europe. It had a lot to do with those who were attempting to require of new believers, the Old Testament customs and practices. The Apostles reacted and stated that they were not in agreement. They felt that the New Covenant had broken the mold and was placing the church on a different path to what was contained in the Old Covenant. By giving the Baptism of the Holy Spirit to those Gentiles, who had not been circumcised, it confirmed that God made no distinction between the new believers and those who had been circumcised.

> "While Peter was still speaking these words, the Holy Spirit fell upon all those who heard the word. And those of the circumcision who believed were astonished, as many as came with Peter, because the gift of the Holy Spirit had been poured out on the Gentiles also. For they heard them speak with tongues and magnify God. Then Peter answered, 'Can anyone forbid water, that these should not be baptized who have received the Holy Spirit just as we have?' And he commanded them to be baptized in the name of the Lord. Then they asked him to stay a few days" (Acts 10:44-48 NKJV).

In continuing to read the decision of the Apostles in Acts 15 we see that they simplified and relaxed the requirements, so that, those who were not from the legalism of the Jewish faith, were able to respond, within the context of who they were, not coming from the same background. Here is how it all developed, step by step.

The early church at Antioch was embroiled in a debate on what should be required of the Gentiles after they have repented.

The church at Antioch of Syria was embroiled in a debate. The legalist Judaizers were spreading dissention and confusion in the church of Antioch. They were trying to move the developing church away from the tenets of: "the just shall live by faith" and "we are redeemed by grace through faith." If they had succeeded, then it would magnetically pull the church back into the law, requiring their faith to be hinged on circumcision and all things physical. It is amazing how legalists keep wanting to "work for their salvation" and do not extend to themselves or others the right of walking in a faith walk.

The leaders in Antioch sent Paul and Barnabas back to the mother church in Jerusalem and to the Apostles for clarification.

The challenge on the table was the fact that the church wasn't just made up of Jews, but also gentiles.[1] This, of course, brought theology into the mix, forcing church leaders to micromanage the requirements to be levied upon the gentiles who would receive the Lord into their hearts?

Upon arriving in Jerusalem, "Barnabas and Paul, were welcomed by the whole church, including especially, the Apostles and Elders."

The legalists who were believers, but still hanging on to their Pharisaical ideals and lifestyles, stood up and insisted that the new gentile believers must not only be circumcised, but must adhere to the Law of Moses.[2] Peter, and then James, launched into comments regarding how the Holy Spirit wanted to restore the Tabernacle of David.[3]

James stated clearly that the gentile believers, who have received Jesus Christ into their hearts, must not have an "Old Covenant Pharisaical theology"[4] imposed upon them. The Apostles recognized that they must function in their theology within the confines of the Divine covenant, given to them by God. Therefore, let this be our decision:

- Do not make coming to Christ a problem in their lives by laying ridiculous measures and requirements upon them. They have turned to God so let them feel good about what they've done.[5]
- Then James said, we should write and tell the new believers to separate themselves from the practice of eating foods offered to idols.[6]
- They must cease any sexual immorality.
- They must also move away from the pagan cultural practice of eating the meat of animals, which have been strangled.
- Finally, they must not drink blood, as the blood is precious and is a carrier of life, which is a gift of God.[7]

The Letter from Jerusalem for Gentile Believers

"Then the apostles and elders together with the whole church in Jerusalem chose delegates, and they sent them to Antioch with Paul and Barnabas to report on this decision. The men chosen were two of the church leaders—Judas (also called Barsabas) and Silas. This is the letter they took with them:

> "This letter is from the apostles and elders, your brothers in Jerusalem. It is written to the gentile believers in Antioch, Syria, and Cilicia. Greetings!
>
> "We understand that some men from here have troubled you and upset you with their teaching, but we did not send them! So, we decided, having come to complete agreement, to send you official representatives, along with our beloved Barnabas and Paul, who have risked their lives for the name of our Lord Jesus Christ. We are sending Judas and Silas to confirm what we have decided concerning your question."
>
> "For it seemed good to the Holy Spirit and to us to lay no greater burden on you than these few requirements: You must abstain from eating food offered to idols, from consuming blood or the meat of strangled animals, and from sexual immorality. If you do this, you will do well. Farewell."[8]

The church of two thousand years ago was very wise in their judicious handling of issues, which arose from the mindset of those who thought like the Pharisees, even though they were believers. Such divisive interjections by these legalists brought confusion into the church of that day, as it does in the 21st century. The apostles kept it simple and consistent with the ideas of the Lord, namely that He wants men everywhere to follow the graciousness of the Lord, when inviting men to abandon their ways and follow after Jesus Christ.[9] Don't make things so complicated but receive new believers when they abandon their fleshly practices and receive Jesus into their lives.

What was happening in David's heart at that time?

There are reasons why the Tabernacle of David is so significant and mentioned by the prophets. It was mentioned by the Prophet Amos and then again by the Apostles in the New Testament Book of Acts. We must look at what was going on in the heart of David, during his lifetime.

We must remember that David was a "Mentoring King" and to him was given the Davidic Covenant by the Lord. God had chosen David because he was a man "after God's heart." David mentored the men who came around him, while he was young, and this continued throughout the years and long after he was king. Also, David became a mentor to the nation to help them in their cultural and national relationship with Israel's God. Up until David, Israel's relationship with God was limited and weak at best.

David had captured Jerusalem, and then made it the nation's capital city. A portion of the city was given an alternative name, or nickname: "The City of David." He then continued his plan by bringing the Ark of the Covenant to Jerusalem, thereby establishing Jerusalem as the spiritual capital of the nation. In all of this, David was exercising the wisdom of a mentor to the nation.

Israel began to develop a relationship with David. Here are some of the significant roles, which define his place as Mentor-King to the nation:

- David, the King of Israel
- David, the Shepherd King
- David, the Worshipping King
- David, the Sweet Psalmist of Israel

- David, the recipient of the Davidic Covenant
- David, the king from whom would come the Messiah

David was Israel's Mentor King

As much as Abraham was the "Father of the Faith," and Moses was the "Law-giver," we see that David, was Israel's "Mentor-King." He can and should be seen as a mentor, in that he gave national identity to Israel, as they searched for their place among the nations.[10] Without David's input, then Israel could eventually have fallen by the wayside, because they would not have seen themselves in a strong and current relationship with God. They watched David as he had no qualms within, when it came to worshipping God. He set the bar high, for all of Israel.

Israel is more than their traditions, culture and language

It is valuable to see Israel, through more lenses than just involving their traditions, culture and language. You must see Israel through the lens of how they responded to God in their religion, if you are to truly grasp their uniqueness.

David recognized that in his day, Israel was functioning under the covenant relating to the Law of Moses, and thereby were in the Old Testament era.

- And yet, he also saw Israel as progressing toward the day when the Messiah would come, and a New Covenant would be given to them.
- He recognized the Tabernacle of Moses, and all the relics of the Old Testament culture, but he also knew that God wanted an "up close and personal relationship" with mankind.

- He did not prefer a people who continued to refuse the idea of venturing close to the mountain of God.
- David perceived that the Heart of God wanted a people who loved God with all their hearts, and who wanted to come to the summit of the mountain of God, move up close and who would cry out for a touch of their master.

David knew that it would be good (necessary) to build a temple for God such as his son, Solomon, would build. However, in his heart of hearts, he also knew that God really wanted his children to lift their hands, long for the presence of the Holy Spirit, and invite Him to live in their hearts.

David never felt that the relationship he had with God required a building, but he did realize that he, himself, would not live forever. He recognized that the nation he led (and would eventually leave behind) needed a meeting place to which they could come, and from which they could meet the requirements given to them by God at Mt. Sinai. During the Old Testament Covenant, a building was in order, but after the Messiah would come, some things would change, "for God is Spirit, so those who worship him must worship in spirit and in truth."[11]

In the New Covenant, or New Testament times, "the just shall live by faith"[12] and "you are the temple of the Holy Ghost."[13]

David had prophetic eyes?

As a prophet,[14] David could see prophetically through a portal, so he knew that the day would come when, not just Hebrews, but gentiles, in all nations everywhere[15] would come to the Lord their God in worship. In that day, no building would hold the hearts of the people to God, but there would be a day when God would, through the Holy Spirit, dwell in the hearts of men everywhere.[16]

All through the Psalms, David cried out with the force of self-challenge, using such terms as "deep calls unto deep"[17], as he summoned Israel to come close to the Father and develop that same "deep calling unto deep" hunger. Although it does not state that David wrote this particular psalm, Spurgeon felt that it had, at least, been spawned by the Heart of David, as it clearly uses David's worship style.[18] In Psalms 42 the author continues by describing how he felt, in the depth of his heart toward God. There was chaos all around the writer as he was experiencing drama, trauma and disappointment, and yet, he felt, deep within, the desire to draw close to God, because, of the principle: "When everything is shaking around you, find something strong and lean up against it."[19]

He spoke of the deer (or hart), and how it thirsts for the cool streams of water, or the water brooks. Then he compares it to how his own heart is thirsting, or panting, and longing to take a cool drink of God and all He brings to him in the form of cool clear and refreshing water:

> "As the deer pants [longingly] for the water brooks, so my soul pants [longingly] for You, O God.[20] Deep calls to deep in the roar of your waterfalls; all your waves and breakers have swept over me."[21]

National identity is generally seen in light of the "cohesive whole, as represented by their own distinctive traditions, culture and language."[22] I must add "religion" to this, when it comes to the nation of Israel. For Israel found its cohesiveness in its traditions, culture, language and religion. Other nations did not go through the same metamorphosis, or change, to define who they would be on the inside. Israel, however, had to go through this, or they would become just like any other nation on earth.

The prophet Amos lived more than 200 hundred years after David lived, and yet felt strongly, that God wanted to introduce, again, what David had in his heart, on this subject of worship. This is what Amos said about what David did regarding the Tabernacle of David:[23]

> "On that day, I will raise up The tabernacle of David, which has fallen down, And repair its damages; I will raise up its ruins, And rebuild it as in the days of old.[24]

Then the Apostles talked of David and his role as the ancestor of Jesus,[25] being a man after God's own heart,[26] being a prophet,[27] and then, in Acts 15, of how the Tabernacle of David would be restored[28], just as Amos had prophesied. We do know that Saint Augustine stated, "The new is in the old concealed; the old is in the new revealed."[29]

In conclusion, the Tabernacle of David represented the New Covenant, which was to come; and when it came, would reflect the open arms of the Messiah, who would welcome to the foot of the cross, not just the Hebrews, but "whomsoever will," including all the gentiles. Redemption was available to all men everywhere. The Law of Moses would pass, the Aaronic priesthood would come to an end, and a new day would come, when all men everywhere could make their way to the cross and be saved.

Once again consider that as a prophet, David, had not tried to recreate the Tabernacle of Moses (a two-room tabernacle), but a New Covenant style of tabernacle (a one-room tabernacle). The significance is that David took the Ark out of storage and made its new home, one of worship, and not just ceremony.

Endnotes

1. Acts 15:7
2. Acts 15:5 NKJV "But some of the sect of the Pharisees who believed rose up, saying, 'It is necessary to circumcise them, and to command them to keep the law of Moses.'"
3. Acts 15:13-18, especially v. 15
4. Old Covenant Pharisaical theology - In the context of the New Covenant, it is imperative not to "cherry pick scripture, to create your own theology." It is best to accept the scriptures as it was given, without trying to sway the church toward Old Testament legalism, or even toward the legalism of your favorite persuasion. I appreciate the freedom of expression and the power we can receive from the Baptism of the Holy Spirit, just as it came to the early church, without trying to box the church into some denominational pigeon hole, which suits the fancy of some, while coming short on early church theology.
5. Acts 15:19-21
6. Note: the gentiles had come from the environment of idols and must separate themselves from such things as "anything to do with idols." Note, also that the Jews had come from unrealistic piety, and now needed to separate themselves from self-righteousness. Salvation would come by grace through faith. The Old covenant was gone and the New Covenant was in.
7. Acts 15:20 - The requirements for the Gentile believers.
8. Acts 15:22-29 NLT
9. Acts 15:20
10. www.en.oxforddictionaries.com/definition/national_identity - National identity is generally seen in light of their "cohesive whole, as represented by distinctive traditions, culture and language." I must add "religion" to this, when it comes to the nation of Israel. For Israel found its cohesiveness in its traditions, culture, language and religion.
11. John 4:24 NLT
12. Hebrews 10:38 NKJV
13. I Corinthians 6:19
14. Acts 2:30

15. Rev. 7:9-10

16. Romans 8:9-11 MSG "But if God himself has taken up residence in your life, you can hardly be thinking more of yourself than of him. Anyone, of course, who has not welcomed this invisible but clearly present God, the Spirit of Christ, won't know what we're talking about. But for you who welcome him, in whom he dwells—even though you still experience all the limitations of sin—you yourself experience life on God's terms. It stands to reason, doesn't it, that if the alive-and-present God who raised Jesus from the dead moves into your life, he'll do the same thing in you that he did in Jesus, bringing you alive to himself? When God lives, and breathes in you (and he does, as surely as he did in Jesus), you are delivered from that dead life. With his Spirit living in you, your body will be as alive as Christ's!

17. Psalm 42:7

18. www.spurgeon.org/treasure/ps042

19. I tried to confirm this quote but could not. I remember something like this from the movie, "San Andreas Fault." The point here is that nothing is stronger than God, so when you face hard situations, get really close to God and lean on Him. If you do, everything will be just fine.

20. Psalm 42:1 AMP

21. Psalm 42:7 NIV

22. www.en.oxforddictionaries.com/definition/national_identity "- National identity"

23. www.encyclopedia.com/philosophy-and-religion - Amos was born in the Judean town of Tekoa, near modern Bethlehem, Israel. His activities probably took place during the reign of Uzziah, also called Azariah, King of Judah (reigned 783-742 B.C.), and Jeroboam II, King of Israel (reigned 786-745).

24. Amos 9:11 NKJV

25. Acts 2:22-30

26. Acts 13:22-23

27. Acts 2:30

28. Acts 15:12-17

29. www.ligonier.org/learn/articles/ancient-promises - Saint Augustine said, "The New Testament is in the Old Testament concealed, the Old Testament is in the New Testament revealed."

Notes